NO EXPERIENCE NECESSARY!

A "Learn by Doing" Guide
for Creating Children's Worship

ELAINE CLANTON HARPINE

MERIWETHER PUBLISHING LTD.
Colorado Springs, Colorado

Meriwether Publishing Ltd., Publisher
Box 7710
Colorado Springs, CO 80933

Editor: Rhonda Wray
Typesetting: Sharon E. Garlock
Art direction: Tom Myers
Back cover and interior photographs: William D. Harpine, Ph.D.
Interior illustrations: Beth A. Tallakson

All Scripture quotations marked (RSV) are taken from the Revised Standard Version, copyright © 1971 by the Division of Christian Education of the National Council of Churches of Christ in the U.S.A. Used by permission. All other Scripture included is the author's paraphrase.

Library of Congress Cataloging-in-Publication Data

Harpine, Elaine Clanton, 1952-
     No experience necessary : a learn by doing guide for creating children's
  worship / by Elaine Clanton Harpine. -- 1st ed.
        p. cm.
     ISBN 0-916260-78-X : $12.95
     1. Worship (Religious education)   I. Title.
  BV1522.H37 1992
  288'.432--dc20   92-30575
                                                                        CIP

Acknowledgments

It is with special gratitude that I say thank you first to my loving husband Bill. Thank you for taking the pictures for the book and for your carpentry expertise, which made the biblical house and children's church feasible projects.

A special thank you to my three wonderful children, David, Virginia, and Christina, for being willing to test every idea. I created this program and wrote the book for the three of you so that you might learn and always remember that worshiping God can be fun and spiritually enriching at the same time.

Thanks also go to each and every child with whom I had the privilege and honor of working while developing and writing this children's worship program. I love each of you dearly.

My thank-yous would not be complete without expressing my gratitude to the parents who helped make this program a fabulous success, especially Chuck Nichols, Jr., who designed and helped build our first children's church. Thank you for the wonderful hours we spent together and the memories we shared.

And finally, I wish to thank the staff and all of our wonderful friends at the First United Methodist Church in Cuyahoga Falls for their help and support in keeping this project alive and flourishing.

Elaine Clanton Harpine, Ph.D.

TABLE OF CONTENTS

PART III

THE WORSHIP EXPERIENCE

PART IV
WRITING THE WORSHIP SERVICE

PART V
WHERE DO WE GO FROM HERE?

INTRODUCTION

It's 9:30 Sunday morning and 32 children between the ages of four and 12 are busily setting up their Children's Church as they prepare to lead the worship service. This is no ordinary service. Today is Children's Day. The children have built their own church featuring paper stained glass windows, a communion table, Bible stand, candleholders, and a cross — all made by their own hands. The children's church stands proud and beautiful at the front of the sanctuary as the children gather to lead the entire congregation in a worship service they wrote themselves.

Sound incredible? This is an accurate description of what can happen with any group of children in any denomination, with any leader, in any church, in only eight months.

You need a group of children between the ages of four and 12 (a group of five or 35 is fine), a leader to work with them, a large classroom, and 30 minutes or an hour each Sunday. The programs are written for 30-minute sessions because that seems to be the typical time frame being used by most churches. If your church has an hour-long session, you will find it easy to combine sessions to fit your needs.

No Experience Necessary! is a complete year-long program and includes special sessions that emphasize religious holidays throughout the year. Just insert the holiday sessions in at the appropriate time of the year to give you an entire year of Sundays of children's worship.

PART I

GETTING STARTED

CHAPTER ONE

HOW TO SET UP A CHILDREN'S WORSHIP PROGRAM

Find a big room, an energetic bunch of children, and let children's worship happen! No experience necessary — all you need is patience and love.

A new family arrives at the big brick church. The doors swing open and a kindly gentleman says, "Welcome, so glad to have you here this morning. And we are especially glad to have you young ladies and young sirs with us today," he says as he kneels to the children's level and shakes the hands of all the children in turn. "We have programs and classes for all ages, but we have a special treat for the children. Just follow the sign on the wall," he says, as he points to a wooden plaque that says: **Come and Follow Me**. "The sign will lead you to our children's worship room upstairs."

Following the plaques through the hallway, the family arrives at a room filled with the sounds of children. Prominently displayed is a large banner saying: **Children's Worship**. Inside they see a table full of children painting a rainbow with brushes, string, sponges, and even their hands on a big piece of cloth. Another table is covered with pieces of wood; a child hammers at one end while another saws at the other end. The sound of bells being played comes from the far corner in front of a structure that looks like a child's size church. A group is sitting together embroidering a banner. And still another group of children is busily drawing and writing a new TV script to explain the Lord's Prayer.

Another friendly smile welcomes the family, as the teacher kneels down to ask the youngest if she and her brother and sister would like to paint. All three eagerly shake their heads yes.

As the children put on painting smocks, the teacher explains that each table contains a sign and explains a part of the worship service — the Call to Worship, Affirmation of Faith, Witness to the World, and so on through the Benediction. Children's worship is a church service in motion. The children go from table to table as they work through each aspect of worship and then conclude with a self-directed, very active 10-minute worship service in their own church.

Sound like a dream? It doesn't have to be. This can be how children are welcomed to your church every Sunday.

Why Children's Worship Is Important

Many churches are still struggling with the old question: "What should we do with the children during worship?" Some churches keep the children in the service; others provide playrooms or Sunday school, and still others offer a combined session, frequently called Junior Church.

Children need action. Children's worship as proposed here in *No Experience Necessary!* provides action with a purpose. Children learn best when they are involved with what they are learning about. They have different needs than adults.

Watch children at play; they are always in motion. Yet we invite children to church to sit and listen to adults talk. It's no wonder many children do not want to go to church.

All you need to use this children's worship program are 30 minutes, a large room with space to move around, at least one teacher willing to try something new, and a group of children — five or 25 will do just fine. With more than 30 children, set up two separate rooms.

Children Love to Worship

I wanted my own children to experience worship instead of just sitting in church feeling restless and bored or being packed off upstairs to play with toys. I was determined to make learning about worship as much fun as being turned loose in a new toy box full of toys, and yet I wanted the time to be very meaningful, spiritual, and educational.

No Experience Necessary! gives you step-by-step instructions on how you can create a children's worship program in your church that will be so exciting that the children will beg to come back the next Sunday. One young lady pleaded with her mother, "Can't we come back next week too? I know we have to go to Grandmother's house, but can't we come here first?"

The program presented in this book will teach your children about worship and will help them enjoy worshiping while they learn.

This program may sound totally different from anything you have seen your church do before. Starting a new program does not mean that anything is wrong with the programs you are already offering on Sunday morning. Your church may already have a dynamic children's program. *No Experience Necessary!* just presents a new way to achieve the same goals. You may just want to add a "new coat of paint" to what your church already offers. As the title indicates, the children really *are* able to build a small church, lead a worship service, and many other activities with no previous experience. They just need a minimum of loving guidance to direct them through each Sunday. Children's worship is like taking your child to a hands-on museum to learn about science, but instead you are taking your child to church to learn about worshiping God. The science museums are set up with dozens and dozens of learning centers. You will set up seven workstations every Sunday.

This children's worship program is designed for children ages four to 12, but you may use any combination of ages. I once thought that children of different ages should never be combined, but the children soon taught me differently. It is a joy to watch 12-year-olds and four-year-olds working side by side, helping each other learn about what it means to be a Christian.

Since this program is designed to be active and geared to the attention span of children, you will not find long, elaborate explanations or lectures. Instead you will find Bible-based, action-oriented programs.

Learning centers are becoming more and more popular in Christian education as a result of their success in elementary school classrooms. Learning centers are tables containing all the supplies and information needed for a given project. Directions are posted by the table so that children may learn on their own, yet be guided. Both teacher and child benefit. I have taken groups of young people who were considered discipline problems and transformed them into productive groups. The learning centers, or *workstations,* keep the young people so busy that they don't have time to get into trouble.

The workstations offer the children a variety of activities and experiences, some active and some quiet. The program is fast-paced, lively, and varied so the children never get bored. Every part of the program leads to a better understanding of worship.

An Inviting New Approach

This book is a practical toolbox of ideas with step-by-step plans. The ideas work and have been tested with lively children just like your own.

This program builds self-esteem, pride, and ownership because each week the children are building and creating their own church and their own worship service. Worship is no longer just a collection of words and songs; worship has meaning.

The children use their five senses to discover and explore what it means to worship. As they touch the wood beneath their sandpaper and

build their church, as they smell the bread they are kneading for the Thanksgiving basket for a needy family, as they taste the cake they decorated with liturgical colors for the Birthday Party, as they see the light shine through the paper stained glass windows that they designed and colored, and as they hear the music made by their own musical instruments, the children learn that worship really is a joyous celebration of God's love.

The children learn to believe in themselves and their abilities. Worship is a time to celebrate. In this program, the children are taught that the church is a place where everyone can share the skills and talents that God has given them. Every single child who wishes to participate is included. No one sits on the sidelines watching the others because he cannot sing or she cannot read very well. It is God's church, and in his church all children are seen to be equal and important.

You are ready to start. As you work with the children, I hope you will discover, as I did, how many wonderful people attend your church. My first children's worship program was supported totally by donations: scraps of wood left over from a new house, fabric and discarded cloth to make banners, household junk for musical instruments, and the skills and love of adult volunteers. The church did not spend one cent. Make your needs known and watch generosity appear.

Getting Organized

Most churches have trouble getting children to arrive on time but, much to my surprise when I first set up this program, some of the children persuaded their parents to bring them early so they could have a little more time, others would leave the church's donut shop to come upstairs, and still others who openly insisted that they "hated" church would come in and don costumes to act out the Bible lesson.

Find a Room and Decide on a Time

Adults may walk into a nice, neat, clean room with a table and little chairs, a small cabinet against the wall for supplies, and a picture of Jesus on the otherwise bare wall and think, "What a nice classroom."

Children, on the other hand, give such comments as: "I don't want to go in there; it looks cold and scary"; "I don't like this room, there's nothing to do in here"; "I don't want to go back to the class again because all they do is just sit around a table and answer questions."

Think about your children on the first day of public school when they go to a new classroom. They are much more eager to go into a classroom that looks lively and interesting than they are a plain room with no catchy bulletin boards or colorful posters. We set the mood for our classes by how we set up our classrooms. Make the room inviting, but don't worry about empty wall space here and there. The entire room will eventually be decorated by the children's artwork. Select a comfortable place and time and then transform it into a children's worship room filled with excitement.

Pick a room with a lot of space to move around. One big room is better than two adjoining rooms. A dingy, unfinished, junk-filled basement or a crowded kitchen annex won't work. You'll want to make the children feel that their room is an important part of the church and not just some far and distant corner where no one else ever goes.

Lots of windows, sunlight, and a pleasant view of the outside world are good. You want plenty of storage or a closet, at least four work tables, and easy access for families.

Getting Approval

Children are ready and willing to try something new, but adults are not always so eager. Start by finding a teacher to be in charge of overseeing the entire program and setting up the workstations. Then you will need volunteers to help at the various workstations. These volunteers may be parents who volunteer one Sunday a month to come in and help or teenagers from your youth group. Have photocopies of the Program Proposal and remind committee members to look at the program, time requested, and use of the room as a child would. You may even want to walk them through the room so they may be able to visualize the end results a bit better.

PROPOSAL FOR CHILDREN'S WORSHIP PROGRAM

Goals:

1. To teach the children about worship as they work in and plan their own service each week.
2. To include all children in the building of their own worship setting: a children's church.
3. To involve the children in the actual planning, writing, and leading of their own Children's Service.
4. To work cooperatively with representatives, both children and adults, from every aspect of our children's programs to build a worship program for all children.
5. To help the children worship in a way they can understand and to help prepare children to participate fully in a sanctuary worship service.

Needs of the Children:

1. Children need active programs.
2. Children learn best by doing.
3. Just like adults, children need to feel ownership to make worship meaningful for them. Both building a church and writing their own worship service to share with the entire congregation develop a sense of ownership.

Proposal:

1. Set up a large room for the Children's Worship Program (See Illustration I.)
2. Have the children build their own church and write a service to share with the entire congregation following the step-by-step detail in *No Experience Necessary!*
3. Children's worship will include every child in our congregation and will pull together and coordinate our entire children's ministry.
4. Children's worship will help the children learn about worship as they experience seasonal programs and weekly services in their children's church.

Advantages:

1. A service including all the children shows them that they are included in the church and family of God.
2. A service showing the talents and spiritual development of all the children will show members the strength and depth

of the children's program.

3. Including people is a great way to encourage new or reluctant members of our church.

4. It will help attract new members, especially families with children, to our church and congregational family by demonstrating the spiritually enriching program we offer to children of all ages.

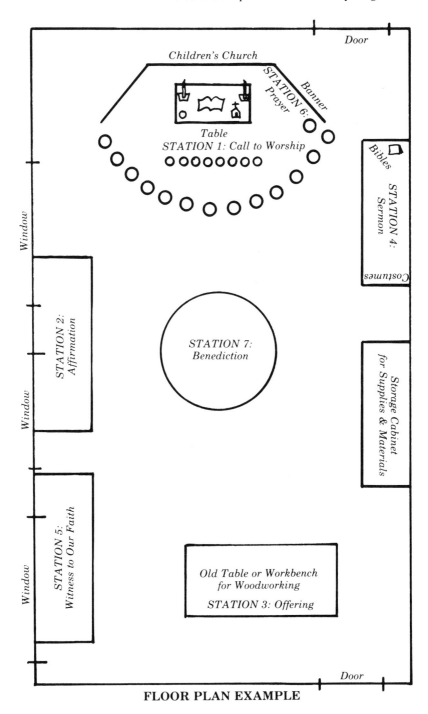

FLOOR PLAN EXAMPLE

Publicizing the Start of Something New

Publicity is essential. You should have an article in each week's church newsletter telling about the upcoming new program for children and the plans to build a children's church. Make it sound exciting to children.

Put forth a list of items and donations needed. Even after the program gets started, write a weekly announcement for your church newsletter or bulletin, or talk about what's happening and invite others to join during the announcement time.

Let Your Love Show Through

Children can be a true joy to work with. You don't have to be a teacher of 20 years' experience to conduct this program. All you need is love. If you love children and genuinely want to help them learn, you are perfect for the job.

Most of all, remember that children want to be included in the life of the church. Many of them are in church every single Sunday. They will not remain children forever. They will not still be children in 20 years. They are only children *today*.

If we fail to meet their needs as children today, few of them will be sitting in church 20 years from now. Today is the only opportunity we will ever have to *minister* to their needs.

CHAPTER TWO

SETTING UP THE WORKSTATIONS

Prepare for the Sundays ahead by setting up the room and gathering supplies, then "let the children come." (Matthew 19:14)

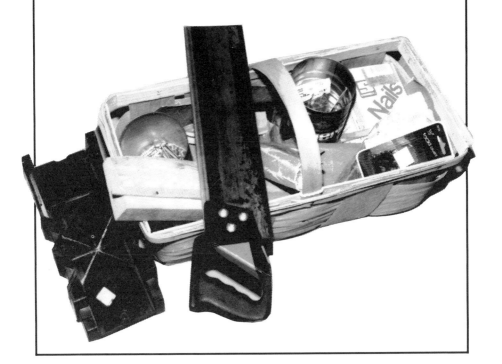

It's a cloudy and rainy Sunday morning outside, yet inside the church the large room is bright and bustling with children and the rhythmic sounds of hammers and saws at work. Two children are measuring the width of one end of the room while others are drawing a sketch of their church.

The children are thrilled about the chance to build their own church. Independently working on this big project instills in the children a genuine sense of pride. They appreciate it more than if it was simply given to them by adults.

Hammers and saws in the church on Sunday? Yes, hammers and saws and children learning to work side by side — taking turns, helping each other, and sharing God's love. This chapter explains what you'll need to do to get ready before the first day.

Getting the Room Ready

Each week you will set up seven workstations for the children. These workstations represent seven basic parts of the worship service. Although the parts of the service used in this book are common to many Protestant denominations, please feel free to adapt the terminology to fit your church's preference.

Set up a little worship center at one end of the room with a circle of chairs. You will also need four to six tables for workstations. (See Illustration I in Chapter 1.) If possible, place them next to the walls to allow space in the middle for "walk-around" room. The walls will come in handy as you hang up sign-up sheets and workstation instructions each week.

Making Signs for the Workstations

Step 1: Make posters or signs for each of the seven workstations using the information below. Since you will use them every week, make signs that will last (by covering them with plastic, for example).

Workstation #1: The ***Call to Worship*** is an open invitation for everyone to come and worship God.

Workstation #2: The ***Affirmation of Faith*** can be a statement or song telling what one person believes or what an entire church says they believe in.

Workstation #3: The ***Offering*** does not always have to be money. It may also be our time or handmade gifts.

Workstation #4: The ***Bible Lesson/Sermon*** teaches a biblical concept or verse and shows how it is important in our lives today.

Workstation #5: When we **Witness to the World** we send messages out to others about our faith.

Workstation #6: ***Prayer*** is a quiet time to ask for understanding and help with our daily problems and to be patient, kind, and understanding with others.

Workstation #7: The ***Benediction*** or closing to the service sends everyone out to share the teachings of Jesus.

Step 2: Once your signs are made, you only need to clip on a new set of directions for each week's activity and, in some cases, post a sign-up sheet. The sign-up sheet on page 353 may be photocopied and used as needed — just fill in the correct information.

Helpful Hints for Gathering Supplies

It's nice but not necessary to have exclusive use of a room. Every piece of the children's church collapses for easy storage. To make workstations easier to set up, have a separate basket or cardboard box for each workstation's supplies.

Keep all of the woodworking sandpaper, nails, hammers, masking tape, etc. in one basket so all you have to set out is the woodworking basket plus the wood for that project.

Also assemble a craft supply basket. Keep it stocked with: glue, construction paper (various colors), scissors, yarn, string, hole punch, pencils, ink pens, crayons, markers, beads and buttons, seeds or pebbles,

shells, straws, paper fasteners, paper plates, stapler and staples, tape, stickers, self-stick name tags, extra paper for drawing and writing, and tissue paper. The craft basket will be needed each week. Another time-saving idea is to have a paint basket or box. Whenever a session calls for paint, all you have to do is set the paint basket on that table. You can also have an instrument box for the musical instruments. Teach the children how to put everything back in the basket for next week, and you are all set up for the following week.

Station 1: The *Call to Worship* workstation is your music station and stays more or less the same each Sunday.

You may use any kind of instruments, including homemade oatmeal box drums, handbells or melody glasses, rhythm instruments, and sing-along tapes.

You can make your own set of melody glasses by getting eight glasses or jars that are exactly the same size and shape. Fill each with water using about ⅛ cup less water in each glass as you go down the line of all eight. Label them C, D, E, F, G, A, B, C. Ask a church musician to tune them and mark fill lines with a grease pencil. Tap the glasses lightly with a spoon to play. A child's toy xylophone will serve the same purpose.

Station 2: The *Affirmation* station changes each week.

Station 3: The *Offering* station is your woodworking station; it is here that the children make the items needed in their church. Safety is the first concern in the woodworking station. Never use more than two hammers or two saws at one time. Hammers and saws should be supervised by an adult and the children need to share. Make a sign saying "Joseph's Carpenter Shop" and post safety rules.

RULES FOR THE WOODWORKING STATION
"The Safe Way Is the Only Way"

1. We only use hand tools. This is the way Jesus would have learned to work with wood.

2. You must share. If there is not enough wood for everyone, then invite someone to work with you.

3. Never fight over tools. The words "I had it first" are never heard here.

4. If you argue, fight, or act unsafely, you will leave the woodworking station for the rest of the time and work at another station.

5. Hammer in one nail and then give someone else a turn.

6. Saw for *one minute*. Then give someone else a turn.

7. Do not put your hands near the saw when someone is sawing.

8. You are *not allowed* to hit your fingers with the hammer. You may hit the nail as many times as you wish, but no fingers please. Hammer slowly and keep your fingers away from the nail.

9. Put your sandpaper back in the basket when you finish.

10. Always put the tools back in the basket at the end of class and clean up your woodworking station.

Station 4: The **Sermon/Bible Lesson** station often pantomimes or acts out the parable or Bible verse as the lesson for the day's worship celebration. You can use simple costumes if you wish. Make them from old, worn-out bed sheets or fabric:

STEP 1: Select a piece of fabric that will drape over the person.

STEP 2: Cut a hole in the middle for the person's head to slip through.

STEP 3: Tie a ribbon, rope, or thin piece of fabric around the person's waist.

STEP 4: Make headpieces from pieces of cloth and a ribbon or band to tie around the head.

Station 5: The **Witness to the World** workstation changes each week and stresses how we tell others what we believe.

Station 6: The **Prayer** workstation stays the same each week. It takes all year to embroider the Lord's Prayer banner.

Station 7: The **Benediction** workstation changes each week and focuses primarily on the message the children take home.

How will you move everyone around to each station in such a short time? Quite simply — you won't. Some children will not make it around to all seven stations; others will want to do everything. Some children will not want to sew and others will not want to saw. Of course, when the children see the activities from each workstation they will want to try more things the next week.

Keep a photo record of the year. Record every step of building your church and the other activities in a photo album or scrapbook. The children will feel a sense of accomplishment when they see how much they've progressed.

Children are always hungry, so ask parents and other volunteers to sign up to bring snacks each Sunday — nothing fancy, just something to nibble on.

Above all, let the children enjoy learning about God and always remind them that worship is a time of celebration and praise.

PART II

BUILDING THE CHURCH

CHAPTER THREE

WORKING WITH THE ARCHITECTS

Just like real-life architects, the children need to make plans before they start to build their church. They will learn the importance of patience and preparation.

SESSION 1

DESIGNING THE CHILDREN'S CHURCH

The Bible Lesson

The Parable of the Two House Builders (Matthew 7:24-27) helps us see that the church is only as special as the people who worship within. This parable lends itself perfectly to the first day of designing the children's church.

What the Children Will Learn Today

The children will learn from the Bible that how they live their lives is the foundation on which the church is built. The foundation of your children's church is love.

Time Needed

Twenty minutes for workstations and 10 minutes for worship.

Supplies Needed

1. Stiff cardboard for church model.

2. Blueprints and pictures of churches to decorate room.

3. Bibles, a snack, and simple biblical costumes if desired.

4. Workstation signs and instructions (see Chapter Two).

5. Scrap wood for making wooden stands.

6. Musical instruments and song book.

7. Woodworking basket: 2 hammers, nails of varying sizes, 2 saws, sandpaper, and scrap wood.

8. Craft supply basket: Usual supplies (see Chapter Two), including beads, paper plates, flat buttons for eyes if you wish, and yarn for hair.

9. Embroidery supply basket and banner: large embroidery needles, scissors, thread of varying colors, and a 37" x 28" piece of aida cloth or other suitable embroidery fabric.

WORKSTATIONS

Workstation 1 — Call to Worship

GETTING READY

The Call to Worship is the music station where the children will practice a song to play for their worship service. Sing-along tapes, melody glasses, or any kind of instrument can be used. Pick an easy song for the children to sing and play. Post a sign-up sheet for those musicians who want to play in today's worship celebration, and copy and post the following instructions for the children:

> Today you'll invite everyone to come and gather for worship with your music. Use the instruments and practice your song.

Workstation 2 — Affirmation of Faith

GETTING READY

Make a sample puppet and post a sign-up sheet for those who would like to present their puppets today, and post the following instructions for the children:

> This morning, I would like you to make an "I Believe" puppet face on a paper plate. It may be a guy with a beard and a hat or a girl with paper curls and tissue paper ribbons. Use your imagination. On the back of your puppet face, write one thing that you believe in — God, love, or whatever seems most important to you. Put your name on the sheet if you would be willing to show us your puppet and read what you wrote on it during the Affirmation.

Workstation 3 — Offering

GETTING READY

Your group may take an offering each Sunday, but they will also make something to give to the church they are building each Sunday. Post a sign-up sheet for volunteers to attach the puppets to the stands in today's service, and copy and post the following instructions for the children:

> The gift you give to God today is your time. Make stands for the paper plate puppets. Cut seven thin boards 20" long and nail onto bigger scraps to form stands. Sand down the rough spots. Bring your finished stand to the worship celebration today.

Workstation 4 — Sermon/Bible Lesson

GETTING READY

If your group is not accustomed to acting out stories, you may want to have an adult help them the first time. Post a sign-up sheet for the actors needed today: builders, wind and rain, and the reader. Copy and post the following instructions for the children:

> Most children think sermons are boring. This is your chance to give an active sermon. Read in the Bible, Matthew 7:24-27. You may dress up in biblical costumes. Decide how you can act out the Bible verses for the worship celebration. Have one member of your group read the verses out loud while the rest of you act out the story. You may use scraps of wood and tools to act out building the two houses if you wish.

Workstation 5 — Witness to the World

GETTING READY

The handprints show that today is the first day of work on the children's church. It takes everyone joining their special talents together. Provide your craft basket and make sure it is well-stocked. Copy and post the following instructions for the children:

> Everyone is important, but often we only think people are important if they are popular. Today we are going to discover something about you.
>
> Take some paper and trace around your hand with a crayon. In the middle of your handprint, write a few words about yourself: you're easy to talk with, kind, forgiving, like to help others, or anything else that comes to mind. Notice that the suggested ideas do not say "prettiest" or "most popular in class." Tape your handprint to your clothes and wear it.

Workstation 6 — Prayer

GETTING READY

The work on the banner represents prayer. The idea is to show the children how much they can accomplish by sewing just one letter or so a Sunday — or in one moment of prayer. This project reminds us that the answers to our prayers are not always immediate. This project is not just for older children; four-year-olds do fine.

Print the Lord's Prayer with a pen across the aida cloth in block letters. Stitch one letter or word to show how it will look. If you do not know how to sew, invite a seamstress in your church to come for a couple of Sundays to help the children. Copy and post the following instructions for the children:

> We are embroidering a Lord's Prayer banner for our church. This is a year-long project. Prayer takes patience. So find a needle and thread and then do a simple stitch on a letter or two. You'll be surprised how much you will get done by doing one letter at a time.

Workstation 7 — Benediction

GETTING READY

Bring along this book (see diagram in Session 3) and some thin cardboard for the children to make a model of a church. This will generate excitement for the actual building of their own church which they will begin next week. Post a sign-up sheet for architects who wish to present their models in today's service, and copy and post the following instructions for the children:

> You are the architects. Look at the plans in *No Experience Necessary!* Either do a drawing or make a stand-up model with the stiff cardboard to show others about the church we are going to build. How many stained glass windows should it have? How large should it be? Show the pictures from the book. Sign up to present your model of the church today for the Benediction.

The Worship Celebration

GETTING READY

Check sign-up sheets. Encourage the children to lead as much as possible, but you will have to help the first few times. Remind your actors to be in costume and ready.

Order of Service

I. Call to Worship — A song by those who signed up.

II. Affirmation — The puppeteers hold up their puppets.

III. Offering — Attach puppets to the top of a sign stand.

IV. Sermon — Read and act out the story. What will be the foundation of the church we are building?

V. Benediction — The architects show their model.

VI. Prayer — Count the number of letters finished on the prayer banner. Close by saying the Lord's Prayer together.

Items to Go Home

Handprints

SESSION 2

LAYING THE FOUNDATION

The Bible Lesson

Jesus told many stories about helping others and sharing kindness. This program puts the children in situations where they have to share, take turns, stop what they are doing to help someone else, and show kindness through their work together. This is what Jesus stressed in Luke 10:25-37.

What the Children Will Learn Today

A church is more than just a building; it's people. Everyone is important, talented, and needed in God's church. Building a church together takes cooperation.

Time Needed

Twenty minutes at the workstations and 10 minutes for worship.

Supplies Needed

1. Workstation signs and supply baskets.
2. Large brown paper grocery bags for everyone.
3. Several copies of the "ME Booklets" or one big poster. (Instructions on page 37.)
4. Wood scraps for collection box (paneling scraps work fine).
5. *Washable* ink pad and old magazines for cutting.
6. Bibles, pencils, extra paper to write on, and a snack.
7. Musical instruments and song book.
8. Craft supply basket: Usual supplies.

WORKSTATIONS

Workstation 1 — Call to Worship

GETTING READY

Provide a selection of a few familiar songs and instruments and post a sign-up sheet for the musicians that want to play today. Copy and post the following instructions for the children:

> Our Call to Worship will be a song of your choice today. Sign the sheet if you want to sing and play in our worship celebration.

Workstations 2 & 5 — Affirmation of Faith and Witness to the World (combined today)

GETTING READY

Help everyone get started. When the older children figure out how to make the "ME Bags," they can help the others. Provide a large brown paper grocery bag for each child in your group and a "ME Booklet" for each team to work from (or large poster for everyone to read). Use the materials in the craft supply basket. Make an example "ME Bag." Copy and post the following instructions for the children:

> You are going to make "ME Bags." They are very easy to make. Decorate your paper sack with each of the answers from the "ME Booklet."

Workstation 3 — Offering

GETTING READY

Follow the plans in the diagram for a simple small wooden church or use a birdhouse kit and add a steeple. This will be your collection container each week. Ask an adult to be the helper, and copy and post the following instructions for the children:

> Today our woodworking shop is going to make a special little church for our offering box. Look at the drawing. Cut as indicated and work with adult help.

If you prefer a simpler project, the children can glue a picture of their proposed church onto a coffee can, then you can cut a slit in the plastic lid (make it wide enough that coins can slide through).

Plan I
Wooden Church Collection Box
(Very Simple)

Step 1: Cut three 5½" x 5½" thin boards or paneling for roof and floor of church.

Step 2: Cut one 4¾" x 4¾" thin board or paneling.

Step 3: Cut the 4¾" board in half following dotted line in drawing. Use a miter box if you have one.

Step 4: Glue church together with wood glue, except for floor of church. Hold pieces together for a few minutes till glue sets.

Step 5: Tape the floor on with duct tape, placing tape on the inside out of sight.

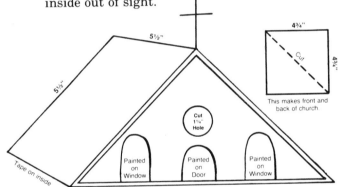

Workstation 4 — Sermon/Bible Lesson

GETTING READY

Post a sign-up sheet for volunteers to act out the story in today's worship. Parts needed are: 1. The Person Who was Robbed, 2. The Priest, 3. The Samaritan, 4. The Robbers, 5. The Levite, and 6. The Innkeeper. Copy and post the following instructions for the children:

Read Luke 10:25-37 out loud. Sign up to play a character. One person may play more than one role. You may dress up in biblical costumes. Practice the story. All acting of biblical stories for our celebrations use only pantomime; therefore, in the fight scene with the robbers, YOU MAY NOT HIT ANYONE, YOU MAY ONLY PRETEND. Think about what Jesus was saying in this story.

Workstation 6 — Prayer

GETTING READY

Copy and post the following instructions for the children:

> Thanks for remembering to stop in the middle of your busy schedule to sew a letter. Praying isn't hard and doesn't take fancy words. We just have to stop and share our feelings with God.

Workstation 7 — Benediction

GETTING READY

Publicity is important and materials are essential. Seek donations for lumber. Be ready with the lumber for next week. Copy and post the following instructions for the children:

> We want to start building next week, and your job is to write a short announcement for our church newsletter to tell what is going on. Include a list of any supplies you still need or request for helpers.

The Worship Celebration

I. Call to Worship — Musicians who signed up play their chosen song.

II. Affirmation/Witness — Ask everyone to model their ME Bags. Have partners tell something special about each other.

III. Offering — Praise the children for their hard work on the church offering container. Tell them they may bring offering money each week to place in the church if they wish and briefly describe how their money will be used.

IV. Sermon — Pantomime the story of The Good Samaritan and discuss what it means for us today.

V. Prayer — Show how many letters have been stitched on the Lord's Prayer banner and then say a prayer of thanksgiving for the children's hard work.

VI. Benediction — Explain that building on the church starts next week. Send the group home with the thought that we should show our love for each other and God by being kind and forgiving, helping others, giving to those in need, and accepting others' ideas.

Items to Go Home

ME Bags

ME BOOKLET
Meet Someone Special

This booklet is about someone very special. There is no one else exactly like this person anywhere in the world. There has never, ever been anyone with the same talents. And no one in the future will be the same. This very special person is *you*.

1. Write your name in a column down the left hand side of the front of your ME Bag. Beside each letter of your name, draw a picture or write words that tell something about you, like this:

   A   Ambitious

   N   Nice

   N   Needs Friends

   You may use your first, middle, or last name.

2. Then find the ink pad and place both thumb prints on the bottom corners of your ME Bag. No one else has the same fingerprints as you!

3. Open your partner's paper bag. Put the bag over your partner's head. With your crayon, gently draw two circles where the eyes should go and draw a line on each side of the bag showing where the shoulder is. Your partner will mark your bag the same way. Cut out the eyes and up the sides of the bag to the shoulder mark. Try your bag on.

4. Draw a mouth on your bag to show how you are feeling.

5. If you could change anything about yourself with a magic wand, write or draw a picture of it.

6. Suppose you were being placed in a make-over machine that would change everything about you but one thing. What one thing would you never want to have changed about yourself? Write or draw this on your bag.

7. Draw on a nose for how honest your answers are: really long for "this is a joke" or short for "this is how I really feel."

8. Complete the Friendship Contract listing what you need from a friend and how you can be a good friend to others. Tape the contract to the back bottom edge of the ME Bag so it will follow you wherever you go.

FRIENDSHIP CONTRACT

I, _____, (Name) agree to do my part to make a new friend or make up with one I haven't been getting along with.

I need _____ from a friend to help me feel important, wanted, and needed.

I agree that every day I will do my best to try to meet the needs of others. I agree to try not to hurt others' feelings and I will do these things to be a good friend to everyone I meet each day: _____.

No matter how long it takes or how many times I have to try, I agree to keep trying to make friends until I am successful.

I will be repaid with the happiness of friendship for my efforts on this _____ _____ of _____ in the year _____.
Day   Month   Year

Signature: _____

CHAPTER FOUR

BUILDING THE CHURCH

The rhythmic sound of hammers and saws that you hear each Sunday are the same sounds that Jesus heard growing up as the son of a carpenter. The children's hands and tools are building more than a project as they work together and learn the value of cooperation and sharing.

SESSION 3

A HUMBLE BEGINNING

The Bible Lesson

Start small (one board at a time) and end up big (the completed church). The mustard seed was used throughout Palestine to describe the smallest of all things (Mark 4:30-32).

What the Children Will Learn Today

This is the first day of building. Make sure you have two adults so both saws can be working full time. The lesson compares building the church to the time and patience of planting a seed.

Time Needed

Twenty minutes for workstations and 10 minutes for worship. (By the end of this chapter, the wooden frame for your children's church is complete and ready to use.)

Supplies Needed

1. Workstation signs and supply baskets.
2. Old magazines for cutting out pictures.
3. Two saws and two adults to work in woodworking station.
4. House plant seeds, potting soil, small plastic containers, small shovels, newspapers for the mess, tray for plants to sit on near a window, and water.
5. Lumber for building the church.
6. Bibles and a snack.
7. Musical instruments and song book.
8. Craft supply basket: Usual supplies.

WORKSTATIONS

Workstation 1 — Call to Worship

GETTING READY

Post a sign-up sheet for the musicians, and post the following instructions for the children:

> Today is a joyous day. We are building our church. Pick a happy song and practice, then sign up if you wish to sing and play in today's celebration.

Workstation 2 — Affirmation of Faith

GETTING READY

The Affirmation gives children a chance to tell their life stories. We need to stop and think about not only the sad but also the good in life. Put out the craft basket and old magazines. Make a sample. The children will enjoy having you tell them something about your own life. Post a sign-up sheet for volunteers to share their pictures and life stories, and copy and post the following instructions for the children:

> Draw pictures, cut out magazine pictures, write, or in some way tell the story of your life from the day you were born until today. Include both happy and sad moments, the places where you have lived, and what you enjoy doing most with your family and friends. Sign the sheet if you would be willing to share your story.

Workstation 3 — Offering

GETTING READY

Copy and post the "Guide Sheet for Building a Church." Leave it hanging up until the church is built. Ask at least two adults to help with the saws. Try to make sure that each child gets a chance to saw today. You will not finish all of the sawing today. Don't worry — while they are waiting for a turn, encourage children to visit other workstations.

Remember, this is a good opportunity to invite carpenters and those handy with building projects to work with the children. Copy and post the following workstation instructions for the children:

> The gift you give to God today is your time and your ability to work with your partner on the church. Take turns and work carefully. Listen to the adults and follow the "Guide Sheet for Building a Church."

GUIDE SHEET FOR BUILDING A CHURCH

Three general rules to follow: (1) Always measure a board twice to make sure you measured correctly, (2) ask an adult to check your work before you saw, and (3) lightly pencil on a piece of masking tape or on each board you cut for the church telling where it belongs (bottom right 72" long or bottom center 46").

Lumber Needed:

a. Lumber, 1" x 2" nominal thickness (measures actually 3/4" thick). These are sold as furring strips, and often go on sale. You need 6 pieces that are 6 feet in length, and 4 pieces that are 8 feet in length.

b. Lumber, 2" x 2" nominal thickness. These are used to add stability to the bottom. The plans call for 3 pieces that are 6 feet in length.

c. 3" hinges. You need four.

d. A box of 1¼" nails. These are short in length so the points won't stick out of the boards.

DIAGRAM OF THE CHURCH

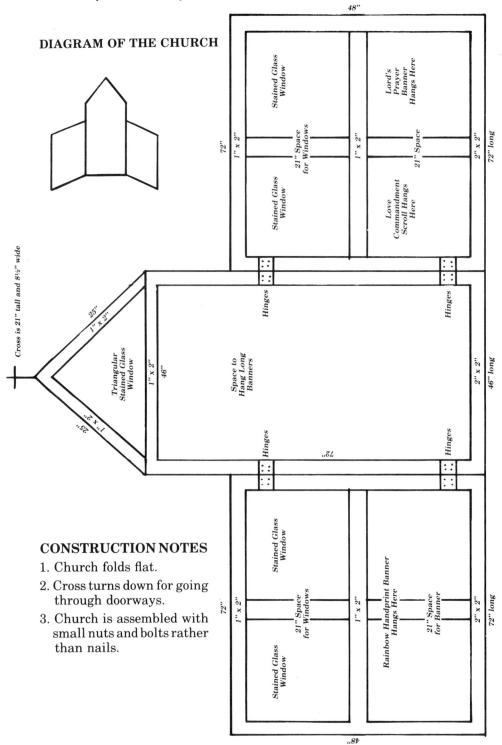

Cross is 21" tall and 8½" wide

CONSTRUCTION NOTES

1. Church folds flat.
2. Cross turns down for going through doorways.
3. Church is assembled with small nuts and bolts rather than nails.

DIAGRAM SHOWING WHERE TO MARK AND CUT BOARDS
(Boards are 3¾" wide by ¼" thick)

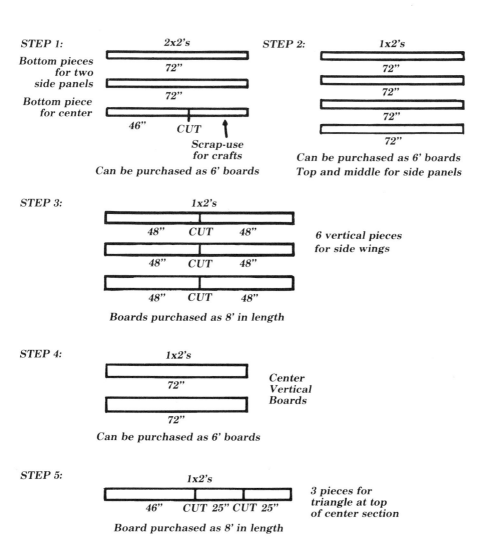

STEP 1:

Bottom pieces for two side panels

Bottom piece for center

2x2's

72"

72"

46"   CUT

Scrap-use for crafts

Can be purchased as 6' boards

STEP 2:

1x2's

72"

72"

72"

72"

Can be purchased as 6' boards
Top and middle for side panels

STEP 3:

1x2's

48"   CUT   48"

48"   CUT   48"

48"   CUT   48"

6 vertical pieces for side wings

Boards purchased as 8' in length

STEP 4:

1x2's

72"

72"

Center Vertical Boards

Can be purchased as 6' boards

STEP 5:

1x2's

46"   CUT 25" CUT 25"

3 pieces for triangle at top of center section

Board purchased as 8' in length

Sawing:

Step 1: Measure and cut two 2" x 2" boards 72" long to go across the bottom. Sometimes you are lucky enough to be able to purchase the exact length you need and won't even have to cut the 72" boards. Measure carefully. Then cut one 2" x 2" board 46" long for the center bottom.

Step 2: Measure and cut (again measure to make sure that you even need to cut the 72" boards) four 1" x 2" boards 72" long for top and middle boards on the side panels. See drawing.

Step 3: Measure and cut six 1" x 2" boards 48" long for each side panel. You now have all of the boards cut for the side panels. Make sure each is properly marked with tape.

Step 4: Measure and cut (if needed) two 1" x 2" boards 72" long for center section of church. Then cut two 1" x 2" boards 25" long for top of church. Mark each piece with tape.

Step 5: Measure and cut one 1" x 2" board 46" long for top.

Save your wood scraps. You will need them at Easter time to make a cross. Mark all boards with tape. You have now finished cutting all of the boards needed to build you children's church. Congratulations!

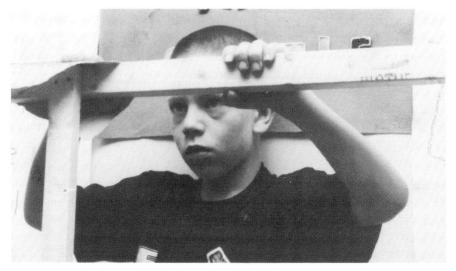

Sanding:

Sand all boards until they are smooth. Do not nail any boards together until they have been sanded completely.

Hammering:

Step 6: Build the church one panel at a time. Start with a side panel. Lay out the top, middle, and bottom 72" side panel boards on the floor. Lay on top the right and left 48" side boards. Use your framing square to make sure all corners are the same. Measure twice before you hammer. Don't worry about fancy corners, just hammer each board down securely. Add a little glue to the corners to make the joints secure. Then, nail on the middle 48" side board to support the middle section of the side panel. Sand all rough spots.

Step 7: Repeat the same process as above for the other side panel.

Step 8: For the center section, measure with framing square and nail together the 72" tall pieces to the 46" bottom board first. Then lay out the triangle for the top. Measure carefully. Nail triangle together first, then connect onto the children's church. Sand any rough spots that remain. Your church is together. Congratulations to all workers!

Step 9: Attaching the hinges will depend somewhat on the type of hinges you secured. But before you attach the hinges, stand the church up with adult help and test out the placement of your hinges. Make sure the church will fold up. Lay the church back on the floor.

Step 10: Attach one hinge according to the package directions and then stand the church up again and test for accuracy before attaching the remaining hinges. If you happen to make a mistake don't worry. Take the hinge off. Attach it correctly. Then you can fill any holes with wood putty before you paint. Stand up your church and rejoice! You have completed the children's church. The next step is painting it.

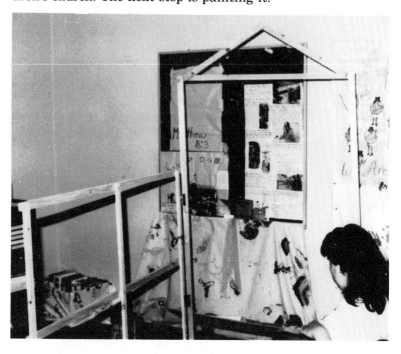

Workstation 4 — Sermon/Bible Lesson

GETTING READY

Today's Bible story is short. Ask questions: What does the story have to do with building a church? Post a sign-up sheet for actors to read and pantomime the Bible verse today.

Include a few craft supplies at this station in case the children want to make paper plate masks today. Copy and post the following instructions for the children:

> Have one of your group read the Bible verse (Mark 4:30-32) out loud so everyone can hear while the rest of you act out the story. Dress up in costumes or even make masks out of paper plates for the birds to wear. Someone can pretend to be the seed that slowly grows into a big tree while the rest are birds fluttering around. The mustard seed starts small but ends up sometimes seven or eight feet tall: a giant among the herbs.

Workstations 5 and 7 — Witness to the World and Benediction

GETTING READY

Occasionally workstations will be combined, particularly when extra space or time is needed for a particular station.

Planting seeds is a popular activity with children. Use flower seeds or even bulbs. Help the children realize how long it takes to grow something from a seed or bulb. Remind them of the care that the young plant needs. Tell them that when the plant grows up, they will be able to give it as a gift to someone who is ill or a shut-in. Children feel very important when they get a chance to do grown-up activities. Copy and post the following instructions for the children:

> We are planting seeds today. We will take care of these seeds until they are large plants to give to someone who is sick or unable to come to church on Sunday. Fill a plastic container carefully with dirt. Press two seeds gently into the dirt till the tip of your fingernail touches the dirt — that's not very far. Water gently with the watering can and then set your container on the tray. Water your plant every week.

Workstation 6 — Prayer

GETTING READY

Copy and post the following instructions for the children:

> Thanks for stopping to work on the Lord's Prayer banner. Prayer, just like this banner, takes patience. Find a needle and thread and do an outline stitch on a letter or two. Count how many letters have been done so far.

The Worship Celebration

I. Call to Worship — A song played by those who signed up.

II. Affirmation — Have those who signed the sheet show and tell one or two items from their life stories as time permits.

III. Offering — Count how many boards were cut and sanded.

IV. Sermon — Encourage the children who signed up to read and act out the story. What does the story mean?

V. Prayer — Praise the work done on the prayer banner. Count the number of letters. Say the Lord's Prayer together.

VI. Benediction — Close with a happy song.

Items to Go Home

Life stories

SESSION 4

THE GIFT WE GIVE TODAY

The Bible Lesson

Children have trouble understanding why they should give an offering. This session teaches about the gifts we offer God (1 Peter 4:10).

What the Children Will Learn Today

Tell the story, "The Best Gift Is You." The shaving cream helps the children visualize change. Afterwards, use shaving cream to clean the tables. The children love it.

Time Needed

Twenty minutes at workstations and 10 minutes for the worship service including five minutes for the story.

Supplies Needed

1. Workstation signs and supply baskets.
2. Lots of sandpaper.
3. Cassette player with religious sing-along tapes.
4. Two hand saws and an adult to manage each.
5. Cardboard for making hand mirrors, aluminum foil.
6. One can each of shaving cream (foam) and shaving gel.
7. Wood and woodworking basket for building the church.
8. Bibles and a snack.
9. Craft supply basket: Usual supplies.

WORKSTATIONS

Workstations 1 and 2 — Call to Worship and Affirmation

GETTING READY

The Call to Worship and Affirmation are combined. Have everyone work together in teams, sing along to the music, and enjoy being together. Fellowship is important in any church. Copy and post the following instructions for the children:

The job today is to get all of the wood sanded smooth. Sometimes doing the job right takes commitment — the willingness to stay with a task till it is finished. Play the tape and sing along as you work.

Workstations 3 and 4 — Offering and Sermon

GETTING READY

You will be tempted to bring more saws so the work can go faster, but unless you have adults to supervise each saw, I would advise against it. Some of the main lessons to learn from building the church are sharing, compromise, and the needs of others. Copy and post the following instructions for the children:

We are continuing where we left off last week in the woodworking shop. Work with a partner. Follow the Guide Sheet in Session 3.

Workstation 6 — Prayer

GETTING READY

Copy and post the following instructions for the children:

Thanks for remembering to stop in the middle of your busy schedule to sew a letter this morning.

Workstations 7 and 5 —
Benediction and Witness

GETTING READY

Gather the craft basket, cardboard, foil, and an example of the mirror. You might also want to provide an actual hand-held mirror for the children to trace around. Copy and post the following instructions for the children:

> You are a very special person. Take a piece of foil and a piece of cardboard. Cut your cardboard into the shape of a mirror. Follow the example or trace around the real mirror or make up your own design. Cut and glue the foil to fit your mirror. Read: 1 Peter 4:10.
>
> On your mirror write or draw a picture of at least three reasons that you are very special. If you can't for some reason think of any reasons, ask a friend to help because you are indeed a very special person.

The Worship Celebration

I. Offering — Start the offering collection by placing money in the church. Ask the children why they bring money each Sunday.

II. Sermon — Read the following story, "The Best Gift Is You," or tell it in your own words. The children love the sound and excitement of watching the shaving cream. Use a big tray. Place a mound of shaving cream on the tray to represent the money being placed in the church in the story — tall mountain for the dollar bill, small circle for the nickels shared, or whatever you can create. Then use the shaving gel to show how Joey felt.

III. Benediction and Witness — Encourage everybody to tell about their mirrors. Add something positive to each person's list on their mirrors. Send the group home with the thought that everyone is special.

Items to Go Home

"I'm a Special Person" Mirror

The Best Gift Is You

The children cheered as each coin was dropped into the small wooden church Sunday morning. They were saving every penny from now till spring to see how many baby chicks they could buy to send to needy farmers in other countries. It was all part of the world service mission project at their church. They already had the money to buy six and they could hardly wait to count the money each Sunday to see how many more would be added.

As the little wooden church was passed around the circle, the children were counting. Everyone clapped and cheered. One child even put in a whole dollar bill. *(Squirt large mound of shaving cream for dollar bill.)* Little Molly said she forgot her money and looked as if she might start to cry, but Lucy quickly reached over and gave Molly one of her nickels. *(Make a small dot for the nickel.)* Molly beamed with pride as the nickel jingled inside the church.

The excitement grew and grew until the wooden church with its steeple standing tall and proud on top came to Joey. Joey just sat there for a minute. He didn't have any money to put in the church. Joey's family was having a hard time right now. Joey's dad had been out of work for almost six months. Joey's mom was due to have another baby any day now, and there just wasn't enough money to go around. Joey felt embarrassed as he sat there fumbling the church back and forth in his hands. He wished he could just melt. *(Plop down some gel to show Joey's feelings.)* Finally, quick as a flash, he thrust the church into the hands of the child sitting next to him and sort of slithered down into his chair. *(Slither more gel here to emphasize Joey's feelings.)*

The children all sat in complete silence. Finally, Ted spoke up and said, "Hey everybody, remember how we said this was going to be a group project and it didn't matter how much you were or were not able to bring each Sunday? Because in the church a penny has the same value as a dollar bill. *(Make two equal sized mounds.)*

And Judy chimed in, "There are many ways to give. For some of us it's easy to say, 'Dad, may I have some money for church?' Or Mom says, 'Here's your quarter. Now be sure you put it in the offering this morning.'

"But Joey, you're the best when it comes to sawing, hammering, and building our church. Why, if it wasn't for you, I would have never gotten that board sawed this morning." *(Slowly start to rub the gel representing Joey and make it begin to foam.)*

The teacher got all excited and said, "God doesn't want us just to bring money to church. God wants us to bring and give ourselves and our talents — that one special thing you can do better than anyone else. If you give money just because it's easy, then it has no meaning. Like when

Jesus said that the woman who dropped in two copper coins worth about a penny actually gave more than all the money the rich people gave because she gave all of what little she had.

"So your gift may be your special ability to draw, to hammer a nail straight, to sing or play an instrument, to share a kind word or a smile, to be a friend to someone who seems to have no friends at all, to seek out and include someone who is feeling lost or left out, to be here every Sunday to help out where you are needed. When you give of yourself, it has more meaning.

"It's true," the teacher went on, "that we need money to reach our mission goal. But we also need kindness and to care about each other's feelings. *(As you talk, work the gel faster to make it lather up into a peak to show Joey feeling more important.)* It builds us up! If you show kindness to others, then kindness will return to you. If you're grumpy and only concerned with what you want and how you feel, then you'll most likely only receive grumpiness from others. If you keep giving kindness without expecting it in return, when you least expect it, you'll find that kindness coming back to you. *(Now stack the shaving foam and add it to Joey's gel until it is as tall as possible and bends over to touch one of the little dots of shaving cream beside it.)*

The teacher told them, "We give a little bit of ourselves each Sunday as we work and build our church together — cooperating, taking turns and sharing; it's our offering to God. So make your offering the best you can give, *(Make loops with the shaving foam to connect all of the dots into one big circle)* not by how much money you bring, but by what you give to others."

SESSION 5

ARE YOU LISTENING?

The Bible Lesson

Today the children will be acting out a very long but important Bible story, Matthew 13:3-8 and 18-23. You will either need two sets of actors or the children will need to play two roles.

Part I, Matthew 13:3-8, is the parable of the Sower and the Seed. Part II, Matthew 13:18-23, explains the importance of listening and applying what you hear.

What the Children Will Learn Today

Continue building the church. The children will also learn from the Bible the importance of listening and will be challenged to think about possible changes in their daily behavior or actions.

Time Needed

Twenty minutes for workstations and 10 minutes for worship.

Supplies Needed

1. Sing-along tapes.
2. Bibles and simple biblical costumes if desired.
3. A snack, pencils, and extra paper.
4. Woodworking basket.
5. Wood as needed for your church.
6. Workstation signs and instructions.
7. Craft supply basket: Usual supplies.

WORKSTATIONS

Workstations 1 and 2 — Call to Worship and Affirmation

GETTING READY

Copy and post the following instructions for the children:

It is not always easy to be a Christian. Often, we are asked to do tasks as Christians which may not seem very exciting but have to be done just the same. Sing along with the music as you work. Always do your best work, even though sanding can be a very boring task.

Workstation 3 — Offering

GETTING READY

Copy and post the following instructions for the children:

Start where you left off on the church last week. Listen to the adult leaders. Work safely.

Workstation 4 — Sermon/Bible Lesson

GETTING READY

Have the children pantomime the Bible story. Ask what the story means for us today. You may have to help more than usual. Post a sign-up sheet for today's celebration with these roles:

Part I: (Matthew 13:3-8) The farmer who plants the seeds, the seed that gets carried away by the birds, the birds, the seed that sprouted in the shallow soil, the hot sunshine, the seed in the thorn bushes, the thorn bushes, or the seed in the good soil.

Part II: (Matthew 13:18-23) Those who do not understand, the "Evil One," those who hear but it doesn't sink in, trouble and persecution, those concerned with making money and the worries of the world, or those who hear the message and understand.

Copy and post the following instructions for the children:

The Sermon today is one of action and talks about how we live as Christians: Matthew 12:3-8 and 18-23. Read out loud.

Part I: Farmers in biblical times took handfuls of seed and just threw them around everywhere on the ground. This was risky for several reasons: the ground of the paths where everyone walked was so hard that nothing could grow, some of the seeds were eaten by the birds, and there have always been weeds. But it was worth the risk because some of the seed would fall in the good soil and grow and produce a crop.

Part II: The different kinds of soil stand for the different ways we live. The hard soil is like those who do not want to understand.

The shallow soil is like those who listen, but when the going gets tough, they give up or leave. The thorny ground stands for people who are so busy making and spending money that they don't have the time to be kind or helpful to others. The good soil represents those who listen and understand. Your pantomime could describe a modern setting — like at your school.

Workstations 5 and 7 — Witness to the World and Benediction

GETTING READY

Provide an example of the "changes" list for the children to follow. Post a sign-up sheet for volunteers to share what they would and would not change, and copy and post the following instructions for the children:

We are going to be given the rare chance to change anything about ourselves that we would like to change — from the color or length of our hair to the way we act or talk.

On a piece of paper, list on the left all the things that you want to have stay the same as they are right now. On the right, list the things you would like to change about yourself, such as how you act when you're angry, how tall you are, or the number of friends you have.

Do Not Change	Changes to Be Made

At the bottom of your paper, draw a picture and/or describe the kind of person you would be after the changes you listed. Tell how you would act and what you would do differently.

Workstation 6 — Prayer

GETTING READY

Copy and post the following instructions for the children:

> We are still embroidering the Lord's Prayer banner. Prayer takes patience. Stitch a letter today.

The Worship Celebration

I. Sermon — Encourage those who signed up to read and act out the Bible story.

II. Prayer and Offering — Praise and count the number of letters finished and talk about your work on the church so far.

III. Witness to the World and Benediction — Close by everyone sharing changes and things they would not change about themselves.

Items to Go Home

Do Not Change and Changes to Be Made lists

SESSION 6

THE CHURCH IS MADE OF MANY PARTS

The Bible Lesson

One of the main lessons to be taught by using hammers, saws, and building projects is the importance of sharing, working together, and thinking about others. This teaches the children how to live a Christian way of life (1 Timothy 6:18-19).

What the Children Will Learn Today

The church is made up of many people, each playing a very important role, and no one person is more important than any other in God's world.

Time Needed

Twenty-five minutes for workstations today and five minutes for worship.

Supples Needed

1. Wood and woodworking basket (include a framing square).
2. Bibles and a snack.
3. Tacky glue for banners.
4. Workstation signs and instructions.
5. Sing-along tapes.
6. Craft supply basket: Usual supplies — be sure to have green construction paper.
7. Alleluia banner supplies — white cloth about 50" x 35" (you may use felt, an old sheet, etc.); glitter.
8. Liturgical green banner supplies: 74" x 35" piece of green felt or green paper, white or gold felt or paper (small amount for symbol).

WORKSTATIONS

Workstations 1 and 2 — Call to Worship and Affirmation

GETTING READY

Have a 74" x 35" green felt or paper banner with white or gold for the symbol. Make pattern or have the children draw one. Copy and post the following instructions for the children:

> We want to have a green banner to hang in our church. Green is a liturgical color used in the church to remind us to study and learn all we can about God. This special time set aside each year for studying the Bible usually occurs during the fall season. You may see the color used in the sanctuary.
>
> A symbol often found in the church is IHS. The early church used the first three Greek letters of Jesus' name to remind early Christians of Jesus and his teachings.
>
> To make the banner, first get a piece of white or gold felt or paper and draw the letters I, H, S on top. Then cut out the letters and glue them onto the bottom of the green banner. It should look something like this: (See Illustration right.)
>
>
>
> *Green Liturgical Banner*
>
> After you finish, make a green bookmark out of paper or scraps for your Bible. Write on your bookmark in your own words why we use the color green in the church. Decorate your bookmark any way you like using the craft basket.

Workstation 3 — Offering

GETTING READY

Try to finish all of the sawing today if possible. Copy and post the following instructions for the children:

> Check the list and make sure that you have cut all of the boards needed for the church. Then check each board to make sure it has been sanded smooth.

Workstations 4 and 5 — Sermon/Bible Lesson and Witness

GETTING READY

Today should be just about the end of the sawing. What better way to start a worship service than to begin putting all of the pieces together? Again have music playing while you work. Post a sign-up sheet for a reader to present 1 Timothy 6:18,19 today. Be sure to have an adult working with each saw and hammer.

Help the children nail the boards together following the plans. Work on one section at a time. Put at least two nails into each joint. An adult should help the children use a framing square to make sure that all of the walls are square and straight; otherwise the church won't stand up properly. A bit of white glue in the joints before you nail will make more permanent joints. But there's no need for fancy joints; just overlap the corners of the boards and hammer away. Copy and post the following instructions for the children:

> We are about to start putting our church together. Read 1 Timothy 6:18-19. Read the step-by-step Guide Sheet, but do not hammer until your adult leader says to. Reread the safety rules. And always remember: hammer twice, then give someone else a turn.

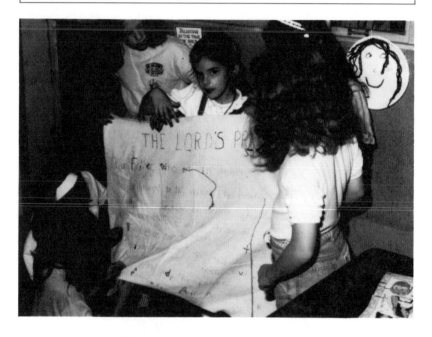

Workstation 6 — Prayer

GETTING READY

Copy and post the following message for the children:

> Don't give up on prayer; keep sewing!

Workstation 7 — Benediction

GETTING READY

You can make banners out of any white fabric. Ask for donations. Keep this banner handy; you will use it often. Copy and post the following instructions for the children:

The Benediction today is a statement of praise: Alleluia! The word alleluia means "Praise God!" in Hebrew and is used often in church services at times of joy, happiness, and celebration. You are going to make a banner today to hang in your new church when complete. Make your banner white with gold letters. White is the color used at times of celebration in the church. Use the materials provided. Measure, mark, and cut your banner into an upside-down triangle shape. It will hang over the green liturgical banner. The lettering can be done very simply by using a pencil to write "Allelulia" down the banner, then going over the letters with glue and glitter. If you use glue and glitter make sure that the banner is completely dry before you hang it. See drawing.

Green Liturgical Banner with Alleluia

The Worship Celebration

I. Sermon — Read and discuss Bible verse.

II. Prayer — Announce how many letters have been sewn on prayer banner and close with the Lord's Prayer.

Items to Go Home

Bible bookmarks

SESSION 7

COMING TOGETHER

The Bible Lesson

We should try to say something positive to another member of the church every time we meet. Unfortunately, positive feelings do not always come out as readily as negative ones. The Bible lesson gives guidelines to follow: Colossians 3:12-17.

What the Children Will Learn Today

Today's lesson is to give everyone an opportunity to share some of their positive ideas and feelings.

Time Needed

Twenty minutes for workstations and 10 minutes for worship today.

Supplies Needed

1. Wood and woodworking basket: 2 hammers, nails, hand drill (no power tools), lots of sandpaper, hinges, screwdriver, and framing square.
2. Bibles, pencils, extra paper, and a snack.
3. Workstation signs and instructions.
4. Musical instruments and song book.
5. Craft supply basket: Usual supplies, plus rulers and yellow construction paper.

WORKSTATIONS

Workstation 1 — Call to Worship

GETTING READY

Post a sign-up sheet for the musicians who want to play in today's worship celebration, and copy and post the following instructions for the children:

> Select a song of friendship for today. Play instruments and have everyone sing along.

Workstations 2 and 4 —
Affirmation of Faith and Sermon

GETTING READY

Copy and post the following instructions for the children:

> Read Colossians 3:12-17. Then write down or draw a picture about a mistake you made with a friend one time and the lesson you learned from your mistake. You do not have to tell anyone about your mistake. Fold your paper and put your mistake in your pocket. Your mistake is just between you and God. Sometime this week, think of a way to correct the wrong you did or at least say "I'm sorry."

Workstation 3 — Offering

GETTING READY

Work on one section at a time. Put at least two nails into each joint. Use a framing square to make sure that all of the walls are square and straight; otherwise the church won't stand up properly. Put glue in the joints before you nail. Then, just overlap the corners of the boards and hammer away. Copy and post the following instructions for the children:

> Today you continue last week's work. Remember that our task is more than just having fun. Working together to build a church is our way of giving a gift. To offer a gift to God is a way of saying thank you for all that he has given us. To use our hands to make that gift has just as much meaning as to drop coins in the collection box. Listen to your adult leader. Do not nail until told to.

Workstations 5 and 7 —
Witness to the World and Benediction

GETTING READY

Photocopy the example or have the young people draw their own suns on yellow paper. Have masking tape on hand. Copy and post the instructions on page 66 for the children:

Sometimes the look we put on our faces can make us feel happy or sad. Look for people and things that make you happy. Try to make others happy. Don't hide from the problems you have, but don't let them take over your life.

Find a partner. Draw a smiling sun with lines for rays. On the lines, write several things you like about your partner. Write down why it is nice to have your partner for a friend. You may only write nice happy thoughts. Then tape your sun on your partner's clothing for all to see. Be prepared to share one thing you wrote during worship today. Everyone will share during today's celebration.

Workstation 6 — Prayer

GETTING READY

Copy and post the following message for the children:

Thanks for not forgetting today.

The Worship Celebration

Each week, give the children a little more responsibility in leading their own Worship Celebration.

I. Call to Worship — A celebration song the musicians have prepared. Everyone sings along.

II. Offering — Emphasize that today's offering is not only the monetary offering they placed in the collection box church, but it is also the church that they are making with their own hands.

III. Prayer — Show how many letters have been stitched and hang the prayer banner on one of the side panels in the church if you can.

IV. Witness and Benediction — Ask everyone to share one positive statement about their partner.

Items to Go Home

Sunshine bags and friendship forgiveness notes

SESSION 8

WE ARE ONE

The Bible Lesson

It's wonderful to have friends and be friends with other people, but what happens when you don't seem to be able to make friends or you lose a friend? Loss can range from the tragedy of death or the seeming unfairness of having them move away to the everyday cruelty of hearing "I don't want to be your friend anymore." Today's Bible verse is Proverbs 18:24.

What the Children Will Learn Today

The children will define friendship and their anger and pain at losing friends, and then they should explore how they can mend broken friendships or establish new friendships.

Time Needed

Twenty minutes for workstations and 10 minutes for worship today.

Supplies Needed

1. Wood and woodworking basket.
2. Bibles and a snack.
3. Workstation signs and instructions.
4. Musical instruments and song book.
5. Craft supply basket: Usual supplies plus circle patterns.
6. Stars or star patterns large enough to write on, Friendship Star Sheet on a big piece of newsprint, paper tube.

WORKSTATIONS

Workstation 1 — Call to Worship

GETTING READY

Post a sign-up sheet for the musicians for today's celebration, and copy and post the following instructions for the children:

> Pick a happy song so that everyone can clap their hands and sing along.

Workstation 2 — Affirmation of Faith

GETTING READY

Make a Friendship Star Chart from a long sheet of newsprint or several sheets of newsprint taped together. Copy the graph and provide a sample star (illustration 8). Get a big wrapping paper tube and write "Lost Friend Capsule" on it. You will put the Star Sheet inside it during the worship service. Post a sign-up sheet for volunteers to pantomime their angry feelings during worship today, and copy and post the following instructions for the children:

I'm Angry...

> Has anyone ever said to you: "You're not my friend anymore" or "You can't be in our group"? Have you ever lost a friend after an argument or had your best friend move away? Or did you ever know someone who died? How did it make you feel?
>
> Use the pattern or make your own star on yellow construction paper. Write your angry feelings and what happened to you down on your star. Place it on the Star Chart measuring your anger: from ferocious like a bellowing lion to sad like a sailboat drifting out into the ocean. Sadness is a kind of anger too; it's just not being acted out right now.
>
> If you would be willing to show us just how angry you are during our "Time Capsule" portion of worship today, sign the sheet.

FRIENDSHIP STAR CHART

Place stars on the column that
most clearly describe your feelings.

Ferocious like a bellowing lion ★

So angry you want to stomp your feet

So mad you slammed the door

So mad you refuse to talk to anyone

Never talk to that person again

Mad but you go over and talk anyway

Angry but forgive them after a few minutes ★

Looking for a new friend ★

Feeling like no one likes you

Needing help

All confused ★

Feeling lost and lonely

Quiet and looking for a place to hide

Sad as a sailboat drifting out to the ocean ★

Workstation 3 — Offering

GETTING READY

Copy and post the following instructions for the children:

Continue working on the church. We're close to being finished!

Workstation 4 — Sermon/Bible Lesson

GETTING READY

Copy and post the following instructions for the children:

> The church is like a family that helps each other. Sort of like in music, each note has a special place and job to do. No one is ever left out.
>
> You may be tired of hearing others in your neighborhood or at school say, "we don't want you on our team." In God's church, no one can ever say, "we don't want you," "you're not welcome here," "get out," "we don't like you," or "go away and leave us alone." God wants and needs everyone in his church, and your children's church is no different. Even if you don't look, think, feel, or even act the same way others do, you are still welcome in God's church. Read Proverbs 18:24. Look around and find someone in our group whom you have mistreated. Maybe you have been unkind or rude toward this person and caused his or her feelings to be hurt. Go over and say you are sorry and think of a way that the two of you might start being better friends. Think of at least two things you really like about this person. If you look hard enough, you can think of something nice to say even about someone you don't really like. Everyone has a good side. So go on, try it!

Workstations 5 and 7 —
Witness to the World and Benediction

GETTING READY

Set out the craft supply basket and objects to draw around for circles (glasses, jar lids, cookie cutters, etc.). Also provide a sample (see illustration). Copy and post the following instructions for the children:

> Cut out a circle. Draw a smiling face on one side, then flip it over and draw a sad face on the other side. On the smiling side, write something that really makes you happy. On the sad side, write something that really makes you sad. Tape on your face, showing the smile or frown to tell us how you feel right now.

Workstation 6 — Prayer

GETTING READY

Copy and post the following message for the children:

> Once you figure out how it is done, prayer is sort of like embroidery; it's not hard at all. It just takes practice. Sit quietly and share your thoughts with God as you sew today.

The Worship Celebration

I. Call to Worship — Be happy and sing together.

II. Affirmation of Faith — Emphasize that we are not always happy. Have those who signed up to pantomime their feelings come forward. Remind them that pantomime does not involve any violence or contact, just gestures and motion. See if others can guess what feeling is being expressed. When everyone has expressed their feelings, anger, and pain over losing friends, roll up the star sheet and place it in the Lost Friend Time Capsule that you made before the meeting. Pretend to time warp it into the past by sliding it into the corner. Explain that we can't change the past but we can change the future, so on we go to the future.

III. Witness to the World — Have group members tell one thing that turns their frowns into smiles when they are sad.

IV. Prayer/Benediction — Close with happy thoughts and a prayer.

Items to Go Home

Smile faces

SESSION 9

PATIENCE AND LOVE

The Bible Lesson

The frame of the children's church will be completed today. In the following weeks, the children will add windows and banner walls to the church until it is filled with the children's beautiful work. The Bible lesson talks about Jesus as a leader and compares Jesus' struggle to be accepted by the people of his day with the problems people face when they try to fit in with groups today.

What the Children Will Learn Today

The church is made up of many people, each playing an important role. No one person is more important than any other in God's world. Today you begin to teach some of the duties the church should fulfill (Matthew 25:31-40 and 45).

Time Needed

Twenty minutes at workstations and 10 minutes for worship.

Supplies Needed

1. Workstation signs and supply baskets.
2. Church.
3. Bibles and simple biblical costumes if desired.
4. Extra paper, pencils, and ingredients for a simple snack.
5. Musical instruments and song book.
6. Woodworking basket: 2 hammers, nails, hand drills (no power tools), screwdrivers if needed, lots of sandpaper, hinges, framing square, and nails.
7. Craft supply basket: Usual supplies plus newsprint.

WORKSTATIONS

Workstation 1 — Call to Worship

GETTING READY

Post a sign-up sheet for the musicians who want to play in today's service, and copy and post the following instructions for the children:

Today your musical invitation will include everyone. Pick a song that everyone can sing. Also, make simple badges to pass out to everyone during the call to worship, saying: "I'm a Builder in God's Church." You can use the blank name tag stickers in the craft supply basket.

Workstation 2 — Affirmation of Faith

GETTING READY

Provide paper and markers or crayons. Post a sign-up sheet for volunteers to act out the story or to hold up a sign in the church as the Bible verses are read, and copy and post the following instructions for the children:

The word *sanctuary* refers to a safe place to gather and worship God, but we do more than just sit in the sanctuary and sing songs and read Bible verses. As our church is completed, we want to discover why we have a church, what its purpose is, and what it is supposed to do. Jesus gave very specific instructions. First, read: Matthew 25:31-40 and 45, then make signs to illustrate each way of helping others discussed in the Bible passages: (1) "I was hungry and you fed me . . ." — make a sign showing hungry people of the world being given food, (2) "thirsty and you gave me a drink . . ." — make a sign showing new water wells being drilled, (3) "I was a stranger and you received me in your home . . ." — make a sign showing blankets, beds, and shelters being set up in a school gymnasium after a bad tornado or hurricane, (4) "naked and you clothed me . . ." — make a sign of someone taking a bag of clothes to a family after a fire, (5) "I was sick and you took care of me . . ." — make a sign showing someone being taken to a hospital, (6) "in prison and you visited me" — make a sign showing people packing coffee cans filled with cookies to be taken as presents to a local prison.

Save the signs made by the children so that they can be hung in the church for Thanksgiving.

Workstation 3 — Offering

GETTING READY

An adult should install the hinges so that the church will fold. The children can help screw in the screws once they are started accurately. Copy and post the following instructions for the children:

Today our woodworking shop is going to finish putting the church together. Continue your work from last week and have the church ready to stand in your worship area for today's worship celebration. Listen to your adult helper so your work can go faster.

Workstation 4 — Sermon/Bible Lesson

GETTING READY

Provide the Bible verses and questions at the workstation. Post a sign-up sheet for volunteers to share their answers during worship, and copy and post the following instructions for the children:

Teachers and parents say, "Don't give in to what the group is doing just because they want you to," "think for yourself," or, "make your own decisions on what is right or wrong." You have probably complained that if you don't do what the rest of the group wants, then they won't be friends with you anymore. Jesus faced the same problems. He had to decide what was right or wrong and how to stand up to group pressure. Read the Bible verses: Matthew 12:1-8, Matthew 23:24 and 28, Matthew 24:9-14, Matthew 22:15-22, Luke 22:1-2, and John 11:53-54. Read first and then answer the questions. Write your answers down and be ready to share them during worship.

(1) How did Jesus act toward the accepted religious leaders (Pharisees) of his time?

(2) Was Jesus a group leader?

(3) (Choose one) Was there peer pressure to be a part of Jesus' group or to stay away from Jesus' group?

Workstation 5 — Witness to the World

GETTING READY

The children will enjoy making their own snack. Select a very simple recipe that only needs to be mixed. Or you may choose to serve a biblical snack of fruits, goat cheese, and bread. The children can arrange the snack on a tray. Post a sign-up sheet for helpers to serve the snack today, and copy and post the instructions on page 76 for the children:

You are in charge of making the snack today. There is no cooking involved. Just read the recipe and follow the directions. Make sure you count correctly so that everyone will have a piece. Present your snack during the worship celebration.

Workstation 6 — Prayer

GETTING READY

Copy the post the following message for the children:

Thanks for remembering to sew today.

Workstation 7 — Benediction

GETTING READY

Set out newsprint for the group to write on. Post a sign-up sheet for someone to read the list of problems during worship today, and copy and post the following instructions for the children:

"You can't be a member of our group. You don't dress right. And besides, you never want to do the things we want to do." Do conversations like these sound familiar to you? If you think about it for a minute, you might be able to imagine the Pharisees saying something similar to Jesus. The Pharisees were the strict religious leaders (the ones in charge) of Judaism at that time. You may also be able to think of some experiences of your own in which groups at school or in your neighborhood left you out because you wouldn't be just like everybody else in the group. Read Luke 11:37-46 and 53-54. Make a list of problems you face at school and in your neighborhood each day.

The Worship Celebration

I. Call to Worship — Sing the song together and pass out badges.

II. Affirmation of Faith — Read Matthew 24:31-40 and 45 and act out or show pictures.

III. Sermon — Give answers to questions from the Bible verses.

IV. Benediction and Prayer — Give a suggestion on how to solve each one. Then pray, asking for God's help with the problems.

Items to Go Home

"I'm a Builder in God's Church" badges

SESSION 10

THE OUTER COVERING

The Bible Lesson

The story shares the same message as the Bible verse: Be the best you can be (2 Thessalonians 2:16-17).

What the Children Will Learn Today

Your group will be unusual indeed if everyone does not want to help paint the church. Divide up into teams to paint the front and back of the church. Paint the top last while others are cleaning up for the story and snack today. Five minute story.

Supplies Needed

1. Paint and paintbrushes.
2. Painting smocks.
3. A snack during the story.
4. Newspapers and church to be painted.
5. A sticker, pencil, or badge which says the children are a part of God's church.

WORKSTATIONS

Stations 1 through 5 are combined today to paint the church.

GETTING READY

Have a painter's cloth or papers down to catch any spills or excess. Use a paint that easily washes off of hands and clothes.

Have extra-large, long-sleeved old shirts or other cover-ups for all painters. Make sure that every painter's clothing is completely covered. If you do not have enough old shirts, you can use your biblical costumes made from old sheets.

Make sure that at least one adult is helping at this station at all times today. Limit your paintbrushes to four or five per side of panel. Rotate painters if necessary so that everyone gets a chance. Have children clean up before going to the snack and story.

Workstation 6 — Prayer

GETTING READY

Copy and post the following instructions for the children:

> When you are tired of painting, read 2 Thessalonians 2:16-17. Then sew a letter or two today.

The Worship Celebration

Read or tell the story "The Sun Up the Mountain." Have everyone help with sound effects.

The Sun Up the Mountain

Who knows what a make-believe story is? *(Pause for answers.)* That's right. The story I want to tell you today is make-believe but it has an important lesson. But in order for me to tell this story, you're going to have to help me. Do you think you can help? *(Pause)* Good! Now what I need you to do is, everyone on this side — stomp your feet every time I say "mountain" and everyone on this side is going to groan every time I say "push." Are you ready? Let's go.

Once upon a time, there was a mountain. Now around this mountain, there were little mountains, some middle-sized mountains, and then the one BIG mountain. The mountain was bigger than all of the other mountains. At the bottom of this mountain was a village with lots of little houses scattered all around. In each house, there lived a person. Some of the people were tall and strong, some were short and small but each person had very special skills. One person was very good at lifting, one was very good at rolling things, and some were even good at climbing.

Each day two people were matched together to do a very important job. Everyone took a turn and everyone knew when it was their turn without even being told. Their job was to PUSH the SUN up the MOUNTAIN. Now this may not seem very important to you, because we just take the sun for granted, but in this village, if someone didn't push the sun up the mountain there wouldn't be any sunlight — it would stay dark all the time. So you can see why it was very important in this village to push the sun up the mountain each day. So day after day, everyone took their turn to push the sun up the mountain.

Well, one day someone forgot. Yes, that's right. Instead of waking up to beautiful sunshine and happiness, the villagers got up, looked around, and saw that the sky was still dark. "Where is the sun?" they asked. "Whose turn was it to push the sun up the mountain?" "Not mine, not mine." The shouts were heard: "My turn is on Tuesday." "I'm on Wednesday. Someone else said, "Well, who will do it today? Who will push the sun up the mountain?" No one answered. *(Pause)* It was quiet all around the village. No one volunteered. Finally, a little voice was heard 'way in the back: "Uh, uh, I — I — I will, or at least I'll try." Everyone stared. It was a little girl. Then they laughed. "You can't push that sun up the mountain; you're too little." "I could if you helped me," she said. But no one answered. "It's not my turn," said a voice in the corner. So the little girl went off all by herself to push the sun up the mountain.

She pushed and she pushed and she pushed but the sun barely budged. "Maybe they're right, maybe I can't do it," she said. "But I can't give up; I'll try again." So she pushed and she pushed and she pushed, and slowly, ever so slowly, the sun started to roll up the mountain. So she pushed and pushed more.

Hooray! At last she had made it. At last the sun was in place and golden light shone on the little village. It wasn't dark anymore! Somehow the little girl had succeeded when she or no one else thought she could just because she had dared to try and try and try again.

So what's the lesson? *(Pause for answers.)* Never think you're too small, never give up, just try, try, try again. And don't be discouraged when others laugh and tease, but do what you know is best and needs to be done. So take that lesson out with you and tell everyone: NEVER GIVE UP. BE THE BEST THAT YOU CAN BE.

Items to Go Home

A sticker, pencil, or badge which says the children are a part of God's church.

CHAPTER FIVE

WALLS THAT TEACH THE CHRISTIAN FAITH

Church construction continues with decorative "walls" that tell about the Fruits of the Spirit and the Ten Commandments. The children will see these important Bible teachings every Sunday. "Whatever is true, whatever is honorable, whatever is just . . . think about these things." (Philippians 4:8, RSV)

SESSION 11

FRUITS OF THE SPIRIT

The Bible Lesson

Combine the commandments with teaching the fruits of the spirit from Galatians. The Bible readings are from Exodus 20:1-17, Matthew 22:36-40, and Galatians 5:22-23.

What the Children Will Learn Today

These two sessions teach the children some principles of our Christian faith in terms that they can understand and use.

Supplies Needed

1. Paper-making supplies: blender, scraps of paper, starch, glue, water, pan, newspapers, screen, and a yardstick.
2. Bibles, "My Feelings" handout, and pencils.
3. Banner: tacky glue and felt or paper — white (74" long, 27½" wide), green (23" long, 18" wide), brown (25" long, 6" wide), and red, pink, purple, yellow, and green scraps for fruit.
4. Workstation signs, instructions, and a snack.
5. Several old spoons and string, instruments, and song book.

WORKSTATIONS

Workstation 1 — Call to Worship

GETTING READY

Today we celebrate that God has made all people different — and special. As an expression of their individuality, the children will make some new and unique musical instruments to add to their collection. Remember to save all of your instruments to use for the children's service in the spring. Include spoons of different sizes and shapes to test the difference in sound. Post a sign-up sheet so the musicians can share their new talent with the group today, and copy and post the following instructions for the children:

> Take two spoons; tie a string around one and use the other to hit the first spoon as it swings on its string. While you sing, play the spoons to the beat. Sign the sheet if you would like to play today.

Workstations 2 and 3 — Affirmation of Faith and Offering

GETTING READY

The paper you make will not dry in time to write on today. Save and use next week. Make two big pieces of paper for scrolls. Save leftover small pieces so children can take one home.

Post a sign-up sheet for someone to read Exodus 20:1-17 and Matthew 22:36-40 in the worship service today. Also, copy and post the following instructions for the children:

Paper in Jesus' day was very expensive, hard to make, and rare. Most children never got a chance to write on paper in their entire lifetimes. They would memorize stories or sing songs from the Scriptures. Read Exodus 20:1-17 and Matthew 22:36-40.

Make two 36" long and 20" wide scrolls. Tear strips of paper (paper sacks, newspapers or even scraps of leftover paper), and

place them in the blender. Add 2 cups of water and 1/4 cup of starch, and 2 tablespoons of white glue. Blend until thoroughly mixed. Pour over a large piece of screen that is sitting in a pan to collect the extra water. Smooth the pulp out onto the screen with a wooden spoon. Lift the screen up and let the water drain through. Place the screen onto a thick stack of newspapers. Place extra newspaper on top. Press down to get extra water out or use a rolling pin to smooth out the paper. Place in the sun to dry till next week. Repeat process for size of scroll needed.

Workstations 4 and 5 —
Sermon/Bible Lesson and Witness

GETTING READY

The banner the children will be making today will be hung in the center of their church. This banner can be made of felt or paper. You may enlarge the patterns ahead of time or, better, have the children look at the pictures and draw creative fruits free hand. Use tacky glue from fabric store to glue felt.

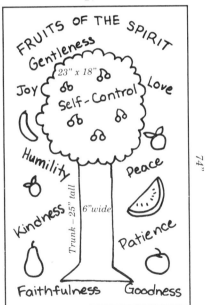

Banner Diagram   *Finished Banner*

Post a sign-up sheet for a volunteer to read Galatians 5:22 in the worship service today, and copy and post the following instructions for the children:

You are going to make a banner to hang in your church to remind you of a special Bible verse, Galatians 5:22. Read the verse and then start to draw.

Start by making a large tree that covers most of the banner (see drawing). Follow the measurements on the drawings. Draw on paper first, then pin your paper pattern onto the felt and cut each piece out. Add fruits around the tree to remind you of each of the characteristics in the Bible verse: peaches, apples, plums, oranges, pineapples, watermelons, grapes, or others of your own choice. As you cut each piece, lay it down into place. Use a long table or the floor to lay the banner on.

When you have all of the pieces laid out the way you want, you can just roll each one back a little to put the glue on the back. Roll them back into place and you're done. Start with the tree. Glue the felt letters last. Hang on top of the liturgical banner in the center of your church when completely dry.

Workstation 6 — Prayer

GETTING READY

Copy and post the following instructions for the children:

We are still embroidering the Lord's Prayer banner. See if you can finish one line today.

Workstation 7 — Benediction

GETTING READY

Have a copy of the "My Feelings" handout for each child. Have older children or adult assistant help younger children. Copy and post the following instructions for the children:

Before we can share with others, we have to think about our feelings. Answer each question in the "My Feelings" handout.

My Feelings

I feel lonely when . . .

I feel sad when . . .

I am scared of . . .

I feel ashamed when . . .

My friends make me feel . . .

My family makes me feel . . .

I am happy when . . .

Two things that I like about myself are . . .

Two ways that I think God can help me in my life . . .

Two ways that I think I can help God . . .

The Worship Celebration

I. Call to Worship — Enter playing instruments.

II. Affirmation/Sermon/Witness — Read the Bible verses.

III. Benediction/Prayer — Share feelings about what makes you happy, then thank God for these things.

Items to Go Home

"My Feelings" handout

SESSION 12

THE TEN COMMANDMENTS TODAY

The Bible Lesson

By having the children write their own version of the commandments, the Ten Commandments take on new meaning. Read: Exodus
20:1-17, Matthew 22:36-40, and Galatians 5:22-23.

What the Children Will Learn Today

Help the children think of the commandments and the fruits of the
spirit as more than just rules. They are guidelines for living.

Supplies Needed

1. Paper made last week and two wooden dowels for scroll.
2. Sandpaper, wood scraps, and wooden thread spools.
3. Bibles; and a snack is nice while they work.
4. Ten Commandments handout and craft supply basket.
5. Workstation signs and instructions.
6. Liquid embroidery from fabric store.
7. Musical instruments and song book.
8. Construction paper (variety of colors) and heart pattern.

WORKSTATIONS

Workstation 1 — Call to Worship

GETTING READY

Provide sandpaper, thread spools, long nails, and an adult helper. Post
a sign-up sheet for musicians for today's Call to Worship, and copy and
post the following instructions for the children:

> The swish-swish sound of sandblocks adds an interesting effect
> to music. Find two pieces of wood with flat sides to rub together.
> Nail an empty thread spool to each block of wood. Glue a piece

of sandpaper to the flat side of each block of wood, then turn them over and nail an empty thread spool into the other side. It is important to let the sandblocks dry completely before using them, so practice singing with other instruments today.

Workstations 2 and 3 —
Affirmation of Faith and Offering

GETTING READY

Furnish liquid embroidery and an adult helper today. Copy and post the following instructions for the children:

Write the words for the fruits of the spirit (Galatians 5:22-23) on the banner. Practice first on a scrap piece of cloth, then on the banner. Start at the top. Do not touch until dry.

Workstation 4 — Sermon/Bible Lesson

GETTING READY

Set out copies of the Ten Commandments handout. Younger children may work alongside older children or draw pictures of what they think each verse means. Post a sign-up sheet for a volunteer to read the Children's Ten Commandments in the worship celebration today, and copy and post the following instructions for the children:

Read Exodus 20:1-17 (the Ten Commandments). Today you are going to put together a children's version. Look up the verses and fill in the blanks of your Ten Commandments handout.

Ten Commandments

1. Worship only _____ (Exodus 20:1-3).

2. Nothing will be more important in your life than _____, not even fancy clothes or toys (Exodus 20:4-6).

3. Do not try to impress your friends by using your _____ in rude talk. Do not curse using your _____ (Exodus 20:7).

4. Sunday is a special day of _____ set aside from work to give special honor to God. Rejoice and celebrate God's love through your kindness to others (Exodus 20:8-11).

5. Help take care of, listen to, and show how much you appreciate your _____ and your _____. Think of ways that you can bring happiness to them (Exodus 20:12).

6. Life is more special than even your favorite toy. You must never hurt, kill, or _____ anyone (Exodus 20:13).

7. Just as marriage is a special promise which brought your parents together, try your best to keep your _____, never promise anything that could hurt someone, and never make a promise unless you really intend to keep it (Exodus 20:14).

8. You must never take anything that does not belong to you. Even if you think you will not get caught or someone dares you to try, do not _____ (Exodus 20:15).

9. Do not tell _____ about another person or accuse someone unless you are completely sure of what you are saying. Never repeat something that someone else said unless you know it to be true yourself (Exodus 20:16).

10. Do not be jealous of someone else's shoes, clothes, toys, or other property. Be proud of who _____ are. Do not measure your worth in terms of money (Exodus 20:17).

Workstation 5 — Witness to the World

GETTING READY

These little baskets are simple enough for even four-year-olds to make. Make a few samples. Adult helper needed. Post a sign-up sheet for volunteers to tell how they can share "fruits" in their lives, and copy and post the following instructions for the children:

> If you let hatred and anger rule your life, you end up always being angry. If jealousy rules, you will be blaming someone else for all your problems. You and you alone are responsible for how you live your life.
>
> Make a Fruits of the Spirit Heart Basket following the step-by-step instructions. Then, fill your empty basket with ideas from Galatians 5:22-23. Draw pictures of fruits and tell how you can share the fruits of the spirit in your daily life at school, home, and at church.

Fruits of the Spirit Heart Baskets

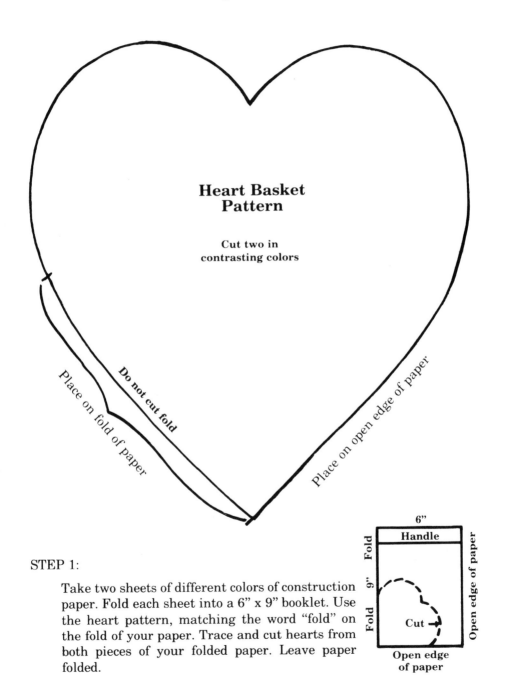

**Heart Basket
Pattern**

**Cut two in
contrasting colors**

Place on fold of paper

Do not cut fold

Place on open edge of paper

STEP 1:

Take two sheets of different colors of construction paper. Fold each sheet into a 6" x 9" booklet. Use the heart pattern, matching the word "fold" on the fold of your paper. Trace and cut hearts from both pieces of your folded paper. Leave paper folded.

6"

Fold

Handle

9"

Fold

Cut →

Open edge of paper

Open edge
of paper

STEP 2:

Open the hearts so that they are lying flat. With a ruler, draw lines on each heart. It is very important that you cut exactly as shown in the diagram. Lay your hearts down on the table as shown; draw lines exactly as they are in the picture.

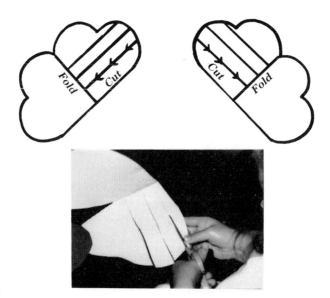

STEP 3:

Use scissors to make three cuts as shown, starting at the rounded edge of the heart and cutting toward the fold line. DO NOT CUT THROUGH THE "FOLD" LINE. Cut both hearts as shown in diagram — Step 3.

STEP 4:

Weave the two front panels of the heart basket together. Weave the cut edges — one over and one under. The hearts will fit together making a little basket.

STEP 5:

Staple or tape loose woven edges together, but do not staple the basket shut. You should be able to put your hand inside your basket when finished. Make a handle out of extra paper and staple it into place.

Finished Basket

Open Inside

Front

Back

Workstation 6 — Prayer

GETTING READY

Copy and post the following message for the children:

> Thanks for remembering the prayer banner.

Workstation 7 — Benediction

GETTING READY

Use the paper made last week. Save the rolled scroll and children's Love Commandment for the spring and Easter services. Hang unrolled scroll in the church. If your scroll did not turn out large enough to fill the space in the church, you can mount it on a piece of wood, large piece of construction paper, or save it till Chapter 7 and make a tissue paper stained glass window to fill the space with the scroll taking the place of the symbol in the middle. Send small pieces of extra paper home with children.

Post a sign-up sheet for someone to read the children's version of the Love Commandment. Also copy and post the following instructions for the children:

> Read Matthew 22:36-40. On plain paper (not the scroll), rewrite in your own words this commandment given to us by Jesus. How

does this commandment fit in at school, at home, and at church? Share your ideas with the others at the Benediction workstation today. Then, put all of your ideas together and write, using markers, in your own words one combined version of the Love Commandment from Matthew. Copy your version of the Love Commandment onto both scrolls. Younger children who cannot write can draw pictures with markers on the scrolls' edges.

Tape one dowel stick to each end of one of the scrolls. Gently roll each end of the scroll so that it meets in the middle. Tie a string around the scroll. Keep the other scroll flat so that it can be hung up in your church.

The Worship Celebration

I. Call to Worship — Ask volunteers to tell how children can share the fruits of the spirit in their daily lives.

II. Sermon/Benediction — Have volunteers read the children's version of the Ten Commandments and the Love Commandment that the children wrote.

Items to Go Home

Heart baskets and small extra samples of paper made last week.

CHAPTER SIX

BUILDING ON THE INSIDE

Before children can think about ministering to the needs of others, they need a way to express who they are wanting or trying to become. Sharing, with hammer and nails, music, or clown ministry, is quite simply witnessing.

SESSION 13
MORE THAN JUST A PRETTY FACE

Clown ministry is not a circus side show but an expression of faith (2 Timothy 1:7-8). The clown as a humble or suffering servant (Luke 17:21) thinks not of self but of the needs of others. The humble servant accepts everything that happens and responds not in anger, but with kindness, joy, happiness, acceptance, and love (John 14:27). The clown's task is described best in the opening lines of the Prayer of St. Francis of Assisi:

Lord, make me an instrument of thy peace:
Where there is hatred, let me sow love;
Where there is injury, pardon;
Where there is doubt, faith;
Where there is despair, hope;
Where there is darkness, light;
Where there is sadness, joy.

(William Neil, ed., *Concise Dictionary of Religious Quotations.* [Grand Rapids, MI: William B. Eerdmans Publishing Company, 1974], p. 148:3.

Clown ministry is not for everyone, yet the shiest, never-can-fit-in individuals come alive under clown make-up.

The Bible Lesson

Building a table, telling a story, or helping and sharing with friends, ". . . the Kingdom of God is within you" (Luke 17:21).

What the Children Will Learn Today

The children will explore what it means to be a Christian through three main workstations: Call to Worship, Affirmation of Faith, and Offering.

Time Needed

Use the same amount of time, but meet for your 10-minute worship celebration first and then the workstations.

Supplies Needed

1. Wood and woodworking basket (hammers, nails, sandpaper, and saws) for building a small table for the church.

2. Water-based clown make-up (whiteface, blue, red, green and yellow), small make-up brushes, cold cream, tissues, hair clips or headbands, a mirror, and simple clown costumes.
3. Bibles, pencils, paper, and a snack.
4. Workstation signs and instructions.
5. Musical instruments and song book.
6. Craft supply basket: Usual supplies, plus paper fasteners and oatmeal containers for drums.
7. A penny for each child.

The Worship Celebration

Pass out paper and a pencil for everyone before you start the story.

Happy Penny

The alarm clock went off — Bzzzzzzzzzzz. Happy Penny rolled over, turned off the alarm, and threw back the covers. She stretched and yawned as she made her way down the hallway toward the kitchen. Happy opened the refrigerator door and leaned back to stare into an almost empty refrigerator. "Now what should I have for breakfast?" she said to herself out loud.

As Happy glanced up at the clock on the wall, she jumped with a start. Forget breakfast — she'd eat something at the hospital.

You see, Happy was a clown. No, not the kind of clown that works in a circus and just does silly gags. Happy was a special clown who went to the children's hospital once a week to tell stories to the children. And today was going to be her first day on the job, so she needed to get going.

Happy raced to her closet, pushed back the doors, and sat down with a big whoosh to decide what to wear. Ah! Cowgirl boots. Now that would be unusual, especially with her cowgirl hat. And she would need something with pockets for her pennies.

Happy used pennies as her calling card. Whenever she met someone new or just wanted to say "How do you do?", Happy would place a penny in the person's hand, politely curtsey, and then, without saying a word, flash a smile. When Happy was working as a clown, she never talked. She told all of her stories with arm and body motions but no words.

At last, Happy pulled just the right outfit from the rack. Her long patchwork quilted skirt would be perfect with her flowery blue blouse and orange vest.

Let's see, now what else did she need? Why, her make-up of course. What would a clown be without make-up?

Decisions . . . decisions! A clown's make-up is sort of like the way you write your name; it tells something about you just by how it looks. And Happy wanted just the right look today.

Should Happy use a complete clown whiteface or just a little rainbow on her cheek with a red nose? Happy couldn't decide.

(Long pause) Perhaps we could help Happy out. *(Another pause)* You each have a piece of paper and a pencil. Draw a circle at the top of your page. We have all seen clowns at the circus, so draw in what you would use for your clown face if you were going out to visit with a group of children in the hospital.

As soon as you have your clown face drawn, hold it up so we all can see. Oh! what great ideas. Now, how about your costume? Would you wear cowgirl boots like Happy? Don't worry if you're not the world's greatest artist. After all, we're drawing clowns. *(Design your own along with the children.)* Look at my stick figure clown! Happy will like it just the same.

Is everyone finished? What great ideas you have given Happy! But wait, you don't have a name. What should your clown name be?

Happy is called Happy Penny because she is always smiling and giving everyone a penny. Happy uses a penny because we often think that a penny is useless and not worth much, but Happy knows that if you put a lot of pennies together, you can even buy someone lunch or help someone who needs a doctor. Happy knows that you cannot always be happy. Sometimes you're sad. *(Pause)*

So when Happy puts on her make-up, she pins up her hair to get it out of the way and puts white clown make-up all over her face. She then paints on colorful rainbows for eyebrows, a perky red smile with dimples on her right cheek, and a big blue teardrop on her left cheek, and bright red lips for the finishing touch.

Happy puts on her long, braided, yellow yarn wig; her cowgirl hat; and off she goes. And you, too, can be a clown. Not just a silly clown, although it is fun to act silly. But a clown with a mission, a clown with a story to tell.

Workstation 1 — Call to Worship

GETTING READY

Musicians can be in clown make-up if they like. Select a serious song for everyone to sing together to contrast with the clowns to illustrate that clown ministry is more than just fun. Set out the craft basket and empty oatmeal containers, and copy and post the following instructions for the children:

Today we are going to make some new instruments to use for a Call to Worship. Decorate an empty oatmeal container to use as a drum.

Decorate each drum so that it tells something about what it means to be a Christian — kind, loving, helpful, or forgiving. Use your imagination to create a special drum. You may use two paper fasteners and string to make a strap.

And remember: Share with your neighbor. Don't pick out the best instrument just for yourself; give others a turn too. Help your neighbors if they are having trouble deciding how to decorate their drum today. Above all else, be kind.

Workstation 2, 4 and 5 — Affirmation of Faith, Sermon and Witness

GETTING READY

If you have never participated in clown ministry before, it is not hard to learn. There are several fine books available, such as *The Clown Ministry Handbook* by Janet Litherland. A list of clown ministry resources may be found at the end of this chapter.

For a group of ten, set up no fewer than three tables with mirrors and make-up. Each table will need whiteface, but everyone may share the colors and brushes.

Be sure you have health forms or information from the children so that you will know if anyone is allergic to make-up.

A letter sent home to parents the week before this session works well:

Dear _____,

Our children will be acting out two parables from the Bible during the children's worship service on _____. The children may participate with or without clown make-up as a part of our clown ministry program. Those wishing to participate need to put together a simple clown costume to bring next week. We're not circus clowns so you don't need the typical polka-dotted outfit with a big ruffled collar. A baggy pair of pants, old dress or skirt, hat, old character-oriented halloween costumes (that are not scary), or basically anything that the children would normally play dress-up in work fine. We will use these costumes for the next four Sundays.

My child _____ may participate joyfully in sharing the message of the humble servant through clown ministry. My child (may/may not) wear clown make-up. Any allergies?

_____

Post a sign-up sheet for actors to pantomime a parable in the street mime three weeks from this Sunday (Session 16). Put the date on the sign-up sheet. Also copy and post the following instructions for the children:

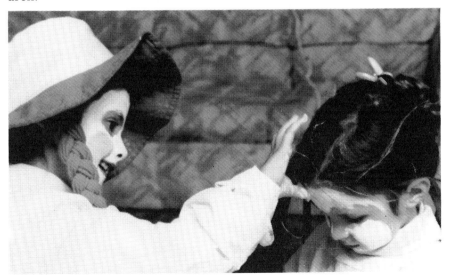

This morning, we are going to follow Happy Penny's example and create our own clown characters.

Use your drawing as an idea, but feel free to change it. Think of what you want to say with your clown face. Who do you want to become? What do you want to share with others?

You may put whiteface on all over your face as Happy did, or you may skip that step and just do face painting. Your make-up can be as much or as little as you wish or even none at all.

Put your costume on before you put any make-up on so that you don't get make-up all over your clothes, and then: Share with your neighbor. If you neighbor is having trouble, stop and help. If your neighbor has been waiting a long time, stop and give your neighbor a turn.

Workstation 3 — Offering

GETTING READY

The children are going to build a table — a simple project. Have the woodworking basket and wood ready.

COMMUNION TABLE

STEP 1: Cut plywood for table top

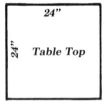

STEP 2: Cut four 22" long 2x4's

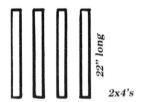

STEP 3: Cut two 2x4's in half to make the frame

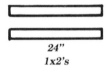

And two:

STEP 4: Nail legs onto frame

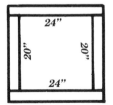

STEP 5: Nail top onto frame

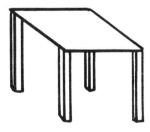

Copy and post the following instructions for the children:

> The gift you give to God today is your time. You are going to make a communion table or altar.
>
> Measure the size and height you want. A table top 24" x 24" with 22" legs will fit nicely into your church.
>
> Make a simple frame out of 2 x 4s. Cut, sand, and nail the boards together to make a 24" x 24" wide frame.
>
> Then cut four 2 x 4s into equal 22" lengths. Sand and nail these onto the frame for the legs of the table. Make sure the legs are even or your table will wobble.
>
> Then put a 24" x 24" piece of plywood on and nail it down for the top. Sand all of the rough spots.

Workstation 6 — Prayer

GETTING READY

Copy and post the following instructions for the children:

> If you are looking for a quiet place, the banner is for you. Think about the words as you sew.

Workstation 7 — Benediction

Tell the children: "We will go out and be happy, like clowns. We will smile and pass out love to everyone we meet." Ask musicians to play their drums and ask two children to carry the Lord's Prayer banner in a recessional.

Items to Go Home

The children may wear their make-up home or they may take it off with cold cream. Send everyone home with a penny from Happy Penny.

SESSION 14

A SERMON
BROUGHT TO LIFE

The role of the clown in the church is to go out and share as a follower of Jesus. "Peace is what I leave with you . . ." (John 14:27)

The Bible Lesson

Today's message lies in the seemingly worthless penny (Matthew 5:1-16). The musicians look at Psalm 100; the carpenters read Matthew 5:15-16, and the clowns will look at two parables that talk about ministry to others: Matthew 13:1-9 and Luke 10:27-37.

What the Children Will Learn Today

You are continuing to teach what it means to be a Christian.

Time Needed

You will use 20 minutes for workstations and 10 minutes for worship. There will be three main workstations today.

Supplies Needed

1. Table, light blue paint, and woodworking basket (hammers, nails, sandpaper, and saws) to build a small table for the church.

2. Water-based clown make-up (whiteface, blue, red, green, and yellow), small make-up brushes, cold cream, tissues, hair clips or headbands, and a mirror.

3. Bibles, clown costumes, props if desired (see Affirmation of of Faith), and a penny for everyone.

4. Workstation signs and instructions.

5. Musical instruments and song book.

6. Craft supply basket: Usual supplies plus margarine boxes, coffee cans, rice, and macaroni (or gravel, if you do not wish to use food items).

WORKSTATIONS

Workstation 1 — Call to Worship

GETTING READY

Collect empty cereal boxes, coffee cans, or margarine boxes. Margarine boxes work especially well. Set out your well-stocked craft basket and a variety of items to put inside the containers which will make a noise when shaken. Post a sign-up sheet for musicians. They will perform today and also in the street mime two weeks from this Sunday (Session 16). Put the date on the sign-up sheet. Also copy and post the following instructions for the children:

> Psalm 100 says, "Make a joyful noise to the Lord," and that is your job today.
>
> Make a simple shaker from a coffee can or margarine box filled with rice, gravel, macaroni, or whatever is available in the craft basket. Make each instrument different. Fill your can or box, tape the end shut so that the contents don't spill out, and then cover it with construction paper.
>
> Read Psalm 100 in the Bible. Decorate your shaker to explain what Psalm 100 means.
>
> Encourage each other to be creative. Decorate your musical instruments your own special way. You may even add crepe paper streamers, jingle bells, or other decorations.
>
> The Call to Worship you practice today will be used as the Call to Worship for the street mime. Take your drums, shakers, and the music and other instruments provided and practice. If you haven't done so already, sign the sheet if you would like to play for the street mime on the date listed.

Workstation 2, 4 and 5 — Affirmation of Faith, Sermon and Witness

GETTING READY

Props are handy for the groups to use in their skits, e.g. a sign saying "HELP" for the hurt man, or packages of seeds for the sower. You may make hair for your clowns by taping yarn to the bottom edges of a paper or regular hat.

Post a sign-up sheet for clown actors for "The Good Samaritan" (Luke 10:27-37) and "The Sower and the Seed." (Matthew 13:1-9). They will perform in today's worship, in next week's carnival, and also in the street mime in two weeks (Session 16). Copy and post the following instructions for the children:

> Roll up your sleeves, put your costume on before you put any make-up on so that you don't get make-up all over your clothes. Put on your clown make-up. You may use the same face as last week or make changes. Use as much or as little make-up as you wish. Read these Bible verses: Matthew 13:1-9 and Luke 10:27-37, then sign up for the part you would like to do. Remember you do not have to wear any make-up at all if you don't want to.

Workstation 3 and 7 — Offering and Benediction

GETTING READY

Get out the table from last week and provide any supplies needed to finish building and painting it. Copy and post the following instructions for the children:

> Finish building your table today and sand it smooth. Then put on a painting shirt. Blue, the color of truth, is used near the altar, so paint your table a light sky blue.

Workstation 6 — Prayer

GETTING READY

Copy and post the following instructions for the children:

> If you are looking for a quiet place to rest today or if you are just waiting for a turn, then sew.

The Worship Celebration

I. Call to Worship — Have the children who signed up do the Call to Worship using their shakers.

II. Offering — If the paint is dry on the table, place it in the children's church. Clowns should be ready to act out their parables.

III. Affirmation/Sermon-Witness — Clowns should be ready to
act out their parables.

Items to Go Home

Give each child a penny at the close of your celebration today. Tell
them that alone, the penny isn't worth much, but if we combine all of
our pennies together with other churches, then the pennies can feed the
hungry, clothe the poor, help the sick, and care for the lonely. Their
mission is to find a way to share their pennies.

SESSION 15

REACH OUT AND SHARE

A Sunday school carnival to raise money for a service project is an excellent way to spread the message of God's love.

The Bible Lesson

Children can learn about the Bible while they play and have fun at a carnival. Use clown ministry to stress how we can all share God's love: Matthew 13:1-9 and Luke 10:30-35.

What the Children Will Learn Today

The children are going to spend their session today setting up for a carnival. You may hold this carnival during your regular Sunday school hour, in the evening, or as a special event. The carnival lets the children practice clowning as they share the Good News (Matthew 28:19-20). Don't maintain silence today. Let the children talk, giggle, and have fun.

Time Needed

Use the entire half hour to prepare for the carnival.

Supplies Needed

1. 1" x 6" pastel-colored construction paper strips for making the paper Friendship Chain (or you may just provide the construction paper and ask the children to cut it into strips).

2. Water-based clown make-up (whiteface, blue, red, green or yellow), small make-up brushes, cold cream, tissues and a mirror.

3. Bibles, biblical costumes and clown costumes.

4. Clown ice-cream snacks — ice cream, ice-cream scoop, ice-cream cones, candies, and a can of whipping cream to decorate ice cream (plus eating utensils).

5. Festive decorations, such as streamers and balloons.

6. String, helium balloon with a blank card for everyone to sign and tag.

7. Craft supply basket: Usual supplies.

8. Strips of cloth, paper bags or trash bags for race.

9. Paper cups, round balloons, and lemonade or punch.

10. Workstation signs and instructions.

WORKSTATIONS

Workstation 1 — Call to Worship

GETTING READY

Set out the pastel construction paper, scissors, rulers, and markers. Everyone at the carnival will sign in by making a Friendship Chain. Post a sign-up sheet for helpers who would be willing to work this station at the carnival, and copy and post the following instructions for the children:

> The Call to Worship prepares the way for what is to come. You are the entrance to the carnival, so make a good impression by decorating with lots of balloons and streamers. Cut strips of paper to use for the chain.
>
> As people arrive, give them each a Friendship Chain strip of paper and tell them to write their names on their paper strip. Then have everyone tape their strips onto the Friendship Chain. Send each person over to the Affirmation of Faith station to make a name tag.

Workstation 2 — Affirmation of Faith

GETTING READY

Place the craft basket at this station today. Post a sign-up sheet for helpers to work this station at the carnival. Copy and post the following instructions for the children:

> You are in charge of name tags. Decorate your station and wear your name tags as examples.
>
> Give everybody a clown face name tag and ask them to draw a clown face to tell what kind of a person they are: happy, shy, friendly, silly, or whatever. Wear your name tags.

Workstation 3 — Offering

GETTING READY

Use your wooden collection church to collect money. The two-legged relay race also gives everyone a chance to share fun with a partner. Use strips of cloth, paper bags, or trash bags, or the partners can just pretend their legs are tied together and try to run in unison. Post a sign-up sheet for helpers to work this station at the carnival. Copy and post the following instructions for the children:

> Set up and lead the two-legged relay race. Make big, colorful "Start" and "Finish" signs. Have a couple of clowns at the finish line to do face painting.
>
> Have everyone find a new partner. Two people each put one leg into a bag and hold onto the bag with one hand. The teams will run a relay race. Make sure you have extra paper bags.

Workstation 4 — Sermon/Bible Lesson

GETTING READY

Have the clown troupe from Session 14 act out the parables in make-up and costume before the carnival starts. Set up your Children's Church with your new table and props in place at one end of the room to be your stage. Blow up balloons and write messages of peace and love on them. Post two sign-up sheets: one for helpers, the other for clowns, to work this station at the carnival. Then copy and post the following instruction for the children:

> As children walk by, give them balloons and invite them to sit down for the clown mime story. Ask the children to guess which Bible story is being acted out.

Workstation 5 — Witness to the World

GETTING READY

Lawn bowling will help everyone develop team spirit. Write the books of the Bible, both Old Testament and New Testament, on cups. Post a sign-up sheet for helpers to work this station at the carnival. Copy and post the following instructions for the children:

> Your task is to set up the lawn bowling game before the carnival starts. You need round balloons. Be sure to have extras.
>
> Make two pyramids, one Old Testament and one New Testament. Stack 10 paper cups per pyramid: four on the bottom, three on the next row, then two, then one. Using the balloons as bowling balls, the object is to knock down all the cups. Have an Old Testament and New Testament team. Give each person three tries and have punch or lemonade to serve in the cups as their prize.

Workstation 6 — Prayer

GETTING READY

For the snack, give each child a scoop of ice cream with an ice-cream cone on top as a hat. Then let everyone decorate their ice cream to look like a clown face.

Set out bowls of candies, nuts, cherries, etc. Provide a can of whipping cream — the children will have fun squirting it on their clowns for hair or eyebrows.

Make paper blue ribbons for everyone that say "God Loves You." Post a sign-up sheet for helpers to work this station at the carnival. Copy and post the following instructions for the children:

> Have everyone decorate a clown face on their ice cream scoops. Give blue ribbon prizes for the most creative, funniest, the one with the most candy or least whipping cream. Make sure that everyone receives a ribbon. And say a prayer of thanks before you eat!

Workstation 7 — Benediction

GETTING READY

Buy a helium balloon. The balloon will symbolize sharing God's love. Make a card that says "We are your neighbors; we love you." When the card has been signed by all the children, you will tie it onto the balloon. Post a sign-up sheet for helpers to work this station at the carnival, and copy and post the following instructions for the children:

> Gather everyone together outside. Make sure that everyone has signed the card. Release the balloon.

Items to Go Home

Send the group home with their balloons, prizes, and memories.

SESSION 16

STREET MIME
TAKE THE MESSAGE
TO THE PEOPLE

Your church may wish to include the children's street mime in the sanctuary or in the hallway before or after worship. Musicians set the mood. Clowns tell the story. And the reporters pass out the newspaper introducing clown ministry.

The Bible Lesson

The parable the children choose to act out. (Refer to Session 14 — they may choose between "The Good Samaritan" or "The Sower and the Seed.")

What the Children Will Learn Today

The object is not a perfect performance, but to share a story from the Bible.

Time Needed

You will use the usual amount of time, but you will divide the time up differently. Allow 10 minutes for the workstations, then 15 minutes for the street mime worship. (Use the extra five minutes to get set up for the street mime.)

Supplies Needed

1. The small table for the church.
2. Water-based clown make-up (whiteface, blue, red, green and yellow), small make-up brushes, cold cream, tissues, hair clips or headbands, a mirror, and the clown costumes.
3. Bibles, "The Clown" handout, and a snack if desired.
4. Workstation signs and instructions.
5. Handmade musical instruments and song to be played.
6. Craft supply basket: Usual supplies (Be sure to have enough construction paper for the newspaper reporter signs).
7. Newspapers about clown ministry (See Offering station).
8. Wardrobe or costume box for dress-up as reporters (ties, jackets, and hats for the boys; dresses, jewelry, and high heels for the girls).

Workstation 1 — Call to Worship

GETTING READY

Today the children will present their street mime. Copy and post the following instructions for the children:

> In big cities you may see musicians playing on street corners. Practice your song and be ready to play for the street mime in 10 minutes.

Workstations 2, 4 and 5 —
Affirmation of Faith, Sermon and Witness

GETTING READY

Check your sign-up sheet from Session 13 to make sure that your cast of clowns are all present. You will need an adult at this station to help everyone get into costume and make-up. If the clowns need longer than the 10 minutes allowed, go ahead and pass out "The Clown" handout to those who are ready so that they can stay busy. Copy and post the following instructions for the children:

> Clowns often take to the street when they are not accepted in theaters. They use the street for a stage. You are a clown with a mission; you have a story to tell.
>
> Put on your clown costume and make-up. Choose which parable you want to perform — either "The Good Samaritan" or "The Sower and the Seed." Practice acting out the parable you have selected for about 10 minutes.

Workstation 3 — Offering

GETTING READY

Even though they are not completely finished, set up the church and table at the front of your sanctuary or in the hallway — wherever your street mime will be. Hang your banners. Be proud and show how hard the children have been working on their church.

Then, turn your carpenters into newspaper reporters. They can wear hats, signs saying "Extra, Extra, Read All About It," or carry a stack of newspapers. They will hand out small, rolled-up newspapers explaining about clown ministry and street mime.

Write your own "Good News Herald" newspaper telling about your clown ministry troupe, its purpose, and what the children are learning from the experience. You don't need a copy for everyone, just enough to get the word spread around.

Copy and post the following instructions for the children:

> The table is finished and you have done a great job. For the next ten minutes, put down your hammers and saws and pretend to be newspaper reporters getting the news out about clown ministry. There was a time when most people purchased their newspapers off the street. Vendors shouted the headlines as they walked.
>
> Roll up each newspaper. Tie a string to hold it in place. Your job is to hand them out during the street mime.
>
> Dress up to make yourself look more like a news reporter. Make a sign: "Good News Herald — Get Your Free Copies Here."

Workstation 6 — Prayer

GETTING READY

Copy and post the following instructions for the children:

> If you have extra time, work on the banner.

Workstation 7 — Benediction

GETTING READY

Copy and post the following instructions for the children:

> The clown handout will help you think about what you are sharing and what it means to share your feelings with others.

Items to Go Home

Send everyone home with "The Clown" handout. Explain to the children that as Christians we experience both sad and happy feelings. Everyone does. The musician shares feelings through music, the clown through make-up and mime, and the news reporter through words written down on paper.

The Clown Handout

We all have feelings. Sometimes we have happy feelings and sometimes we have sad or angry feelings. Clowns put on costumes and make-up to tell how they feel. Draw a face for the clown in the picture below that shows how you feel most of the time — sad, happy, confused . . .

In each of the balloons soaring high over the clown's head, draw a picture of something that would make you happy. Beside the broken balloons on the bottom of the page, draw something that makes you sad.

CLOWN MINISTRY RESOURCES

Books:

Litherland, Janet. *The Clown Ministry Handbook*. Colorado Springs, CO: Meriwether Publishing Ltd., 1985.
The original book of clown ministry basics with skits for service and worship. Includes helpful information on costumes, props, make-up, and more.

Perrone, Stephen P. and James P. Spata. *Send in His Clowns*. Colorado Springs, CO: Meriwether Publishing Ltd., 1985.
A workshop manual for training clown ministers with many ideas and activities which may be adapted for children.

Filmstrips:

Zapel, Ted. *Clowning for Kids*. Colorado Springs, CO: Contemporary Drama Service, 1981.
This 12-minute filmstrip shows and tells how elementary school children can discover the joys of being a clown. Tells the basic clown types, how to put on make-up, how to improvise with costumes, how to make people laugh, and how to use funny props.

Skit Collections:

Barone, Joe. *We're All Clowns at Christmas* and *The Wonderful Easter Gift*. Colorado Springs, CO: Contemporary Drama Service, 1991.
These two seasonal skit collections were written especially for groups of young children. One or two adults supply the dialog while pint-sized clowns pantomime along. Three scripts per collection.

Make-up:

Clown White — Easy to apply. May be removed with soap and water. (Ben Nye)

Rainbow Wheel — Red, blue, black, orange, yellow, and green. (Ben Nye)

Ben Nye's Klown Kit — Clown white; rainbow wheel; red ball nose; brushes, pencils, and applicators; make-up remover, color instructions, and more.

All of the above items are available from Meriwether Publishing Ltd. or Contemporary Drama Service, Box 7710, Colorado Springs, CO 80933.

CHAPTER SEVEN

MAKING STAINED GLASS WINDOWS

Like the church walls in Chapter 5, these "stained glass" windows are also spiritual reminders with their child-drawn images of Jesus and his love.

Follow the step-by-step directions in these five sessions to draw your own windows, or use the simplified tissue paper windows as described in the Benediction of Session 21.

SESSION 17
DRAW A STORY FROM THE BIBLE

The Bible Lesson

The children at each workstation will be reading Bible verses and drawing pictures about each verse on their windows.

What the Children Will Learn Today

You want the children to appreciate the beauty of the windows while understanding that each window tells a story.

Time Needed

Twenty-five minutes for workstations and five minutes for worship. Don't expect the children to finish all the drawings today. The next four sessions allows time for them to finish.

Supplies Needed

1. Wood and woodworking basket (hammers, nails, sandpaper, and saws) for building a small Bible stand for the church.
2. Artist sketch paper or newsprint works best for windows. You need five large sheets, 24" x 71", or smaller sheets that can be put together to make the size needed. (Do not use poster board or tape the pages together, just work on each paper individually.) You will also need pencils, extra paper, and gum erasers (available in art supply stores).
3. Bibles, workstation signs (leave stations 1, 2, 3, 4, 5, and 7 in place for next Sunday, too), and a snack.
4. Sing-along tapes or records to play in background.
5. "God Loves You" stickers or make paper badges.
6. Books and pictures of stained glass windows for ideas.

WORKSTATIONS

Workstation 1 — Call to Worship

GETTING READY

Have long sheets of paper large enough for each window or use several smaller sheets and put them together in Session 21. Post a sign-up sheet for someone to share about his or her drawing and then hang it in the church. Copy and post the following instructions for the children:

> Today we are going to make the (paper) stained glass windows for our church. Stained glass windows were used in the early Christian churches as picture books are used — to tell a story. Each window represents a different Bible verse(s). Read Proverbs 16:23, 24 and Psalm 100, then draw a picture that explains your Bible verses. Many windows are just a collection of different colors and shapes; so after you draw whatever picture you want in the middle, fill in the edges with different shapes.

Workstation 2 — Affirmation of Faith

GETTING READY

Some children will compare their drawing and coloring skills to others. The lesson that continues throughout this chapter is that no one is better than anyone else. We all have something special to contribute to the project and to life. Post a sign-up sheet. You need someone to tell about his or her drawing and hang it in the church. Copy and post the following instructions for the children:

> When artists design stained glass windows, the first thing they do is make a sketch of what they want the window to look like. This is your job today too. First, read Matthew 5:1-12, then draw a picture describing what you think the Bible verses mean. Some windows do not have pictures of people on them; instead, they are just a collection of different shapes put together in a special pattern to make a Christian symbol.

Workstation 3 — Offering

GETTING READY

There will always be someone who doesn't want to draw, but there is more than one job to be done to build a church. Post a sign-up sheet for someone to report on the progress of the Bible stand. (It will take five Sundays to finish.) Copy and post the following instructions for the children:

Building a Bible Stand

Step 1: Cut board and trim.   Step 2: Cut angle for 2 x 4.

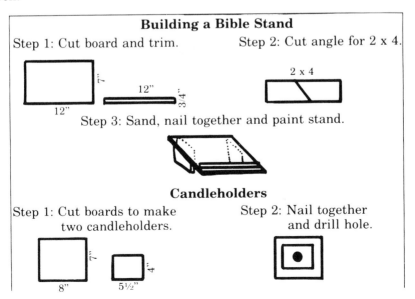

Step 3: Sand, nail together and paint stand.

Candleholders

Step 1: Cut boards to make   Step 2: Nail together
      two candleholders.   and drill hole.

The first Christians did not have Bibles to read; they would listen to someone read from a scroll or just sit and listen to someone tell a story. Letters between friends and leaders of the early church were often read during worship services. Read a letter from Paul: Philippians 4:1-4. Then, build a Bible stand to hold our Bible. You will need one board 12" x 7", a piece of trim 3/4" x 12", and a 2 x 4 cut on an angle to make the stand.

Workstation 4 — Sermon/Bible Lesson

GETTING READY

The best way to teach children how to use their Bibles is to give them lots of practice. Measure the center triangular window beforehand, so that the children will know the size. Post a sign-up sheet for someone to tell about his or her drawing and hang it in the church today. Copy and post the following instructions for the children:

You are responsible for making the center window for the front of your church. Read the Bible verses: Luke 2:4-7, Mark 1:16-17, Luke 9:15-17, Mark 10:13-16, John 12:12-13, Mark 11:15-16, John 19:16, and Luke 24:1-7. You want to tell the story of the life of Jesus through pictures. Draw pictures of some of the various events that happened in his life. Then fill in the extra spaces by drawing clouds, sky, grass squares, or whatever else fits into your picture. Stained glass windows are made of different shapes and colors of glass, so make your pictures a collection of different shapes.

Workstation 5 — Witness to the World

GETTING READY

Picture books illustrating Christian symbols can be helpful. Post a sign-up sheet for someone to tell about his or her drawing and hang it in the church today. Copy and post the following instructions for the children:

> Stained glass windows use color and light to create a picture which tells a story. Read Matthew 6:22-23 and John 8:12. Draw a picture which explains the importance of Jesus in your life today. You may draw a symbol of light on your window. Be creative and remember that different shapes of colored glass make up the pictures on stained glass windows.

Workstation 6 — Prayer

GETTING READY

Copy and post the following instructions for the children:

> Take a moment to rest and sew a letter.

Workstation 7 — Benediction

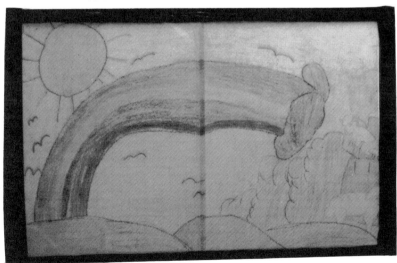

GETTING READY

Find pictures illustrating Psalm 23. Post a sign-up sheet for someone to tell about his or her drawing and hang it in the church. Copy and post the following instructions for the children:

Read Psalm 23. Draw a picture for a stained glass window to hang in your church to explain the meaning of this familiar Psalm.

The Worship Celebration

I. Call to Worship — Person who signed up tells about his or her drawing from Proverbs 16:23, 24 and Psalm 100, then hangs it in the church.

II. Affirmation of Faith — Person who signed up tells about his or her drawing on Matthew 5:1-12, then hangs it in the church.

III. Offering — Person who signed up shares about the progress that has been made on the Bible stand.

IV. Sermon — Person who signed up tells about his or her drawing on the life of Jesus, then hangs it in the church.

V. Witness to the World — Person who signed up tells about his or her drawing from Matthew 6:22-23 with the symbol of light, then hangs it in the church.

VI. Benediction — Person who signed up tells about his or her drawing on Psalm 23, then hangs it in the church.

VII. Give each child a different color or shape "God Loves You" sticker because they have really worked hard today. Make sure that no two pieces are the same. Explain that even though we are all different, we are all an equal part of the same church. We are all children of God.

Items to Go Home

Stickers or make your own "God Loves You" badge.

SESSION 18

YOU ARE THE LIGHT

The Bible Lesson

Having to color, sew, or build a project together as a group and accept the imperfections of others' work is hard for children. Teach the importance of completing a difficult task (Matthew 5:14-16).

What the Children Will Learn Today

I use stories throughout this book because I find children more willing to listen to a story. "The Flower Court" explains that everyone is special in a fun way that children can remember.

The set-up is the same as last week for the windows, except the Prayer workstation includes making clay hand lamps.

Time Needed

Twenty minutes for workstations and 10 minutes for story.

Supplies Needed

1. Wood and woodworking basket.
2. Stained glass window drawings, Bibles, and a snack.
3. Workstation signs and instructions (five copies of new instructions, plus last week's instructions for stations 1, 2, 3, 4, 5 and 7).
4. Sing-along tapes or records.
5. Crayons, pencils, and gum erasers.
6. Clay for lamps (self-drying or oven baked).

WORKSTATIONS

All workstations are the same as last week.

GETTING READY

Place all windows at their appropriate workstations and make sure the instructions from last week are still up in stations 1, 2, 3, 4, 5, and 7. Copy and post the following instructions at stations 1, 2, 4, 5, and 7:

Finish drawing any windows that were not finished last week. Finish all of your drawings before you start to color. Outline each square or shape with a black crayon. All windows must be ready to color next week. If you finish drawing and outlining, then go over to the lamp station and make a clay hand lamp.

Making hand lamps and stained glass windows shows the contrast between life in biblical times and today.

Workstation 3 — Offering

GETTING READY

Copy and post the following instructions for the children:

Work on the Bible stand and candleholders. Continue where you left off last week. Make sure all boards are sanded smooth.

Workstation 6 — Prayer

GETTING READY

Set out pictures of Old Testament and New Testament hand lamps. Follow the directions on the clay you purchase. Copy and post the following instructions for the children:

Sit and sew for a few minutes today. Then read Matthew 5:14-16. When Jesus was a boy, the main source of light in the house was a small clay hand lamp filled with oil. It didn't give out much light. Stained glass windows need light to show their true beauty.

Clay is stiff. Take a piece of clay and shape it into a round ball. Then form a bowl with a spout for the lamp. Look at the example. Place lamp on foil to dry.

The Worship Celebration

Read or tell the story "The Flower Court."

Items to Go Home

Hand lamps.

The Flower Court

One day three children went out into a field behind their house in search of the most beautiful flower they could find to honor a very special guest who was coming for dinner that evening.

Michael asked Samantha, "What kind of flower are you going to look for?" Samantha shook her head with a look of puzzlement on her face. "I'm not really sure," she said, "but it has to be delicate and fluttering in the breeze and pale in color."

Michael then turned to Caesandra, who everyone just called "Candy" because Caesandra always seemed to be too much of a name for someone so tiny. "I suppose you are looking for something delicate and perfect, too," he said with just a touch of sarcasm.

"No, no," she replied. "I'm looking for . . . ," her sentence trailed behind her as she wandered off dragging her basket across the tops of the flowers.

Michael was left alone to shake his head in disbelief. Why him? Two sisters! Why couldn't they have been two brothers? The two girls were always pretending they were twins and wanting everything exactly the same. It made him feel totally left out.

Michael stomped out across the field, tossing his basket higher and higher into the air as he walked, never noticing the flowers crushed beneath his feet.

All the while, the girls stood holding hands and examining each and every flower with precise care. "No, that one wouldn't do, there was a brown spot on it," said one. "That one's too big," said the other, as they brushed past a flower bent over from its own weight.

Finally, the two girls sat down, exhausted. Candy collapsed onto the ground, sinking into a bed of towering flowers as Samantha went on to look alone.

In the meantime, Michael had stopped to attack a young tree that was next to the stream that bubbled and gurgled its way through the field. The young tree wasn't bothering Michael. Michael didn't mean to bother the tree either — not really. It was just that the tree was there. And Michael was very bored looking for flowers — excuse me, "one special flower, perfect in every way," he mimicked Samantha, pointing his nose up into the air.

As you might have guessed, Michael and Samantha didn't exactly get along. Candy was all right, she was little, and besides that, Michael loved to make Samantha scream with jealousy by being really nice to Candy so that Candy would play with him for a while instead of playing with Samantha. Samantha couldn't stand for Candy to play with anyone but her.

But Michael's mind was on this tree right now; he wanted to see if he could make it bend all the way over and touch the water. As for his flower, he could pick one up on the way home.

In the midst of all of this flower searching, Candy had fallen asleep in the middle of the field of flowers. Only the handle of her basket could be seen peeking ever so slightly over the tops of the flowers.

As Candy slept, she dreamed of a courtroom (just like the one she had seen on television the night before), but this time the courtroom was filled with flower people.

The judge sat wearing a long, flowing, pink judicial-looking robe pounding Daddy's hammer on top of a sewing machine table strewn with ribbons and pink and purple flowery fabric.

As Candy looked around the courtroom, she could see each flower very intricately. There were powder blue bachelor buttons on wiry stems looking as if a strong breeze would blow the fringed petals everywhere. There were ever-so-pink butterfly flowers covered with delicate spokes of petals. The purple heliotrope looked to her just like purple broccoli in bloom. There were peace roses, mother's favorite, with each velvety yellow petal having just a touch of pink to tease. There was the stately iris. And the tiny coral bells seemed to ring and tinkle as they sat waiting their turn.

Each flower in turn went before the judge. The judge would ask in his deep, low, but kindly voice, "And just why do you think you should be selected as the prettiest flower of the field?"

Each flower presented its case, telling about its radiant beauty, the fragrance that it alone could provide, and expounding endlessly how no other flower could compare.

The judge listened patiently to each flower. All the flowers in the packed courtroom had taken a turn to tell how they were better than everyone else and how they and only they would be the right flower to be crowned "Perfect Flower of the Year." The flower selected would reign supreme over all the other flowers of the garden as the most beautiful and best ever.

The judge leaned back in his shiny leather chair with its slight squeak when it tilted backwards and sighed a long, breathy sigh. And finally, after what seemed like hours of endless silence, the judge slowly began to speak.

"I can't choose," he said, and then stopped with a long pause. "There is no one flower absolutely and always prettier than the other. It all depends on what you like, your favorite color, or what you think looks pretty. There is no one better fragrance. Again, it all depends on . . ." He paused.

"The beauty of the flowers lies in how they're different. How each one looks different than another, how each one smells different than the other, how each one grows differently than the rest, how each one needs different tending than its neighbor. The most beautiful flower of all is when all the flowers are together side by side, hand in hand, touching each other and helping in whatever way they can — the tall flowers standing tall and proud behind the low-lying new flowers to provide them shade, or the strong flowers serving as stakes on which the vines and young tendrils can anchor themselves. This and this alone is the beauty of being a flower."

As the judge raised Daddy's hammer to pound the finality of his decision, Candy heard a loud bell clanging off in the distance, which sounded amazingly similar to the bell Mother always rang to tell them it was time to return home for dinner.

Wanting desperately to return to her dream, Candy put the sound of the bell out of her mind, rolled over amid the flowers, breathed deeply their fragrant smell, and returned once more to the courtroom filled with flowers.

Meanwhile, the dinner bell really was clanging to call the children home for dinner. Arriving first, Michael immediately announced that he had found this fabulous tree and had decided to bring a leaf instead of a flower because it reminded him of . . . *(Pause)* Samantha broke into the middle of what was about to be one of Michael's hour-long, never-ending, nonstop explanations.

Looking totally disappointed and exhausted, her hair stringing down from her barrette, which was just about to fall out onto the ground, letting her long auburn brown hair fall every which way, Samantha said breathlessly, "I couldn't find what I wanted. Could I have a little more time? Just one more chance to go and look again. I know I can find just the right flower before dinner, and I'll bring one for you too, Candy."

Candy! Where was Candy? They had completely forgotten about Candy. Samantha started running as fast as she could, throwing her beloved basket aside as the wailed, "Candy! Candy! Wake up!"

Again in the courtroom of flowers, the judge in Candy's dream opened his mouth to speak, but all Candy could hear was her name being repeated over and over: "Candy! Candy! Candy!"

Still half-asleep and wanting to finish her wonderful dream of the flower court, Candy ever-so-softly pushed herself up with her arms till her eyes could just barely peek over the heads of the flowers that surrounded her on the ground. She was safe here, she thought. She could sink back down into the flowers and dream again. But then there was the call, "Candy! Where are you?"

This time Candy sat all the way up — just in time, too, for it was at that very moment that Samantha came bounding through the flowers, her hair streaming behind her and her long skirts parting the flowers as she ran, she almost landed right on top of little Caesandra hidden among the flowers.

"Candy! Are you all right?" Samantha inquired, throwing both arms around Candy and knocking her back down to the ground.

"Fine," Candy answered with a yawn. "Samantha!" Candy barked all of a sudden. "You stepped on my basket."

"I'm sorry. I was just so worried. I . . . I had forgotten about you," said Samantha.

"I had the most wonderful dream about flowers," said Candy. "There was . . ." Candy was about to explain all about the flower court and the judge with Daddy's hammer when their mom and Michael arrived. Mother picked Candy up and asked, "Are you all right, Candy?" Candy answered "Yes!" again, but this time she began to sound a little irritated at having been asked the same question over and over again.

"Good," her mother said, hugging and kissing each of the children. "Then bring your flowers and let's go home for dinner," said their mother.

"We can't," said Candy, continuing without even taking a breath so no one would have a chance to interrupt her and take away her turn to speak. "There is no one flower prettier than another, just like there is no one person prettier than another or better than another," Candy said, as she gasped for breath.

"You can never be better, you can only be different, and the part of you that makes you different than everyone else is what makes you beautiful — not more beautiful than someone else, just beautiful in your own special way. That's what the judge said," Candy explained.

"What judge?" said Michael.

"The judge in the Flower Court," snapped Candy.

"You must have been dreaming," their mother explained. "Must have been," whispered Michael softly.

"Well, in that case," said Samantha, "we'll have to collect one of each kind of flower so no one is left out. Come on," she shouted, as she turned and started back out into the field.

"Not tonight," her mother said, as she reached for Samantha's arm.

"It's time for dinner, bath, and bed. Tomorrow you may pick all of the flowers you wish. And besides, we have company. Tonight, instead of a special flower to sit in the middle of our table, we will have a special story."

"Candy," her mother said, looking down at her youngest child lying nestled in her arms, "will you tell us your story?"

Candy proudly pranced to the dinner table and proceeded to tell in elaborate detail all about the judge and the flower court in between reminders from her mom and dad to pause and eat as well.

That night, when all three children had been kissed, hugged, and tucked into bed, Candy sank her little head onto her pillow and smiled as she closed her eyes to dream more about the Judge with Daddy's hammer and the beautiful, flower-bedecked courtroom of her dream.

SESSION 19

USE GOD'S COLORS TO COLOR YOUR WORLD

The Bible Lesson

The Bible lesson talks about five different colors as used in the Bible: 2 Chronicles 5:12-13, Jude 13-16, Ephesians 4:31-32, Mark 15:17-18, Exodus 35:5, Matthew 6:5-7, and Numbers 15:38-39.

What the Children Will Learn Today

Set-up is the same. Place each window at its appropriate station with crayons. Do not use markers. The oil will not work with markers. Have sing-along tapes playing while the children work.

Time Needed

Twenty-five minutes for workstations and five for worship.

Supplies Needed

1. Wood and woodworking basket.
2. Bibles, a snack and sing-along tapes.
3. Workstation signs and instructions.
4. Craft supply basket: Usual supplies plus — a crayon sharpener and gum erasers — and be sure to have a good supply of crayons.
5. "I'm an Important Person" stickers (may be handmade).

WORKSTATIONS

Workstation 1 — Call to Worship

GETTING READY

Copy and post the following instructions for the children:

> Read 2 Chronicles 5:12-13. The Levite musicians dressed in white as a symbol of purity and being ready to serve God. The white dove is still used as a symbol of peace today. Color your

window and use as many different crayons as you can find. Press down hard when you color so the colors will shine through. Color the entire window. Outline each design with black crayon.

Workstation 2 — Affirmation of Faith

GETTING READY

Copy and post the following instructions for the children:

Black is the color of darkness and often refers to disaster, trouble, or death. Read Jude 13 and 16. Outline each design in black. Then color the entire window in beautiful, bright colors. Use only crayons — no markers. Color hard so that the colors will show through when the window is hung up.

Workstation 3 — Offering

GETTING READY

Use small finishing nails when nailing the trim onto the stand. Copy and post the following instructions for the children:

Read Ephesians 4:31-32. Then, start where you left off last week and finish building the Bible stand. Sand all of the edges completely smooth.

If you finish before the worship service, start to work on the candleholders. Cut to 7" x 8" boards and two 5" long 2 x 4s. Take turns with the saw. Then, sand smooth.

Workstation 4 — Sermon/Bible Lesson

GETTING READY

Copy and post the following instructions for the children:

Purple is often used for people who have power or for a kingship. Read Mark 15:17-18. Color your window completely today. Use only crayons. Press down hard with your crayons so that the color will show up when the light shines through. Outline the designs with a black crayon to represent lead in a real stained glass window.

Workstation 5 — Witness to the World

GETTING READY

Copy and post the following instructions for the children:

Read Exodus 35:5. We often think that gold or money is all we have that is special enough to give to God, but actually how we live our lives is a much better gift to offer to God. Color your window with crayons and think about all the gifts that God has given you. Press down hard, color the entire window, and outline in black.

Workstation 6 — Prayer

GETTING READY

Copy and post the following instructions for the children:

Read Matthew 6:5-7, then pick a special color of yarn to sew a letter with today.

Workstation 7 — Benediction

GETTING READY

Copy and post the following instructions for the children:

Blue is a color often used for God. Blue stands for the truth. Read Numbers 15:38-39. Color your window, making it beautiful. Outline each design in black. Use only crayons and color hard so that the colors will show through. Color your window completely today.

The Worship Celebration

Hang the windows in the church and explain the meaning of the Bible colors.

Items to Go Home

Hand out "I'm an Important Person" stickers. If time permits, the children may make their own using the self-stick name tags in the craft supply basket.

SESSION 20

OIL TO HELP US SEE BETTER

The Bible Lesson

Working together and making decisions as a group is the best way to teach that everyone is equal and has a contribution to make (Luke 11:33-36).

What the Children Will Learn Today

If some of the groups did not finish coloring their windows last week, make sure they finish coloring first. You need to make sure that all windows are finished today.

Time Needed

Twenty-five minutes for workstations and five minutes for worship today.

Supplies Needed

1. Wood and woodworking basket.
2. Bibles and a snack.
3. Workstation signs and instructions.
4. Musical instruments and song book.
5. Newspapers, crayons, cooking oil, brushes and windows.
6. Crepe paper streamers of various colors.

WORKSTATIONS

Workstation 1 — Call to Worship

GETTING READY

Find a song for the children to sing or play about colors and light (e.g. "Jesus Loves the Little Children" or "This Little Light of Mine"). Post a sign-up sheet for musicians to lead this song in the worship celebration. Copy and post the following instructions for the children:

Every Sunday is a day of celebration — a day to celebrate God's love. Practice and be ready to lead the group in a joyous Call to Worship.

Workstation 2 — Affirmation of Faith

GETTING READY

All windows must be colored and oiled today. You cannot oil a window until it is completely colored. Check the windows before they go to be oiled, because color cannot be added to a window after it is oiled. Make sure the colors are dark enough and that every square has been outlined in black. Copy and post the following instructions for the children:

If you did not finish coloring your window last week, you must finish coloring the entire window before starting to put oil on the window. Check to make sure you colored each square dark enough for the color to show through. Make sure you outlined each square with black crayon to give the effect of the lead. It's hard work to create these beautiful (paper) stained glass windows, but it's worth it. Keep up the good work.

Workstation 3 — Offering

GETTING READY

Do not use electric power tools; use a brace and bit. You can also use cordless electric candles instead of wax for fire safety. Just drill the hole needed for your particular candles. Copy and post the following instructions for the children:

Finish the Bible stand and candleholders. Have both of your projects ready to paint next week. Work with an adult helper to drill holes for the candles. Safety first!

Workstations 4, 5 and 7 —
Sermon, Witness and Benediction

GETTING READY

Make sure pictures have been completely colored before oiling. Set up long tables where all of the pictures can be oiled. Cover the tables with lots of newspaper. Copy and post the following instructions for the children:

Your job today is to oil the stained glass window pictures that you colored last week. First, make sure that the picture has been colored completely. Then take a paintbrush and brush oil over the entire paper. Keep the window on the newspaper and let it dry till next week. If you finish before worship time, go help someone else or sew.

Workstation 6 — Prayer

GETTING READY

Copy and post the following instructions for the children:

Sew a L, I, G, H, or T letter on the prayer banner today.

The Worship Celebration

I. Call to Worship — Sing the color or light song.

II. Prayer — Count the letters that are finished on the Lord's Prayer banner.

III. Benediction — Celebrate the completion of the stained glass windows.

Items to Go Home

Send everyone home in flowing colors. Tie streamers of different colors onto belt loops or anything the children choose. The colorful streamers will blow in the breeze as they walk.

SESSION 21

SHOW THE WORLD GOD'S LOVE IN ACTION

The Bible Lesson

While you have a joyous atmosphere of excitement over finishing the stained glass windows for your church, share one of Jesus' special lessons on humility. Jesus told this story while at a joyous celebration (Luke 14:7-11).

What the Children Will Learn Today

While the children should be proud of their accomplishments, today's lesson reminds us that everyone is special. By showing someone else's importance rather than our own, we will begin to see our own real importance in life.

Time Needed

Allow 25 minutes for the workstations and five minutes for worship.

Supplies Needed

1. Paint and painting cover-ups.
2. Bibles and a special snack for today's celebration.
3. Workstation signs and instructions.
4. Musical instruments and song book.
5. Craft basket: Usual supplies, plus clear contact paper, black plastic tape, thumbtacks, and black construction paper.
6. Different colors of dark (reds, blues) tissue paper.

WORKSTATIONS

Workstation 1 — Call to Worship

GETTING READY

Post a sign-up sheet for the musicians for today's service, and copy and post the following instructions for the children:

Pick a joyous song to lead today in celebration of work well done.

Workstation 2 — Affirmation of Faith

GETTING READY

The children are being placed in situations where they have to share, take turns, stop what they are doing to help someone else, and show kindness through their work together. Provide the clear contact paper and scissors, and copy and post the following instructions for the children:

The last step in making your own (paper) stained glass windows is to cover your drawings that you oiled last week with clear contact paper. Measure and cut the contact paper to fit about one inch larger than the picture all the way around. Do one piece of clear contact paper at a time. Work slowly to avoid bubbles and wrinkles. Start with a corner and work your way down. Then cut another piece of clear contact paper the same size as the first and cover the other side of the window. Send the windows over to the church to be installed.

Workstation 3 — Offering

GETTING READY

Emphasize that today's offering is not only the monetary offering the children placed in the collection box church, but also their church that they are making with their own hands. Provide black tape, thumbtacks, paint, and brushes. Copy and post the following instructions for the children:

> You are in charge of installing the (paper) stained glass windows in your church today. After the windows are covered with clear contact paper, thumbtack each window into place. Then seal the edges with the black plastic tape to make a window frame. Work slowly. You may also paint your Bible stand and candleholders today.

Workstations 4 and 5 —
Sermon and Witness

GETTING READY

Jesus told this story of humility (Luke 14:7-11) at a grand feast. In the middle of the festivities, Jesus reminded everyone of the need to be humble. Post a sign-up sheet for those actors who want to pantomime this story. (Parts: bride, host, groom, other guests, musicians, and a reader.) Copy and post the following instructions for the children:

> The sermon sets the scene for a great feast (Luke 14:7-11). During Jesus' life, when someone was invited to a big dinner or wedding party, there would often be a long, low table in the center of the room. The host sat at the head of the table with the guests gathered around the other three sides. The wedding couple and family would be the honored guests and would sit to the right and left of the host. Place cards would not have been used as they are today. Jesus tells in his story that we should not just sit down in the places of honor at the right or left of the host, but instead we should go down to the end of the table and sit in the most humble of places so that we might be asked to move up into a place of more importance. If we assume our own importance, then we might be embarrassed if we had to move down.
>
> You and your friends should be able to have a lot of fun with this story. Dress everyone in biblical costumes for a wedding feast. Use a mat for the table. Set the table and have guests coming in as music is played on the drums or tambourine. Have the guests scurry around to find a place to sit near the food and the host. Then the bride and groom come in, expecting to sit in the places of honor. Make everyone stand up and move down to make room for them.
>
> Have someone read out loud while you act out the story.

Workstation 6 — Prayer

GETTING READY

Copy and post the following instructions for the children:

How many letters have been stitched so far? Sew one or two more today to add to the list.

Workstation 7 — Benediction

GETTING READY

Have the contact paper measured and cut ahead of time. Also provide black construction paper and several different colors of tissue paper. Red, blue, and other dark colors work best for this window. Either provide a sample finished window or a frame the children can use as a pattern. Copy and post the following instructions for the children:

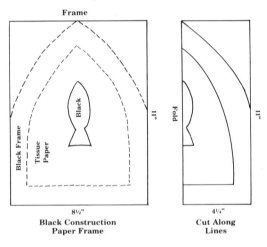

Everyone loves stained glass windows, but you are more important than even the prettiest windows anywhere in the world. As a reminder of just how special you really are, take a piece of clear contact paper, peel the paper off, and lay the contact paper down on the table — sticky side up. Cut or tear small pieces of tissue paper in as many different colors as you like. Arrange the small squares and triangles of tissue paper on the sticky side of the contact paper. Cover the entire piece of contact paper with these tissue paper shapes. When your window is covered with tissue paper, cut a fish symbol or other symbol of your choice from black construction paper. Then place another piece of clear contact paper over your tissue and symbol. Take another piece of black construction paper and fold into a 4¼" x 11" frame. Use pattern and trace window frame. Cut out your frame and glue it down.

The Worship Celebration

I. Call to Worship — A celebration song the musicians have prepared.

II. Sermon — At the end of the Bible story (Luke 14:7-11), ask how we can show humility in our children's church. Offer suggestions.

III. Benediction — Send the group home with the thought that we should show our love for each other and God by helping others to feel important and special. Remind the children that being humble does not mean being critical of yourself. Be proud but not boastful.

Items to Go Home

Tissue paper stained glass windows.

PART III

THE WORSHIP
EXPERIENCE

CHAPTER EIGHT

THE MISSION OF THE CHURCH

As the children make a Thanksgiving basket for a needy family, they see that Thanksgiving is not only a time to receive and give thanks, but it is also a time to give so that others may be thankful.

Giving Thanks at Thanksgiving

You will want to adapt the church holiday programs in the next four chapters to fit your church's traditions and calendar, since it is hard to predict at what stage of building your children's church the holidays will occur in any given year. Just insert these holiday programs when appropriate.

SESSION 22
SHOWING WE CARE

The Bible Lesson

The lesson today is a story about Thanksgiving. Every child is invited to participate (Matthew 25:34-40 and 45).

What the Children Will Learn Today

Help the children reach out and share with others. Celebrate God's love both in and out of the church.

Time Needed

Twenty minutes for workstations and 10 minutes for the worship service.

Supplies Needed

1. Old magazines to cut pictures from.
2. Bibles and a snack, if desired.
3. Craft supply basket: Usual supplies plus tempera paint, painting covers-ups, and brushes.
4. An international song to play and sing.
5. Felt board, basket, and pictures of food for telling story — turkey, potatoes, salad, and so on.
6. Two or three cardboard boxes the size of grocery cartons and paper to cover each that the children can draw on.
7. Workstation signs and instructions.

WORKSTATIONS
Workstation 1 — Call to Worship

GETTING READY

Select a song from another country to remind the children that there are hungry people at home and around the world. Post a sign-up sheet for musicians who will play this song in today's celebration, and copy and post the following instructions for the children:

> Take the instruments and practice a musical invitation from another country. Sign the sheet if you would like to play and lead the singing today.

Workstations 2, 3, 4 and 5 —
Affirmation, Offering, Sermon, Witness

GETTING READY

It is hard to find a basket large enough to put all of the food into, so a cardboard box for the children to decorate works fine. Have cover-ups for all painters. Post a sign-up sheet for a volunteer to present the food box during the offering today. Also, copy and post the following instructions for the children:

> Our lesson today is sharing your time and your ideas with others. To decorate these cardboard boxes, cover them with paper. Then draw pictures, paint, or write things you are thankful for on each box.

Workstation 6 — Prayer

GETTING READY

Copy and post the following instructions for the children:

> Find a needle and thread and work on a letter or two. Count how many letters you alone have done so far. Count how many letters have been done by the group. You are a very important member of the group.

Workstation 7 — Benediction

GETTING READY

Have everyone cut out pictures and bring them to the closing worship celebration. Use these pictures for the story and then pass them out for the children to take home.

You may photocopy the example note or write your own, but it is very important to send *written* communication home. Small children often misunderstand what you say.

Adult Sunday school classes are often excited to donate money to such a worthwhile children's project. Copy and post the following instructions for the children:

> This morning, cut pictures from old magazines to put together a grand Thanksgiving dinner. Your picture dinner should have all of your favorites. It should contain nutritious food from the four basic food groups, and it should make up a yummy meal that anyone would want to eat. Bring the meal you have planned to worship.

The Worship Celebration

I. Call to Worship/Affirmation — Musicians play foreign song while boxes are brought forward.

II. Sermon — Set up the felt board and tell the story "The Thanksgiving Basket." Have cut-out food pictures in a small basket in your lap to tell the story. Improvise a bit, depending on what foods the children have cut out too.

III. Benediction — Place the pictures the children cut from magazines in the box and ask the children to pick one to take home before they leave. Give the reminders to the parents.

The Thanksgiving Basket

What are you going to eat at your house for Thanksgiving? *(Respond to the children's answers.)* Turkey! How many like turkey and dressing? I do, too. So I'll put up a picture of a turkey cooked and ready for Thanksgiving.

What else do you like to eat at Thanksgiving? Did I hear someone say sweet potatoes? Yes, we have some sweet potatoes and some mashed potatoes. *(Put pictures of these — or whatever it is that the children say — on the felt board beside the turkey.)*

What else do we need? Green beans, peas, carrots — some vegetables. You didn't say "yuk," did you? Even though we don't like carrots as well as we like chocolate cake, we do need vegetables.

Speaking of chocolate cake, we have desserts — cookies, pies, cakes, ice cream. Everything you can imagine. And yes, we do have peanut butter and jelly. We must always remember the peanut butter. *(Put up a big picture of peanut butter.)*

Now, is there anything missing? *(Respond to the answers you receive from the children.)* How about fruit salad?

Bread! We don't have any bread for our dinner yet. We must have some bread. Yummy homemade dinner rolls.

And I'd like something to drink; maybe some juice or milk.

Well, what do you think? Is this going to be a grand Thanksgiving dinner? I think so, too.

Thinking about Thanksgiving reminds me of a story I want to tell about a little girl named Amanda.

Amanda wasn't planning a big Thanksgiving dinner like we just did. No, she wasn't planning on anything for Thanksgiving. Her mom had said there wouldn't be enough money to buy a turkey this year, but maybe they could get some bologna.

But all of the children at Amanda's school were talking about going here or there for Thanksgiving and who was going to have the largest turkey. Somehow it just didn't seem fair. Amanda didn't care if they had the largest turkey or not, but for just one year, it really would be nice if her family could have a turkey too — just a little tiny one would do.

Instead, Amanda and her four brothers, mom, and dad would have bologna and cheese sandwiches for Thanksgiving. Bologna is OK, but it's not the same as having a turkey for Thanksgiving.

One afternoon, right after she came home from school, there was a knock at the door. Amanda's mother opened the door to find a kind gentleman standing at the door holding this nicely decorated box filled with food. He said, "Hello, I'm from the church around the corner. Our children have prepared this Thanksgiving basket to share. Your neighbor is a member of our church and said your husband had been laid off from work. It would make the children of our church very happy if we could share this food with you." There was a long pause. Amanda's mother stepped backwards and motioned for the gentleman still holding the heavy box to come inside.

"This sure is kind of you," Amanda's mother said. The man smiled and said, "We're just glad to help out a fellow neighbor."

As the gentleman set the box down on the kitchen table he said, "Just a minute — there's another box."

The man with the kindest smile Amanda had ever seen brought in another box of food. There were fresh baked dinner rolls, pies, sweet potatoes, fruits and vegetables of every kind, and there sitting in the bottom of the second box was the biggest, most beautiful turkey Amanda had ever seen.

Amanda could hardly believe her eyes. As she heard her mother say "thank you" over and over, Amanda thought about Thanksgiving. But this time, instead of bologna and cheese, Amanda saw turkey and dressing, just like everybody else would be eating. And when she went back to school on Monday, and everyone asked what she did for Thanksgiving,

Amanda was going to stand up proud and tall, and say she had the best Thanksgiving ever. And when the teacher asked her to tell one thing that she was thankful for, Amanda was going to say, "My new friends around the corner." *(Pause)*

We're going to be making a Thanksgiving basket to share with a family in our neighborhood this Thanksgiving. If you would like to, you may bring something to put in our basket next week. There are several pictures here for you to choose from. *(Point to the box.)* Now, even if you can't bring a food item or a nickel or dime to put in the food box, come next week and help us make bread, a pie, and some cookies. Because giving your time is just as important as giving money and food. And sharing with others is what Thanksgiving is all about.

Items to Go Home

Food pictures and a note explaining the Thanksgiving project.

Dear Parents,

We are preparing a food basket to go to a needy family for Thanksgiving. The children do not have to donate anything to the basket. Those who wish may bring the food item that they selected today, and some money to help purchase a turkey. Next Sunday, the children will mix and prepare bread, a pie, and cookies. (The children will NOT use a stove.) Thank you!

SESSION 23

THANKSGIVING BASKET

The Bible Lesson

The Bible lesson today (Matthew 25:34-40 and 45) is too long for most children to sit still for, so it is simplified.

What the Children Will Learn Today

The mission of the church is to serve the needs of others by sharing what we have.

Time Needed

Twenty minutes at workstations and 10 minutes for worship.

Supplies Needed

1. Workstation signs, instructions, and supply baskets.
2. Decorated cardboard boxes for food.
3. Do not serve a snack today.
4. Recipes and ingredients for bread, cookies, and pie.
5. Bibles and the pictures made in Session 9, Chapter 4.
6. Sing-along tapes (playing in the background while the children work).

WORKSTATIONS

Workstations 1 and 2 —
Call to Worship and Affirmation

GETTING READY

Waxed paper on the tables makes clean-up a lot easier. Heat milk ahead of time. Keep the milk and margarine warm till needed by wrapping a towel around the container. Post a sign-up sheet for a volunteer to place the bread next to the boxes, and copy and post the following instructions for the children:

Why do you think Jesus said he was the "Bread of Life"? Talk it over as you make bread today. If you need to add extra flour, add only one tablespoon at a time. Then, knead before adding more.

Never Fail Bread Recipe

2 eggs	½ cup milk
4½ cups flour	½ cup water
½ cup sugar	½ cup margarine
2 teaspoons salt	2 packages quick-rise yeast

Oven temperature: 350 degrees

Heat water, milk, and margarine in a pan till it starts to bubble. Do not let it boil. Set aside to cool.

Stir eggs, flour, sugar, salt, and yeast together in a bowl. Add milk mixture to flour, salt, yeast, and sugar.

Knead bread dough by hand. Knead again and again until very smooth and elastic. Roll into balls or make into any shape.

Place each ball of dough in a buttered round pie pan, muffin tins, or on a buttered cookie sheet. You should have about 12 round balls of dough. Cover and let rise again for one or two hours.

Bake in oven at 350 degrees for approximately 30 minutes or until golden brown.

Workstation 3 — Offering

GETTING READY

Do not serve a snack today to make the point that, although we are preparing a very nice dinner for one family and we will be eating a Thanksgiving dinner of our own, many people in our own town and around the world are hungry this Thanksgiving. Post a sign-up sheet for volunteers to place the cookies inside the box in worship today. Copy and post the following instructions for the children:

No cooking involved; just mix.

No Bake Cookie Recipe

1 cup dried fruits, peanuts, raisins, coconut, or nuts

5 cups of dry cereal (any variety)

1½ cups of peanut butter

½ cup of honey

Mix all ingredients together. Press down into a buttered aluminum pie pan. Let chill in the refrigerator for two hours.

Workstation 4 — Sermon/Bible Lesson

GETTING READY

Hang the liturgical green banner and the Alleluia banner before the children arrive. Have the pictures from Session 9, Chapter 4 for the children to put up. Copy and post the following instructions for the children:

Read Matthew 25:34-40 and 45. Then hang up the pictures in your church for Thanksgiving decorations.

Workstation 5 — Witness to the World

GETTING READY

This simple, no-crust recipe is easy for children to make. You may need to help younger children peel the apples. Post a sign-up sheet for a volunteer to place the pie next to the box in worship today. Copy and post the following instructions for the children:

> Read the recipe and follow the directions. I will do the cooking later.
>
> ## No-Crust Apple Pie Recipe
>
> 5 apples   ½ cup softened margarine
>
> 1 tablespoon lemon juice   ¾ cup brown sugar
>
> 1 cup oatmeal
>
> Peel, core, and cut all of the apples into thin quarter-moon-shaped wedges. Place the apples in the aluminum pie pan and sprinkle the lemon juice over the apples.
>
> Mix the oatmeal, brown sugar, and softened margarine in a bowl. With your hands, crumble the oatmeal mixture over the top of the apples. Make sure the apples are completely covered.
>
> Cook at 325 degrees for 45 minutes or until bubbly and golden brown.

Workstation 6 — Prayer

GETTING READY

Copy and post the following message for the children:

> Thanks for remembering to stop in the middle of your busy schedule to sew a letter today.

Workstation 7 — Benediction

GETTING READY

A continuous drawing shows that we all have important parts to play in the total picture of life, no matter how big or how small. Bring extra canned goods or ask an adult or youth Sunday school class if they would like to contribute so the children who forget to bring something will have items for the box. Set the craft supply basket out, and copy and post the following instructions for the children:

> The Benediction today is a card to send with our Thanksgiving basket. Have everyone sign the card on the inside and add to the picture on the cover.

The picture on the cover of our card will be a continuous drawing. Start with one person drawing a simple line somewhere on the front cover; the second person adds to that line, and so on, attempting to make a picture, figure, or something out of the line. By working together, we can make something beautiful!

The Worship Celebration

I. Call to Worship — As the musicians play their song, have the children bring the canned food items forward one by one and place them in the box. The older children bring the bread, pie, and snack forward and place them next to the box.

II. Offering — Explain to the children: "Did anyone notice that we have been very busy cooking all this food and we haven't even had our own snack today? Well, there is a very special reason why we aren't having a snack today. It's to remind us that right now as we sit here with all this food, some people have absolutely nothing to eat and others have only a little bit. Most of us have no idea what it means to be really hungry. But we need to pause today to remember those who do go hungry every day."

III. Prayer/Benediction — Close by saying the Lord's Prayer together.

Items to Go Home

The children will love it if your Thanksgiving basket is so full that it overflows. Send the children home with the thought that we show our love for each other and God by helping others.

NOTE: If your church has a special Thanksgiving service where food is brought forward and dedicated, the children will enjoy participating. One year our church held a community Thanksgiving service and food was brought and placed in a wheelbarrow to be given later to those in need. The children loved taking their warm, freshly baked bread up to the front of the sanctuary. The children knew they were truly participating in the service. If the box is too heavy for the children to carry, they can place it in a wagon and pull the box up to the front.

CHAPTER NINE

AN ADVENT WORKSHOP

The Advent sessions and the Christmas Eve service (led by the children) include religious traditions of the past and present: the children make Advent calendars and wreaths, design Christments, and act out the Nativity story. Also included is a Christmas tradition of the future: the Peace Garden.

SESSION 24

THE FIRST SUNDAY IN ADVENT (HOPE)

The Bible Lesson

The message from Luke 2:14: We HOPE for PEACE. We celebrate with JOY at the prospect of PEACE. We remember the LOVE and compassion that is necessary to bring about PEACE. And we strive for the kind of FAITH that will hopefully someday lead us to PEACE. And we begin the story by reading Luke 2:4-6.

What the Children Will Learn Today

Today you will be teaching the children the meaning of the Advent wreath and calendar.

Time Needed

Twenty minutes for workstations and 10 minutes for worship.

Supplies Needed

1. Advent wreath-making materials (artificial greenery, five white battery-operated candles, and green Styrofoam for the base.

2. Advent Home Worship booklet (Parts I-IV) for every child.

3. Bibles and a snack.

4. Banner-making supplies for purple liturgical banner (35" x 72" purple and ¼ yard white felt and white glitter).

5. Workstation signs and instructions.

6. Copies of the Christmas Eve service for each workstation.

7. Musical instruments and song book.

8. Tree pattern for the Advent calendar.

9. Craft supply basket: Usual supplies plus gold glitter, gold stars, a ruler, and two sheets of green construction paper per child.

10. Brown, blue, and yellow construction paper for everyone.

11. Washable purple tempera paint, string, old catalog or phone book, and paper to make covers for Advent Home Worship booklets.

WORKSTATIONS

Workstation 1 — Call to Worship

GETTING READY

The children will practice the same Call to Worship they will use for Christmas Eve. (Service is on page 171.) Take the Call to Worship right from the script; mark it in red, and select a simple song for the children to play. It is not necessary to purchase instruments. Melody glasses or a child's toy xylophone work fine. Post a sign-up sheet for these parts: Narrator (someone who reads well out loud); Busy Shopper (an acting part with only a few lines); and Musicians (at least four). Put a note on the sign-up sheet to remind the children that they will play these parts every Sunday until Christmas Eve, and also in the Christmas Eve service. Copy and post the following instructions for the children:

> The Call to Worship you practice today will be the Call to Worship for the Christmas Eve service. Practice the part marked in red.

Workstation 2 — Affirmation of Faith

GETTING READY

Make an Advent wreath today. Instead of using lit candles, use the battery-operated candles available around Christmas. Mark in red the portion of the Home Worship booklet to be used today. Post a sign-up sheet for someone to read the Narrator's statement from the Home Worship booklet today, and copy and post the following instructions for the children:

> Make an Advent wreath for our church. First, someone should read the part marked in red. Then shape the greenery into a circle. Gently place five white candles in the Styrofoam base and put the base inside the wreath. Put your wreath on the small table in the center of our church. The candles are white because white is the color for Christmas and for times of celebration in the church.

Workstation 3 — Offering

GETTING READY

You may want to collect an offering during Advent for the baby layette or peace tree (don't forget adult donations). Have patterns for tracing and copies of the Home Worship booklet for every child. An adult helper is needed here today. Copy and post the following instructions for the children:

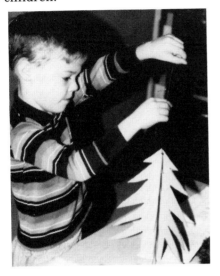

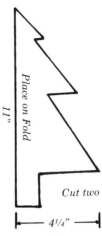

11"

Place on Fold

Cut two

|— 4¼" —|

Christmas Tree Pattern

Make an Advent calendar to keep track of the number of days till Christmas. Your calendar will be a Christment tree. The word Christment is derived from CHRIST and ornaMENT. Christments are ornaments that symbolize Christ. They may be found in your Home Worship booklet. You will color and glue a new one to your tree every day until Christmas.

Fold two pieces of green paper in half lengthwise so that they measure 4¼" x 11". Place the tree pattern against the fold of your paper. Trace and cut out two trees. Staple the two trees together at the fold (see example).

Punch a hole at the top and tie a string. Each day, cut out, color, and glue a symbol as listed in your Advent Worship booklet. Today's symbol is the candle of hope. Color the candle white with a yellow flame and then glue the candle onto the top of the tree.

Workstation 4 — Bible Lesson/Sermon

GETTING READY

Our Sermon for Advent is the story of the birth of Jesus. The Nativity picture is put together in stages; a different part is added each Sunday: the straw and stars, then the animals . . . have patterns and example. You will need the craft supply basket. Post a sign-up sheet for a reader to share Matthew 2:6 and Luke 2:4-6 in the worship celebration today, and copy and post the following instructions for the children:

11"

4"

Blue

4½"

Light Brown

Salt dough cave

14" long

Shepherds Yellow straw Donkey Sheep Mary Joseph Sheep Cow Wise men Camel

Nativity Picture

Throughout the four weeks of Advent we will be reading the Christmas story. Read Matthew 2:6 and Luke 2:4-6 from the Bible. To make your own Nativity scene, each Sunday you will add another part to your picture. Today, make the straw, sky, and stars. Cut yellow construction paper into itty bitty tiny slivers and glue them down across the bottom of the brown construction paper to make the straw.

Cut a strip of blue paper about 3" x 11" and glue lengthwise across the top of the brown paper. Stick some stars onto the blue sky of your paper Nativity. Put your name on the back. Hang your finished picture in the church.

Workstation 5 — Witness to the World

GETTING READY

The banner the children make today can be used during both Advent and Lent. Enlarge a pattern or have the children draw their own. Copy and post the following instructions for the children:

Make a new banner to hang in your church. Make the banner purple, which is the color for Advent reminding us to get ready.

The early Greek Christians often used the "X" (CHI) and the "P" (RHO), the first letters of Christ in Greek. "Christ" is the Greek word for "Messiah." Messiah is the Hebrew word for "appointed one." Today Christians use this symbol to tell people that they follow Jesus.

Measure and cut your banner if it isn't done already to 72" long and 35" wide. Make a big X and P for the symbol from gold glitter or white felt. Place the symbol on the bottom of the banner. Hang banner in your church when dry.

Workstation 6 — Prayer

GETTING READY

Copy and post the following instructions for the children:

Continue embroidering. We will be praying the Lord's Prayer together at the close of each worship celebration in Advent. Think about the words as you sew.

Workstation 7 — Benediction

GETTING READY

Have a Home Worship booklet copied for each child. Set out the catalog, paper, string, and tempera paint. An adult helper is needed today. Copy and post the following instructions for the children:

The benediction sends everyone out to share God's message of HOPE. Make a cover for your Advent Home Worship booklet. Put on a painting smock. Select two pieces of paper. Place a piece of string in the paint. Use just a little bit of paint. Place the string between the two pieces of paper. Put a heavy catalog on top of your paper. With the weight of the book on your paper, pull your string out. Remove the catalog. Open your paper and see your creation! No two pictures are exactly alike just as no two people are exactly alike. Let your paper dry and staple the Home Worship booklet inside to take home.

The Worship Celebration

Each Sunday before Christmas, the children will be lighting the Advent wreath as well as practicing for the Christmas Eve service. Their worship celebrations will be based on the Home Worship booklet services.

I. Call to Worship — Those who signed the Call to Worship sign-up sheet should enter playing their instruments. For today, use the Call to Worship from the Christmas Eve service as your opening to today's children's service.

II. Bible Lesson/Sermon — Follow with the Narrator's statement from the Home Worship booklet (First Sunday in Advent) and the lighting of the Advent Wreath.

III. Benediction — Make sure the readers are ready, then close with the Bible verses: Matthew 2:6 and Luke 2:4-6.

Items to Go Home

Send home Advent Home Worship booklets and Advent calendars.

HOME WORSHIP BOOKLET
(Part I)

To Parents: Advent was first celebrated in the seventh century and grew out of several different traditions and customs. You might see Advent wreaths with (1) three purple candles, one pink, and a white Christ candle, (2) four purple and a white Christ candle, (3) four blue and a white Christ candle, (4) four white candles and a red Christ Candle, or (5) all white candles. The meaning of the candles is often different, too, depending upon the days of fasting that the traditions come from.

Make the tradition your own. Make Advent a special time of preparation for Christmas for you and your family.

Advent Wreath: You'll need (1) a plain artificial evergreen wreath (to reduce the fire hazard) to represent eternity, the continuation of life, undying faith, and the endless flow of time, (2) five candles; use any of the colors listed above, and (3) a frame or candleholder for the candles. The traditional meanings of the candles (in order) are: 1. Hope, 2. Joy, 3. Love, 4. Faith. The Christ candle is the fifth one. Light a new candle each Sunday along with the candle from the preceding weeks.

Advent Calendar: The children have made Advent calendars in the shape of Christment trees. See the sheet of attached symbols to cut out, color, and place on the tree each day.

Set aside a special time for family worship during Advent. Bible passages and a narrated part of the story are written for each day of the week. Sing a favorite Christmas carol. Have someone read the Bible lesson and narration. Color and glue that day's Christian symbol on the Advent calendar as it is being described in the narration. Close with the Lord's Prayer.

The Meaning of Christmas
Home Worship for the First Week of Advent

Add a Christmas carol and the Lord's Prayer to each day's worship.

First Sunday in Advent: the Candle of Hope

CALL TO WORSHIP: Sing a favorite Christmas carol.

NARRATOR: **Advent is a time of spiritual preparation; a time spent getting ready for Christmas. A plain evergreen wreath is shaped into a circle to show that God's love lasts forever. The Christ candle sits in the center surrounded by the four Advent candles: Hope, Joy, Love, and Faith. This week we**

light the candle of Hope, which reminds us to get ready and wait for the birth of Jesus.

BIBLE LESSON: Matthew 2:6 and Luke 2:4-6

BENEDICTION: Lord's Prayer

Monday

NARRATOR: We add a new symbol each day to our Advent Calendar. Today we add the "Advent Rose" to remind us of the human birth of Jesus. The rose represents the hope of the Jewish people for a Messiah. "Messiah" is the Hebrew word for "chosen one" or leader. The rose comes from the prophecy that "the desert would blossom as the rose."

BIBLE LESSON: Isaiah 35:1-2

Tuesday

NARRATOR: The early Christians used the fish symbol as a secret sign of friendship. These secret symbols identified other Christians and often led early Christians to safe houses for the night and to secret places of worship.

BIBLE LESSON: Romans 13:8-10

Wednesday

NARRATOR: The fish was so popular because the Greek word for fish (Ichthus) is how the phrase IXOYC is formed: I-Jesus, X-Christ, O-God, Y-Son, and C-Savior.

BIBLE LESSON: Isaiah 2:2-4

Thursday

NARRATOR: The Tau Cross represents Moses' staff and promises.

BIBLE LESSON: Jeremiah 33:14-16

Friday

NARRATOR: Four Tau Crosses joined together remind us of the Old Testament prophecies of a Savior in Isaiah.

BIBLE LESSON: Isaiah 60:18-20

Saturday

NARRATOR: The cross with the heart sends God's
  love.
BIBLE LESSON: Mark 13:33-37

Christments to Cut and Color for the Advent Calendar

CAST
(In Order of Appearance)

Narrator*

Busy Shopper

Stagehand

Town Crier

Child 1

Child 2

Child 3

Child 4

Mary**

Joseph**

Innkeeper**

Bible Reader 1

Wise Men**

Bible Reader 2

Angel

Reader 1

Reader 2

Reader 3

Reader 4

Reader 5

Reader 6

Reader 7

Extras

(Shepherds [one line], Musicians for Call to Worship and Benediction, and Stagehands to help decorate the sanctuary.)

You may double or triple up on parts if your group is small. If you are working with a large group, include as many children as possible in the cast or extras. Remember, your goal is not to stage a perfect performance, but to include every child.

*You may use the same narrator all the way through the service, or you may use five narrators — a different one for each scene that calls for a narrator. Encourage your older, reliable children to sign up for the narrator parts.

**These are nonspeaking roles, and therefore may be performed by the younger children.

PROPS

Stack of wrapped gifts for Busy Shopper

Bell for Town Crier

Stick Donkey for Mary

Wreaths, greenery, candles and an Advent wreath (made by the children) for the Stagehands to decorate the sanctuary

Manger

Gifts for the Wise Men

Bibles for the two Bible Readers and the Angel

Wagon with small live evergreen tree ("Live Christment Tree" for the Peace Garden)

Christments which the children have made (including special Christment for top of tree)

Popcorn, needle, and thread for Stagehands to string and place on tree

COSTUMES

Use the biblical costumes you have on hand (or bathrobes) for the sermon portion of the script where the Nativity story is enacted. Mary, Joseph, the Innkeeper, Shepherds, and the Wise Men should be in costume. The Wise Men may also wear simple crowns made of cardboard and covered with foil and the Shepherds may carry canes or crooks. The angel's costume should be a white robe — cardboard wings optional.

Christmas Traditions Past and Present: Christmas Eve Worship Celebration

CALL TO WORSHIP

(CHILDREN play instruments — piano, flute, bells, or whatever — for 15 minutes before service begins as an introit. Then, have a child play piano in the background as two children arrive, one carrying an impossible stack of packages. The packages finally topple and fall.)

NARRATOR: Well, it sure looks like you're ready for Christmas.

BUSY SHOPPER: Oh, I guess so. We have our tree and everything.

NARRATOR: Did you ever wonder how all this got started — trees, candles, Christmas carols?

BUSY SHOPPER: Are you kidding? I get tired just thinking about Christmas.

NARRATOR: Why?

BUSY SHOPPER: Why! Because there's so much to do.

NARRATOR: But Christmas should be a happy time — a Celebration of Love from start to finish.

BUSY SHOPPER: *(Just sits and shakes head no.)* **You must be living in a dream world.**

NARRATOR: After all, that's why we do all of this decorating and stuff, isn't it?

BUSY SHOPPER: Oh, I guess . . .

NARRATOR: Wait! I hear something . . . *(Pause to sound of bells.)* **It's carolers! Maybe they'll cheer you up.** *(The two gather up packages and walk off in the direction of the bells.)*

(CHILDREN walk in playing instruments — jingle bells, shakers, oatmeal box drums — and singing. Stage is quiet during first verse — just music. STAGEHANDS enter on second verse, carrying in Nativity set. Speak when music stops.)

AFFIRMATION OF FAITH

NARRATOR: That's what Christmas means to me.

STAGEHAND: Me, too. Christmas is about the baby Jesus.

NARRATOR: Did you know that the Pilgrims didn't even celebrate Christmas?

TOWN CRIER: *(Walks across the front ringing bell and shouting.)* **No Christmas! No Christmas! No Christmas!**

CHILD 1: No candles?

CHILD 2: No music?

CHILD 3: No Christmas tree?

CHILD 4: No presents?

NARRATOR: Nothing! Just wash the clothes, scrub the floors, plant the crops, and sermons on Sunday as usual. *(Long moan from all CHILDREN)* Later, as living in the new world got easier, the colonists decorated their homes with evergreens, berries, and fruits found near their home. *(STAGEHANDS enter and decorate the church and communion table with wreaths and candles.)* And almost two hundred years later, one of our very favorite Christmas carols was written in Philadelphia.

SERMON/BIBLE LESSON

Congregational Hymn: "O Little Town of Bethlehem" (First verse)
(If any of the CHILDREN are learning to play Christmas carols, let them play the first time through and then have an adult take over the piano and accompany the singing. CHILDREN play instruments — shakers, drums, jingle bells — and sing with the congregation. As singing starts, MARY and JOSEPH enter with MARY riding on a (stick horse) donkey, arrive at the inn, are turned away by the INNKEEPER, and finally settle into the stable.)

NARRATOR: The Nativity scene has long been used to retell the story of Jesus' birth. From French New Orleans came the tradition of having a crèche with Mary, Joseph, and the baby Jesus in every home.

BIBLE READER 1: Luke 2:6-7. *(STAGEHANDS bring stuffed animals and place in the Nativity scene.)*

NARRATOR: In the Southwest, the early settlers celebrated with the Spanish custom of looking for the "Babe of Bethlehem." *(Child pianist plays first verse of hymn while SHEPHERDS go through congregation asking, "Do you know where the baby Jesus is?" They eventually arrive at the Nativity.)*

Congregational Hymn: "O Little Town of Bethlehem" (First verse)

NARRATOR: But not all celebrations were so grand. Sometimes the gifts were simple handmade expressions of love; other times they were very expensive expressions of wealth. Gifts sometimes came in groups of three to remind everyone of the wise men and their three gifts: gold for a king; frankincense for a special servant and leader of the church, and myrrh to symbolize his faith. *(WISE MEN arrive at Nativity with their gifts in hand.)*

BIBLE READER 2: Matthew 2:2.

NARRATOR: Martin Luther placed a tree behind the Nativity in his church in Germany because he wanted to teach the children the beauty of the night Jesus was born. The German settlers brought the tradition of the Christmas tree with them to their Midwestern farms.

(STAGEHANDS enter pulling a wagon with a small live tree. Two other STAGEHANDS sit next to the tree and string popcorn. They continue to string popcorn until Chrisments are hung. As they finish a string of popcorn, they place it on the tree.)

NARRATOR: *(Continued)* These trees were often covered with tiny burning candles and an angel on top. The angel's message to the shepherds is passed from person to person as a peace token of "salaam" in Mideastern churches. We would like to share in that tradition tonight.

(ANGEL reads Bible verse [Luke 2:14] and then takes place at Nativity. NARRATOR goes over to the closest member of the congregation and initiates the sharing of peace while pianist plays first verse. All CHILDREN, except those in the Nativity scene, go out to share with congregation.)

Congregational Hymn: (First verse)

WITNESS TO THE WORLD

NARRATOR: The early settlers decorated not only their homes but also their churches. Advent wreaths were hung from the ceiling and one candle was lit for each Sunday before Christmas.

(STAGEHANDS set up an Advent wreath in church. Children hang Chrisments on the tree while READERS read. Send a CHILD to invite any children sitting in congregation to come and hang Chrisments.)

NARRATOR: *(Continued)* The tradition of making and hanging

Christments was started to remind us of the birth of Jesus, his life and teachings, and of the struggle of the early Christians.

READER 1:   The Advent rose reminds us of his humanity.

READER 2:   The cross tells the story of his life.

READER 3:   The crown tells of his kingship and victory through the power of love.

READER 4:   Three entwined fish represent God's love, Jesus teaching us to love, and the Spirit which helps us to love.

READER 5:   The fish was drawn on jewelry and utensils as a sign of friendship.

READER 6:   The Greek initials for Christ and a cross on the mast of a sailing ship symbolize the church.

PRAYER

READER 7:   And tonight, we, the children, add a new symbol to the list — one of our own design. We have designed this symbol to represent the children who follow Jesus. As we hang our symbol on the tree, will you please join us in praying "The Lord's Prayer"? *(This is the symbol the CHILDREN make in Session 27. Hang on top of the tree.)*

OFFERING

NARRATOR: We, the children, would also like to start a new Christmas tradition. We would like to plant a peace garden. Our live evergreen Christment tree will be the first to be planted. This spring we will add flowers that we grow from seeds, a bird feeder, and tulip bulbs in the fall. The tree is a prayer for peace for every child, whether rich or poor, alone or part of a family, afraid or happy, hungry or satisfied, searching or content. And tonight we place under our peace tree a gift for a newborn baby, so that as we celebrate the birth of Jesus, we may share his love with others.

BENEDICTION

Congregational Hymn: (First Verse only)

(Close with melody glasses or other instrument playing simple tune.)

SESSION 25

THE SECOND SUNDAY IN ADVENT (JOY)

The Bible Lesson

The Christmas story from Isaiah 35:1-2 and Matthew 1:21.

What the Children Will Learn Today

Think of one child in your group who does not seem to fit in. To help even one child brings JOY to Christmas.

Time Needed

Twenty minutes for workstations and 10 minutes for worship today.

Supplies Needed

1. Advent log materials (artificial greenery, foam for the base and candles: three purple, one pink, and a white Christ candle). Reuse the greenery from last week or bring extra.
2. Advent Home Worship booklet (Part II) and Bibles.
3. Salt, flour, water, mixing bowl, spoon, and measuring cup.
4. Gold pipe cleaners with white, clear, gold, or yellow stringing beads to make Christian symbols.
5. A snack if desired.
6. Workstation signs and instructions.
7. Copies of the Christmas Eve service for each workstation.
8. Musical instruments and song book.
9. Cardboard boxes and brown grocery bags for Nativity set.
10. Craft supply basket: The usual collection of supplies plus paper plates, big roll of paper, white construction paper, paints, brushes, or other supplies for making wrapping paper.
11. Animal patterns to trace around for the stable, and texture substances for animals — ground coffee, sand, paint, sandpaper, or scraps of fake fur for Nativity scene pictures.

WORKSTATIONS

Workstation 1 — Call to Worship

GETTING READY

The children will practice the Call to Worship from the "Christmas Traditions Past and Present" service each week. Copy and post the following instructions for the children:

> Practice the same Call to Worship you did last week. Be ready to play for our service today.

Workstation 2 — Affirmation of Faith

GETTING READY

Today we are making an Advent log. You may use an actual piece of a log or Styrofoam covered with greenery. Post a sign-up sheet for today's celebration and the Christmas Eve service for the following parts: Narrator (keep the same person from last week), Stagehand (speaking part), and Stagehands (to decorate church).

Also, ask someone in the group to read the Narrator's statement from the Home Worship booklet today. Copy and post the following instructions for the children:

> Today we are making an Advent log using the materials on the table. Place three purple candles in the log to symbolize the Sundays of Advent. The pink candle stands for JOY and may be lit either the second or third Sunday in Advent. It was originally used to mark the end of a period of fasting — going without food. Smaller white candles are placed between the purple and pink to represent each day of the week. A large white Christ candle goes in the center. Practice singing "O Little Town of Bethlehem" as you work. Sign up for parts in the Christmas Eve service (marked in red).

Workstation 3 — Offering

GETTING READY

Even four-year-olds can thread beads onto a pipe cleaner, but you will have to shape it for them. You can create your own symbols or just make the simple fish described. If you have a Christment tree in your classroom, that is a perfect place to store all of the fish being made till Christmas Eve. Have at least one adult helper at the Christment workstation at all times. Copy and post the following instructions for the children:

> Christments are made in many ways. We are using beads and pipe cleaners. To make a fish: (1) fill a pipe cleaner with beads — leave half inch at each end, (2) bend the tips of the pipe cleaner over to keep the beads from falling off, (3) bend the pipe cleaner in half — making two equal lengths, (4) one third of the way up from the open ends of the pipe cleaner, twist together, and (5) then shape with your fingers to get the simple designs of a fish. Make two fish today; one to take home and one to hang up in class.

Workstation 4 — Bible Lesson/Sermon

GETTING READY

Continue the Nativity project from the last session. Have patterns or pictures available. Mix up a simple salt dough recipe of 2 cups of flour, 1 cup of salt, and 1 cup of water, or use a recipe of your own choosing. You will need one recipe for about 10 children. Bake the salt dough in your oven at 325 degrees for 15 to 20 minutes till it is golden brown so it will be hard and easy to glue down next week. Post a sign-up sheet for someone to read Isaiah 35:1-2 and Matthew 1:21 in today's worship, and copy and post the following instructions for the children:

Have someone read the Bible verses: Isaiah 35:1-2 and Matthew 1:21. Then, trace around the animal patterns for the cow and donkey on a piece of brown construction paper. Glue the animals lying down in the straw. Save room for baby Jesus, Mary, and Joseph in the middle. You may give your animals a special look. Put the glue down first, then sprinkle coffee or sand on top of the glue. Also, cut animals out of sandpaper or glue fuzzy fake fur on your animal.

Next, make the stable or cave where Jesus was born. We are making a "C" shaped cave out of salt dough. Roll the salt dough into a ball and then roll it out into a long snake around a paper plate to shape the "C". For now, place your salt dough "C" on the foil-covered baking sheet. Next week, you will glue the cave onto your scene.

Workstation 5 — Witness to the World

GETTING READY

Today the children are making wrapping paper. Use for baby layette package and children's gifts to parents. Use craft supply basket. Copy and post the following instructions for the children:

This is the "Busy Shopper" station today, but instead of thinking of things you want, we are going to work on gifts to give to others. There is a long piece of white paper on the table; this will be our wrapping paper. Decorate the paper using the supplies provided. Let the paint dry today; wrap the packages later.

Workstation 6 — Prayer

GETTING READY

Copy and post the following instructions for the children:

Keep working on our banner.

Workstation 7 — Benediction

GETTING READY

Use big boxes — moving boxes work great. Have the boxes cut open so the children will only need to cover them with paper. Supply a paper bag or two. Copy and post the following instructions for the children:

You are in charge of building the Nativity scene for our Christmas service. History tells us that Jesus was most likely born in a cave that had been dug in a nearby hill. Even though Jesus was very special, he was born in the most humble of places. Cut and glue the plain brown paper bag over any words or pictures on the box. Make the cave look a little raggedy.

The Worship Celebration

I. Call to Worship — Use the Call to Worship from the Christmas Eve Service (found in Session 24).

II. Sermon/Bible Lesson — Use the Narrator's part and the lighting of the Advent wreath from the Home Worship booklet (second Sunday of Advent).

III. Use the Affirmation from the Christmas Eve service.

IV. Benediction — Close by singing "O Little Town of Bethlehem."

Items to Go Home

Send everyone home with one of their fish Christments.

HOME WORSHIP BOOKLET
(Part II)

The Meaning of Christmas
Second Week of Advent

Sing a Christmas carol each day, and close with the Lord's Prayer.

Second Sunday in Advent: The Candle of Joy

(Joy may be celebrated on the second or third Sunday.)

CALL TO WORSHP: Sing a favorite Christmas carol.

NARRATOR: We light the candle of Hope and the candle of Joy. Even today, the simple sign of the fish says that we are followers of Jesus.

BIBLE LESSON: Isaiah 35:1-2 and Matthew 1:21

BENEDICTION: Lord's Prayer

Monday

NARRATOR: A candle symbolizes Christ as the light of the world.

BIBLE LESSON: Philippians 1:3-4

Tuesday

NARRATOR: The Star of David is the Creator's star. The six points symbolize the six days of creation.

BIBLE LESSON: Genesis 1:31 and 2:1-4

Wednesday

NARRATOR: The early Greek Christians made monograms or symbols of the first three letters of Jesus' name (Iota Eta Sigma).

BIBLE LESSON: Isaiah: 11:1-2

Thursday

NARRATOR: The first letter in Jesus (I) and in Christ (X) formed a star.

BIBLE LESSON: Isaiah 40:3

Friday

NARRATOR: **The CHI and RHO (X and P) were the Greek initials for Christ.**
BIBLE LESSON: Matthew 3:1-3

Saturday

NARRATOR: **The ship symbolizes the Church of Jesus Christ.**
BIBLE LESSON: Malachi 3:1-3

SESSION 26

THE THIRD SUNDAY IN ADVENT (LOVE)

The Bible Lesson

Continue the Christmas story from Luke 1:46-55.

What the Children Will Learn Today

The children will experience the excitement of preparing for Christmas by being loving and accepting.

Time Needed

Allow 20 minutes for workstations and 10 minutes for worship.

Supplies Needed

1. Advent wreath materials (greenery, foam for the base and candles: four white and one red Christ candle.
2. Advent Home Worship booklet (Part III).
3. Craft supply basket, Bibles, and a snack.
4. Pipe cleaners and beads for making Christian symbols.
5. Workstation signs and instructions.
6. Copies of the Christmas Eve service for each workstation.
7. Musical instruments and song book.
8. Baked salt dough caves for Nativity pictures.
9. Each child's Nativity scene — pictures of Mary and Joseph.
10. Stiff piece of cardboard for each Nativity backing.

WORKSTATIONS

Workstation 1 — Call to Worship

GETTING READY

Prepare the same materials as the last two weeks. Copy and post the following instructions for the children:

> Practice is the same as last week. Be ready to do the entire Call to Worship for our service.

Workstation 2 — Affirmation of Faith

GETTING READY

Gather materials or reuse wreath from earlier Advent wreaths. Remind the Narrator that he or she is reading the Narrator's statement from the Home Worship booklet in today's worship. Copy and post the following instructions for the children:

> We are making an Advent wreath with a red center Christ candle. Red candles may also be used on an Advent log like last week — just replace the purple and pink candles with red. Or white candles may be put on a wreath with a red center Christ candle. Use the materials on the table and make an Advent wreath today.
>
> Red is the liturgical color for the Holy Spirit. "Christ" is the Greek word for Messiah, meaning "anointed one" or "chosen one." Jesus was a common name given to many Jewish boys of Jesus' time (Colossians 4:11). Jesus means "savior." Therefore, the red Christ candle symbolizes that Jesus Christ is our chosen savior.

Workstations 3 and 5 — Offering and Witness

GETTING READY

Have at least one adult helper at the Christment station today. Supply the pipe cleaners and beads. Post a sign-up sheet for the Narrator (or use the same Narrator in each scene) and seven readers for today's worship and also Christmas Eve. Copy and post the following instructions for the children:

> We are still making Christments. Fill the pipe cleaner with beads. Then, bend the pipe cleaner to form a fish or any other symbol you wish to make. Remember that you may create your own Christian symbol. Make two or three symbols today to share with others.

Workstation 4 — Bible Lesson/Sermon

GETTING READY

We are continuing the Nativity. Photocopy the figures or draw your own. Set out the craft supply basket. The big salt dough letter "C" the children made for the cave last week should be glued down over the straw and under the stars to provide shelter for the animals and baby Jesus. Help the children get it in the right place. Post a sign-up sheet for these parts: Narrator (unless you want to use the same narrator in each scene), Bible Reader 1, Bible Reader 2, and the Angel. Those who sign up will read from the Christmas Eve script for today's worship celebration and on Christmas Eve as well. Copy and post the following instructions for the children:

> Read Luke 1:46-55. You will add Mary, Joseph, and the cave to the Nativity. Color Mary and Joseph and glue them into place. Save room for baby Jesus in the middle. Before you glue down the salt dough cave you made last week, glue your picture onto a stiff piece of cardboard to keep it from tearing. Don't forget to put your name on the back. Put the cave over the animals and people. Ask for help if you need it.

Workstation 6 — Prayer

GETTING READY

Post a sign-up sheet for the part of Reader 7 for today's worship and also Christmas Eve. Copy and post the following message for the children:

> Keep up the good work!

Workstation 7 — Benediction

GETTING READY

Today the children are designing their own Christment. If you have any books on Christian symbols, make these available. The children are just drawing a picture of the Christment today. Post a sign-up sheet for someone to show the picture and explain what it means at today's worship service. Copy and post the following instructions for the children:

> As a group, design a new symbol to be placed on top of the Peace tree. Think of a design that tells something about you as children who follow Jesus. You only need to draw a picture today. We'll make the symbol later.

The Worship Celebration

1. Start with the Narrator's paragraph and lighting of the Advent wreath from the Home Worship booklet for the third Sunday.

II. Sermon, Witness, and Prayer — Use these portions from the Christmas Eve service (reading only — no acting).

III. Benediction — Have the children present their Christment design. Hang the picture of the design on the church. Tell the children that they will make the Christment next week to hang on top of the tree.

Items to Go Home

Send the children's extra Christment drawings home.

HOME WORSHIP BOOKLET
(Part III)

The Meaning of Christmas
The Third Week of Advent

Sing a Christmas carol each day and close with the Lord's Prayer.

Third Sunday in Advent: The Candle of Love

CALL TO WORSHIP: Select a favorite Christmas carol to sing.

NARRATOR: The circle of the Advent wreath reminds us that Jesus is the Light of the World. As we light the first, second, and third candles, let them remind us of the true meaning of Christmas: the innocence of a baby lying in a manger, peace and good will for all, and the loving kindness of God.

BIBLE LESSON: Luke 1:46-55

BENEDICTION: Lord's Prayer

Monday

NARRATOR: The crown reminds us that Jesus won through humility and the power of love, and not by money or power.

BIBLE LESSON: Romans 1:2

Tuesday

NARRATOR: Although we do not know the exact shape of the cross on which Jesus died, we use the Latin cross today.

BIBLE LESSON: 1 Thessalonians 5:14-18

Wednesday

NARRATOR: Many symbols are added to the cross to tell the story of Jesus' life and teachings. What do you think they mean?

BIBLE LESSON: Romans 15:13

Thursday

NARRATOR: A cross made into a shepherd's crook reminds us that Jesus was the Good Shepherd.

BIBLE LESSON: Philippians 4:4

Friday

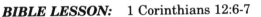

NARRATOR: The triangle is the oldest and most common symbol for the Trinity: The Father, the Son, and the Holy Spirit.

BIBLE LESSON: 1 Corinthians 12:6-7

Saturday

NARRATOR: The triangle and circle are combined to symbolize that God's love will never end.

BIBLE LESSON: Ephesians 4:2-3

SESSION 27

THE FOURTH SUNDAY IN ADVENT (FAITH)

Today the children will put all of the pieces of the Christmas Eve service together.

The Bible Lesson

We continue reading the Christmas story from Luke 2:6-14 and Matthew 2:1-2 and 9-10.

What the Children Will Learn Today

The lesson from this service is to share God's love with everyone by including each child as a participant and not just an observer.

Time Needed

You will only have 10 minutes at the workstations today to allow 20 minutes for the celebration.

Supplies Needed

1. Advent wreath materials (greenery, foam for the base, and candles: four blue and one white Christ candle).
2. Advent Home Worship booklet (Part IV).
3. Bibles and a snack if desired.
4. Pipe cleaners and beads for making Christian symbols.
5. Workstation signs and instructions.
6. Copies of the Christmas Eve service for each workstation.
7. Musical instruments and song book.
8. Nativity scenes for each child — add the baby Jesus, shepherds, wise men, sheep, and even a camel if desired.
9. Craft basket: Usual supplies plus cotton for sheep and coffee, fake fur, or sandpaper for camel.
10. Biblical costumes for the Nativity play.

WORKSTATIONS

Workstation 1 — Call to Worship

GETTING READY

Post a "reminder" sign-up sheet for the Call to Worship — for today and Christmas Eve. Copy and post the following instructions for the children:

> Practice is the same as last week. Be ready to do the entire Call to Worship for our service.

Workstation 2 — Affirmation of Faith

GETTING READY

Post a sign-up sheet for someone to read the Narrator's Affirmation portion from the Home Worship booklet — today and on Christmas Eve. Furnish new supplies, or you may reuse materials from the last Advent wreath. Copy and post the following instructions for the children:

> Blue, the liturgical color for truth, is often seen around the altar. Use the materials available and make an Advent wreath with a white center Christ candle and four blue candles.

Workstation 3 — Offering

GETTING READY

Station at least one adult at the Christment station to help. Provide the pipe cleaners and beads, and copy and post the following instructions for the children:

> Today you are going to make a Christment from your own original design that you drew last week. Work together. Fill the pipe cleaner with beads. Then bend the pipe cleaner to form the Christian symbol you wish to make. When you finish, you may also make some more fish or other symbols. Make some of your own creative symbols.

Workstation 4 — Bible Lesson/Sermon

GETTING READY

Round up the necessary costumes for the Nativity play (sermon portion of the Christmas Eve service). The children will present it during today's worship celebration. You may need to help them get dressed. Post a sign-up sheet for the following parts for today's celebration and the Christmas Eve service: Bible Reader I, Bible Reader II, Mary, Joseph, Innkeeper, Shepherds (remember — both girls and boys can be shepherds), Angel (you may have more than one angel), Wise Men.

Add a note telling them they should be in costume and ready to act out the story of the first Christmas in the service today. The children will also finish their Nativity pictures. Furnish the necessary materials, and copy and post the following instructions:

Today you will finish reading the story of Jesus' birth and you will finish your Nativity picture. Read in the Bible Luke 2:6-14 and Matthew 2:1-2 and 9-10.

Add shepherds, wise men, and the baby Jesus. Use pictures provided or draw your own.

Workstation 6 — Prayer

GETTING READY

Copy and post the following instructions for the children:

> Announce how many letters were completed during Advent at the Worship Celebration today.

Workstations 5 and 7 —
Witness and Benediction

GETTING READY

Furnish wrapping paper, the craft supply basket, and the baby layette for the children to wrap. Copy and post the following instructions:

> Your task is to wrap your Nativity scene as a gift for your parents. Use the paper you made earlier or design you own.
>
> We are also going to give a gift to a newborn baby during the offering in our Christmas Eve service. Arrange all of the baby items in the box. Wrap the package and have it ready for the worship service today.

The Worship Celebration

I. Start with the Narrator statement and lighting of the Advent Wreath from the Home Worship booklet for the fourth Sunday.

II. Today practice the first 20 minutes of the Christmas Eve service (through the sermon), minus the congregational hymns. Practice both reading and acting parts today.

Items to Go Home

Send everyone home with their wrapped Nativity gift for their parents.

HOME WORSHIP BOOKLET
(Part IV)

The Meaning of Christmas
Fourth Week of Advent

Sing Christmas carols each day, and close with the Lord's Prayer.

Fourth Sunday in Advent: The Candle of Faith

(The number of days in the Fourth Week of Advent vary depending upon the day of Christmas Eve and Christmas. Just use the days needed. On Christmas Eve and Christmas Day, light all five candles.)

CALL TO WORSHIP: Select a favorite Christmas carol to sing.

NARRATOR: **The Fourth Sunday in Advent represents Faith. As we light the first, second, third, and fourth candles let us remember the poor, the homeless, those who are sad and lonely, the sick, the hungry children around the world, and those who just need a friend.**

BIBLE LESSON: Luke 2:6-7 and 14 and Matthew 2:2

BENEDICTION: Lord's Prayer

FAITH

Monday

NARRATOR: **An "M" is sometimes added to the cross to remind us of Mary, the Mother of Jesus.**

BIBLE LESSON: Luke 2:1-7

Tuesday

NARRATOR: **Small white lilies-of-the-valley are sometimes placed on a cross to remind us to be humble.**

BIBLE LESSON: Luke 2:8-14

Wednesday

NARRATOR: **Sheep and shepherds remind us that all are welcome in God's family. You need not be rich or famous.**

BIBLE LESSON: Luke 2:15-20

Thursday

NARRATOR: A star is often placed above the Nativity scene to remind us that Jesus is the Light of the World and shows us the way to live our lives in peace.

BIBLE LESSON: Matthew 2:1-2

Friday

NARRATOR: A small evergreen tree has been chosen this year as our symbol of Peace. Just as the Peace Tree will stay green year round, our hope for peace will be in our daily prayers.

BIBLE LESSON: Matthew 2:3-8

Saturday

NARRATOR: We HOPE for PEACE. We celebrate with JOY at the prospect of PEACE. We remember the LOVE and compassion that is necessary to bring about PEACE. And we strive for the kind of FAITH symbolized by the butterfly that will lead us to PEACE.

BIBLE LESSON: Matthew 2:9-10

CHAPTER TEN

A LENTEN WORKSHOP

P laying an original game, Outcast; building an altar; and sharing a Seder meal teach the children about Lent. On Easter they decorate hollow eggs, a symbolic reminder of the empty tomb. These activities culminate in an Easter celebration of drama and song shared with the congregation.

SESSION 28
REPENT

The Bible Lesson

The Lenten workshop uses one of the Bible verses from the worship service each week. Today's verse is Psalm 95:6.

What the Children Will Learn Today

The children will learn about Lent and the meaning of the word REPENT.

Time Needed

Use 15 minutes in workstations and 15 minutes for worship.

Supplies Needed

1. Workstation signs and instructions.
2. Musical instruments and songs to be used.
3. Copy of Easter worship service and Bibles.
4. ½ yard of white felt for the Lent overlay banner and pins to hang it.
5. Collection containers and Lenten offering calendars — one for each child.
6. Craft basket: Usual supplies plus glitter, stars and extra paper or construction paper.
7. Three copies of the "Getting Ready for Easter" skit (from the Easter service), props (cleaning supplies like brooms, buckets, feather dusters, etc.) and costumes (if desired).
8. Wood scraps and woodworking basket.
9. Seven candles and candleholders.

WORKSTATIONS

Workstation 1 — Call to Worship

GETTING READY

The Call to Worship today is the same as it will be for the Easter service. Set out a copy of the service marked in red from the Introit to the First Congregational Hymn. Post a sign-up sheet for a reader and musicians. These volunteers will be needed both today and in the Easter service. Copy and post the following instructions for the children:

> You are working on the Call to Worship for our Easter service. Look at the copy of the service marked in red. Read Psalm 100. Try the instruments and decide how you can "make a joyful noise to the Lord."

Workstation 2 — Affirmation of Faith

GETTING READY

Cut the ½ yard of white felt into a triangular shape to fit over the purple Liturgical banner from Session 24. Hang up the purple banner in the church. Post a sign-up sheet for helpers to hang the Lent overlay banner on top of the purple Liturgical banner and for a reader to share Psalm 95:6. These helpers are needed today and in the Easter service. Copy and post the following instructions for the children:

> Today you will make a banner. Turn the white felt triangle so the point is down, and then write these seven words for Lent:
>
> | R | F | S | F | H | G | L |
> |---|---|---|---|---|---|---|
> | E | A | A | O | A | R | O |
> | P | I | C | R | P | A | V |
> | E | T | R | G | P | C | E |
> | N | H | I | I | I | E | |
> | T | | F | V | N | | |
> | | | I | E | E | | |
> | | | C | | S | | |
> | | | E | | S | | |
>
> Use a pencil and don't press too hard. Then put glue on the letters and sprinkle glitter on top.

Purple Liturgical Banner (from Session 24)

Lent Overlay

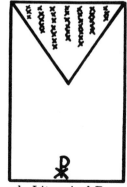

Purple Liturgical Banner With Lent Overlay

Workstations 3 and 7 —
Offering and Benediction

GETTING READY

The children will make collection containers and use the Lenten offering calendar. You may use old boxes, coffee cans, or any kind of container. Have adult helper cut holes in the lids for the money. Set out the craft supply basket for decorating the containers, and copy and post the following instructions for the children:

> During Lent we will be collecting a special offering. Pick a container and decorate it with the supplies here. Bring your collection container back Easter Sunday.

Workstation 4 — Sermon/Bible Lesson

GETTING READY

Have props (cleaning supplies) and costumes (old dress-up clothes if desired) ready for the children to practice the skit. Post a sign-up sheet for three "workers" to be in the skit today. Copy and post the following instructions for the children:

> Today's sermon will be a skit. We need three volunteers. You do not have to memorize your lines. You can just read off the paper and have fun.

GETTING READY FOR EASTER

The Meaning of Lent

(Workers are dusting and cleaning the communion table and Bible. They set up the candles and candleholders made in Session 19.)

WORKER 1: We need something special on the altar today so everyone will know that today is the first Sunday in Lent.

WORKER 2: We have plenty of dust.

WORKER 1: No, not dust!

WORKER 3: We could have a crown of thorns, bread and cup, and then some purple candles, since purple is the color for Lent.

WORKER 2: That's a neat idea. And each candle could stand for something special to think about during Lent.

WORKER 1: Well, the first candle could remind us to REPENT. Being sorry for the wrong things we do is important in preparing for Easter.

WORKER 2: The second candle should mention **FAITH.**

WORKER 3: We can't leave out **SACRIFICE.**

WORKER 1: And the fourth candle can be to **FORGIVE.**

WORKER 2: Can we also mention something happy? Easter brings joy, new life, and **HAPPINESS** too.

WORKER 3: And we can't forget **GRACE.**

WORKER 1: And Easter Sunday itself can stand for **LOVE.**

WORKER 2: We could place all of the candles on that cross we made from wood scraps when we were just goofing around.

WORKER 3: My Mom might help me make a crown. We have a bush in our front yard that has thorns all over it.

WORKER 1: I'll make the bread and bring a cup we have from home.

EVERYONE: *(In unison)* **I LIKE IT. LET'S GO.** *(WORKERS exit.)*

Workstation 6 — Witness to the World

GETTING READY

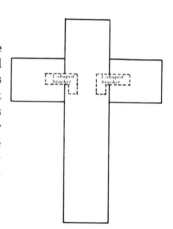

At this station, the children build the cross mentioned in the skit. Use flat L-shaped metal brackets, glue, or nails to attach the arms of the cross. The cross can be painted or left plain and rugged-looking. Provide the scraps and let the children be creative. An adult helper is needed today. The cross will be used in the Easter service cross-building pantomime. Copy and post the following instructions for the children:

> You are going to build a cross today to use later in the Easter service. Make your cross from the scraps. There are no exact measurements today so you decide. You will place the cross on the communion table when you are finished.

Workstation 6 — Prayer

GETTING READY

Add a little enthusiasm to the embroidery project. Encourage the group to finish all of a certain letter each Sunday. Today they will try to

sew all the "R's" since today's session, Repent starts with an "R." Copy
and post the following instructions for the children:

> Can you and your friends finish all of the "R's" in the Lord's
> Prayer today?

The Worship Celebration

   I. Call to Worship.

  II. Affirmation of Faith — Read the Bible verse, Psalm 95:6,
and hang the banner. (Often felt will stick to other felt on
its own, but you may need to thumbtack the white overlay
banner to the purple banner.)

 III. Sermon — Present the skit.

 IV. Prayer — Announce the letters finished on the Lord's
Prayer banner.

  V. Offering — Explain the Lenten Offering Calendar and then
send everyone home with their collection containers.

 VI. Assignment — Tell someone "I'm sorry" this week.

Items to Go Home

Lent Offering calendar and collection containers.

LENT OFFERING CALENDAR

	SUNDAY	MONDAY	TUESDAY	WEDNESDAY	THURSDAY	FRIDAY	SATURDAY
1st Sunday in Lent		1¢ for each TV in your house	1¢ for each record and/or tape you own	**Ash Wednesday** 1¢ for each meal you eat today	1¢ for each minute of free time today	1¢ for each mile you drive in your car today	1¢ for each TV show you watch today
2nd Sunday in Lent		1¢ for each piece of bread you eat today	1¢ for each cola or soft drink you have today	1¢ for each cookie you eat today	1¢ for each candy bar you eat today	1¢ for each potato chip you eat today	1¢ for a computer
3rd Sunday in Lent		1¢ for a microwave	1¢ for an oven	1¢ for a mixer	1¢ for a dishwasher	1¢ for a refrigerator	1¢ for each glass of milk you drink today
4th Sunday in Lent		1¢ for each room in your house	1¢ for each bed in your house	1¢ for each chair in your house	1¢ for each book you own	1¢ for each mirror in your house	1¢ for a washing machine
5th Sunday in Lent		1¢ for each gallon of water used today	1¢ for each light in your house	1¢ for each flower in your yard today	1¢ for each hour of sunshine today	1¢ for each bird you see today	1¢ for each sink and faucet in your house
6th Sunday in Lent Palm Sunday		1¢ for each time you have the privilege to pray today	1¢ for each mile you walk today	1¢ for each hour of sleep today	**Maundy Thursday** 1¢ for each of your friends	**Good Friday** 1¢ for each year of your age	1¢ for each Bible you own
Easter Sunday	*Pause and place a penny in the Lenten Offering for each of the luxuries and privileges you enjoy every day.*						1¢ for each member of your family

EASTER SERVICE

*CAST**
(In Order of Appearance)

Musicians
Call to Worship Reader
Reader 1
Reader 2
Reader 3
Reader 4
Reader 5
Reader
("One Life to Give")
Mary
Carpenters
Preaching Jesus
Fishermen
Reader
("The Good Samaritan")
Clowns
(Man, Robbers, Priest, Levite, Samaritan, Innkeeper)
3 Readers
(Lord's Prayer dialog)
Carpenters
Reader
("The Sower and the Seed")
Clowns
(Farmer, Birds, Scorched Plants, Plants Choked by Thorns, Good Plants)
(Same clowns may be in both skits)
Reader
(Prayer for Peace)

*The children sign up for these parts throughout the Lenten Workshop.

PRODUCTION NOTES

SCENERY

For "One Life to Give": manger; rocker; boat built in Session 33, Offering workstation; biblical house built in Session 33, Call to Worship workstation.

PROPS

For "One Life to Give": baby doll; sandpaper; wood; net; paper fish (if made in Session 33, Affirmation of Faith workstation).

Clown skits: cross made in Session 28, Witness to the World workstation; hammers; sign saying "help" for hurt man, a package of seeds for the sower, and other optional props (see Session 14); pennies, paper flowers, balloons with messages of peace and love, and newspapers about clown ministry to hand out to the congregation.

Other: peace ribbon made in the worship celebration of Session 31; Love/ Peace candle made in Session 34, Call to Worship workstation; instruments; Bibles.

COSTUMES

The clown troupe should wear their clown faces and dress-up clothes. See Chapter Six for make-up tips. The actors for "One Life to Give" should wear biblical costumes. If your group is small and some of the clowns are needed to appear in "One Life to Give," it's OK for them to have their clown faces on — just be sure they are wearing a biblical robe and head-piece also. The carpenters do not need special costumes and, since they are pantomiming, it would be perfectly fine for the clowns with their made-up faces to double as carpenters.

INTROIT: Have any children who have been taking lessons — piano, flute, or any other instruments — collectively play a 15- to 20-minute introit.

CALL TO WORSHIP: Chime — Use two spoons, melody glasses, or anything else you have that will make a chime sound. Strike 12 times to mark the start of the worship service.

READER: Come and let us join together to celebrate God's love. This is the Lord's house and we, his followers, have come together today to sing praises to him.

Clap your hands and let your light shine so that all can see that you are a follower of Jesus. Do not let hatred, anger, or any quarrels grow between you and your neighbor. Let us join together as brothers and sisters in Christ to worship God, our creator.

Sing along with us to celebrate his love. And take that joy and spread the good news everywhere you go and to everyone you meet. Come on, let's celebrate!
(Entrance: All children enter from the back of the church, shaking and playing some kind of instrument or carrying banners. Have the group play a simple song together when everyone has assembled at the

front of the sanctuary.)

CONGREGATIONAL HYMN: Selection of your choice.

AFFIRMATION OF FAITH: Readers of Scripture passages.

> *(Children's songs based on Bible passages are available; you may select Bible verses to fit songs you know. Have someone read a verse and then have all sing a song if desired.)*

READER 1:   *(Old Testament)* **Psalm 95:6.**

READER 2:   *(New Testament)* **Philippians 4:4.**

READER 3:   *(New Testament)* **Galatians 5:22.**

READER 4:   *(New Testament)* **Philippians 4:13.**

READER 5:   *(New Testament)* **Matthew 6:33.**

OFFERING: Special Music: Invite a neighboring church choir or another group from your own church to come and share their love through their music as the offertory.

CONGREGATIONAL RESPONSE: Use an upbeat song that everyone can join in and sing — nothing solemn.

SERMON: "One Life to Give"

> *(ACTORS pantomime as the words are read. MARY is holding the baby doll and is seated on a rocker in the biblical house next to a manger. CARPENTERS stand by the tools. PREACHER JESUS is Off-stage until he is mentioned. The FISHERMEN are by the boat. MARY rocks the baby.)*

READER: **His life began as a tiny baby born in the most humble of surroundings.** *(MARY places doll in manger and exits. CARPENTERS pantomime sanding the wood.)* **He worked alongside his father, Joseph, in the carpenter shop, learning to sand and plane wood until it was smooth and ready to use.** *(CARPENTERS exit. PREACHER JESUS enters and crosses to boat, pantomimes speaking to FISHERMEN as they "fish" with their net.)* **At the age of thirty, which was late in life at the time, he began to travel around from town to town preaching to the common people. He was not liked by the Pharisees. He did not live in a fancy house. He did not even own a horse. He walked on his bare feet or in sandals everywhere he went. His life ended many centuries ago. But today, we in our fast cars and busy households still remember. And it can easily be said that there has never been anyone before or since who has changed life on our planet Earth as did Jesus.**

(FISHERMEN, PREACHING JESUS, and READER exit. CLOWN

TROUPE enters.)

THE GOOD SAMARITAN

READER: Luke 10:27-37. *(CLOWNS pantomime along and exit when done.)*

CONGREGATIONAL HYMN: Song of your choosing on what it means to be a Christian.

PRAYER: Lord's Prayer dialog with three READERS from Session 29, Sermon workstation.

Pray the Lord's Prayer together.

Song: Select a song for the children to sing about prayer.

WITNESS TO THE WORLD: Cross-Building Pantomime: CARPEN-TERS (or clown carpenters) take hammers (actually pound wood) and pretend to "build" the cross that was made in Session 28, Witness to the World workstation. They should refrain from speaking during the "building." When done, they should hold it up and then set it in a visible place.

THE SOWER AND THE SEED

READER: **Matthew 13:1-9.** *(CLOWNS pantomime along and then hand out pennies, paper flowers, balloons with messages of peace and love, or newspapers about clown ministry after the skit as they exit. The children who aren't part of the clown troupe may help with this also.)*

BENEDICTION: Chant: Instrumentalists walk around the sanctuary ringing bells and saying "he is alive," "he has risen," or "he lives." The others should join in and shout softly at first and then end with one big shout. Then there is silence as the bells are rung.

Peace Circle: The congregation should form a big circle around the sanctuary. You may sing a song about peace if desired, such as "Let There Be Peace on Earth." Appoint someone to turn the "Love" candle around to the "Peace" side. Pass the Peace ribbon around the circle.

READER: **Prayer for peace.** *(From Session 31, Benediction worksta-tion. All exit playing instruments following the prayer.)*

SESSION 29
FAITH

The Bible Lesson

The Bible verses being used today combine a parable from the Old Testament (Isaiah 5:1-7), the parable retold by Jesus (Matthew 21:33-45), and a verse from the worship service (Galatians 5:22) to tell how we are to live.

What the Children Will Learn Today

Today's workstations recreate a synagogue school to form a transition from Jesus as a little boy about their age to Jesus as a grown man.

Time Needed

Spend 20 minutes in workstations and 10 minutes in worship.

Supplies Needed

1. Workstation signs and instructions.
2. Several pans filled with sand or a sand table.
3. Playdough or salt dough and sharpened sticks or pencils.
4. Old candles, broken pieces of brown crayons, and newspapers.
5. Craft basket: Usual supplies plus straws or sticks.
6. Brown paper bags and paper plates, one per child.
7. Lord's Prayer handout and Bibles.

WORKSTATIONS
Workstation 1 — Call to Worship

GETTING READY

Prepare a sand table or two or three pans of sand and set out pencils or sticks. Then copy and post the following instructions for the children:

> Today you will write in sand. This is how children learned to write in Bible times. Our text is a parable from the Old Testament that Jesus may have studied as a boy (Isaiah 5:1-7). Read the Bible verses out loud. What did God expect the people of Israel to do? Reread verse 7. Use a stick to write the words in the sand.

Workstation 2 — Affirmation of Faith

GETTING READY

A big step for Bible-times children was when they began using clay tablets to write on instead of sand. (Similar to when modern-day children move from elementary school to junior high.) Playdough is easier to write on than salt dough and if left uncovered will harden. Copy and post the following instructions for the children:

> After a Bible-times boy had practiced writing hı letters in the sand, he would move up to writing on clay tablets. Roll some clay into a ball. Press it into a flat tablet. Read Matthew 21:33-45. Take a sharpened stick (pencil) and write on your clay tablet what Jesus is asking you to do. For help, see Matthew 21:43.

Workstation 4 — Sermon/Bible Lesson

GETTING READY

The fill-in-the-blanks handout will help the children write their own ideas about the Lord's Prayer. Save for Easter. Post a sign-up sheet for three children to act out this dialog both today and in the Easter service, and copy and post the following instructions for the children:

> Pretend that you and a friend are listening to the radio while reading the comics. Then you hear on the radio that instead of your favorite music, someone is going to be reading the Lord's Prayer. Write what you would say about each line as the prayer is read.

READER 1: Good morning and welcome to KTBT's morning program called "Teaching About Prayer" from Matthew 6:5-14. It says in Matthew that when we pray we should not be like the hypocrites! They are only interested in impressing other people with their meaningless, skillful words.

READER 2:   Hypocrites! Who said we're hypocrites?

READER 3:   He didn't say we were hypocrites.

READER 1:   Instead, Matthew Chapter 6 says that we should find a quiet place and pray our simple words to our Father.

READER 2:

READER 1:   Simply pray: Our Father, who art in heaven, hallowed be thy name.

READER 3:

READER 1:   Thy Kingdom come; thy will be done on earth as it is in heaven.

READER 2:   What kingdom?

READER 3:

READER 1:   Give us this day our daily bread;

READER 3:

READER 1:   And forgive us our trespasses, as we forgive those who trespass against us.

READER 2:

READER 3:

READER 1:   And lead us not into temptation,

READER 2:

READER 3:

READER 1:   but deliver us from evil.

READER 2:

READER 1:   For thine is the kingdom, and the power, and the glory, forever. Amen.

READER 2:   OK, maybe we should give it a try.

Workstation 5 — Witness to the World

GETTING READY

A wax tablet was the highest level of learning in synagogue school (like high school). A simple wax tablet is easy to make. Make these yourself ahead of time. Cut corrugated cardboard into 3" x 5" tablets, one for each child. Place a thick layer of newspapers inside a large metal roasting pan. Arrange cardboard on newspaper so that they do not touch. Melt old candles, wax, and brown crayons in a pan on the stove at very low heat, just until everything is melted. Make sure your kitchen is well-ventilated and don't let the wax overheat. Using tongs, dip each piece of cardboard into the melted wax. Place on newspaper. Then, after the first layer cools, with a ladle gently and carefully pour more wax onto each piece of cardboard. Let cool, then add more wax. Let cool again and add a third layer. Lastly, dip each tablet in the melted wax quickly to give a smooth thick surface. Copy and post the following instructions for the children:

> Since you cannot erase what you write on wax, young people were not given wax tablets until they had practiced many years on sand and clay. Take only one wax tablet. Look up Galatians 5:22-23. Write on your wax tablet one of the "Fruits of the Spirit" and your name.

Workstation 6 — Prayer

GETTING READY

Copy and post the following instructions for the children:

> All girls, and the boys learning to be tent makers, would have learned to sew, as did the apostle Paul. Call your friends over and do the "F's" for Faith.

Workstation 7 and 3 — Benediction and Offering

GETTING READY

The children will make paper scrolls out of brown paper bags. Set out the bags, straws or sticks, a bowl of water, and the craft supply basket. Copy and post the following instructions for the children:

> Cut a 6" x 10" piece of plain brown paper. Sprinkle the pieces with water to make them damp but not wet. Crumble the piece of paper into a ball and straighten it out again. This makes the paper look like what they would have used for scrolls in Bible times. Tape or glue a stick or straw to each 6" edge of the paper.

With a marker, write Isaiah 5:1-7, Matthew 21:33-45, and Galatians 5:22. Then roll the paper from each end at the same time onto the straws. Tie together with a string.

The Worship Celebration

I. Sermon — Present the Lord's Prayer Dialog.

II. Benediction — Close by singing a congregational hymn from the Easter Service.

Items to Go Home

Clay and wax tablets and brown paper scrolls.

SESSION 30
SACRIFICE

The Bible Lesson

Children will read Bible verses on the themes of: repentance, faith, sacrifice, forgiveness, happiness, grace, and love.

What the Children Will Learn Today

At each workstation, the children are building part of an altar. You want the children to learn why we have an altar.

Time Needed

Use 20 minutes for workstations and 10 minutes for worship. If a group finishes early, send them to do all the "S's" on the Lord's Prayer banner.

Supplies Needed

1. Magazines and old church curriculum materials.
2. Seven cardboard boxes of varying sizes that can be stacked on top of each other.
3. Bibles, Bible dictionary, and a snack for the children while they work.
4. Construction paper and paper strips for worship.
6. Craft basket: Usual supplies plus stars, name tags to use as Love badges, or even stickers that say "God loves you."

WORKSTATIONS

Workstation 1 — Call to Worship

GETTING READY

Today the children will build an altar out of cardboard boxes of varying sizes. Each box will be decorated as a collage using magazine pictures that illustrate a particular theme. Put glue, scissors, and magazines at each station or at one centrally located table, along with the craft supply basket and paper for children who want to draw their own pictures. Remind them that they may exchange magazines with each other if they wish.

This station will decorate the largest box with the theme of "repent."

Post a sign-up sheet for a helper to put the "repent" box into place and then read Exodus 20:24 in the worship celebration today. Copy and post the following instructions for the children:

> You are to build an altar today. Your box is to be the foundation or bottom block of the altar. Decorate your box with pictures in a collage that covers the entire box. *Do not seal the open flap shut so we can add a surprise later.* Look up the word REPENT in your Bible dictionary. Read Exodus 20:24. Cut out pictures that explain what you think REPENT means.

Workstation 2 — Affirmation of Faith

GETTING READY

Use a slightly smaller box than the "repent" box for the "faith" box. Using a box that is just a bit smaller than the previous box will keep the altar from toppling as you build upwards. Post a sign-up sheet for a helper to add the "faith" box to the altar and read 2 Samuel 24:24-25 in the worship celebration today. Copy and post the following instructions for the children:

> You are designing the second block of an altar we are building today. You are to cover this box with pictures and words that explain what the word FAITH means to you. Read 2 Samuel 24:24-25. Cut out pictures and make a collage covering the box, but *leave the flap open for a surprise later.*

Workstation 3 — Offering

GETTING READY

Use a box slightly smaller than the "faith" box for the "sacrifice" box. Post a sign-up sheet for a helper to add the "sacrifice" box to the altar and read Hosea 6:6. Copy and post the following instructions for the children:

> The altar we are building will be built out of collage-covered boxes. For your box, cut out pictures, words, and letters to show what the word SACRIFICE means. Read Hosea 6:6 and use your Bible dictionary. Leave the flap open so we can put in a surprise later.

Workstation 4 — Sermon/Bible Lesson

GETTING READY

Use a box slightly smaller than the "sacrifice" box for the "forgive" box. Post a sign-up sheet for a helper to add the "forgive" box to the altar and read Matthew 9:13. Copy and post the following instructions for the children:

> In today's worship celebration, you will build an altar out of collage-covered boxes. Decorate your box with pictures and words that tell what the word FORGIVE means to you. Use your Bible dictionary and read the Bible verse (Matthew 9:13) if you need help. Leave the flap open so we can put in a surprise later.

Workstation 5 — Witness to the World

GETTING READY

Use a box slightly smaller than the "forgive" box for the "happiness" box. Post a sign-up sheet for a helper to add the "happiness" box to the altar and read Matthew 5:23 in worship today. Copy and post the following instructions for the children:

> Today we will build an altar out of boxes. Read Matthew 5:23. Decorate your box with pictures and words which tell what HAPPINESS means. Think of what it means when someone tells you that "true happiness is within you." Leave the flap open so that we can add a surprise later.

Workstation 6 — Prayer

GETTING READY

Use a box that is slightly smaller than the "happiness" box for the "grace" box. Post a sign-up sheet for a helper to add the "grace" box to the altar and read Mark 12:41-44 in today's worship. Be prepared with examples to help the children define Grace. Copy and post the following instructions for the children:

> Your group is in charge of making the GRACE block to go on the altar we are building. You may decorate your block with pictures. If you cannot find pictures to describe what you feel the word GRACE means, then write a prayer, a poem, or write your feelings and thoughts about GRACE. Read Mark 12:41-44 and use your Bible dictionary for help.

Workstation 7 — Benediction

GETTING READY

Use the smallest box for the "love" box. Encourage the children to make it a unique shape or somehow different than the other boxes. Post a sign-up sheet for a helper to put the "love" box on the top of the altar and read Mark 12:33 today. Print "love" on badges and have them ready to hand out in the worship celebration today. Copy and post the following instructions for the children:

> You are in charge of creating the top for our altar. Read Mark 12:33. Cover your block with pictures, words, or anything that expresses God's LOVE. Your box is closed shut because God's love is inside each of us.

The Worship Celebration

I. Have the children build the altar one block at a time.

II. Pass out paper and pencils and ask the children to write a response as each Bible verse is read: how they would REPENT (say "I'm sorry"), show their FAITH, offer a SACRIFICE to God (by putting part of their spending money in a collection for food for hungry children instead of buying something they want), show FORGIVEness to someone who teased them, how they can be HAPPY people, and explain what God's GRACE gives to them. Then everyone should write on their Love badges a way to show LOVE.

III. Place the paper responses inside the appropriate block. Seal the block with tape; write the word for that block on the tape.

Items to Go Home

Love badges should be worn home to share with others.

SESSION 31

FORGIVE

The Bible Lesson

In teaching the meaning of forgiveness, we also teach how good it feels to be forgiven: Philippians 4:13.

What the Children Will Learn Today

Saying "I'm sorry" is very hard for children, but forgiving someone who has hurt their feelings is even harder.

Time Needed

Use 20 minutes for workstations and 10 minutes for worship.

Supplies Needed

1. Workstation signs and instructions.

2. Musical instruments and songs of peace.

3. Felt or paper for making banner in the following lengths: 40" of blue, 20" of dark pink, 17" of pink, 14½" of pale pink, 12" of purple, 7" of yellow, 10" of light brown, 19" of dark brown, 14" of dark green, 27" of light green, and 16" of white. Felt used should be the standard 36½" wide.

4. Two bottles of "tacky" glue (found in fabric stores).

5. Craft supply basket: Usual supplies plus gold glitter, sharp scissors for cutting felt, white streamers, and anything else needed.

6. Wood scraps for cross and Bibles.

WORKSTATIONS

Workstation 1 — Call to Worship

GETTING READY

Select some songs on the theme of peace for the children to choose from. Post a sign-up sheet for today and also for the Easter service for musicians to lead the Call to Worship and for someone to lead the Benediction. Copy and post the following instructions for the children:

Practice and be ready to play the Call to Worship for the Easter service in our worship celebration today. Decide on a song for the Benediction. The closing theme is PEACE because Jesus said he came to share his Peace with us (John 14:27).

Workstations 2 and 3 — Affirmation of Faith and Offering

GETTING READY

This banner looks complicated, but the cutting actually follows very simple lines. Enlarge the patterns ahead of time or have the children draw each piece freehand. "Tacky" glue is suggested for gluing the pieces together. An adult is needed today to help. Copy and post the following instructions for the children:

Banners are often used in the church to announce special occasions or to convey special messages. You are going to make a banner to hang in your church for Easter.

Start at the top with the sky and work your way down to the grass. Follow the measurements on the drawings. Draw each piece on paper before you lay it down on the felt and begin to trace and cut. If you make a mistake you can redraw that piece on the paper before you cut the felt.

Work on a long table or on the floor. Pin the pattern onto the felt, then cut each piece out. As you cut a piece, lay it down into place. Cut and put into place the sky, clouds, and then each piece of the rainbow. Tuck the edges of the sun in between the mountain and the rainbow. Put the lakes and streams between the trees and the mountain. Then add the dirt and finally the grass.

Easter Banner

This banner fits together like a puzzle.
Cut each piece separately, then glue each piece together.

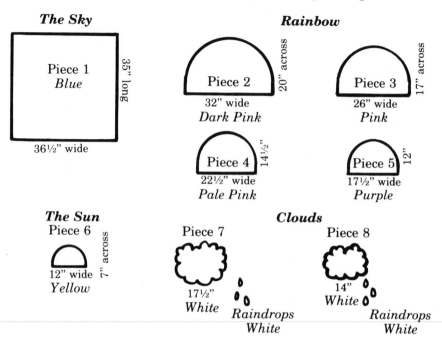

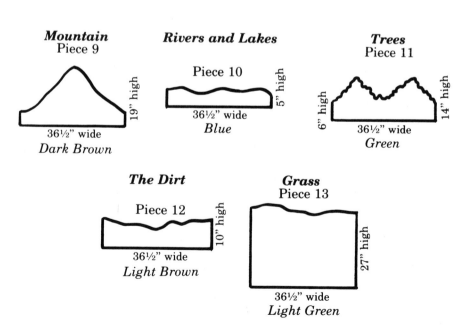

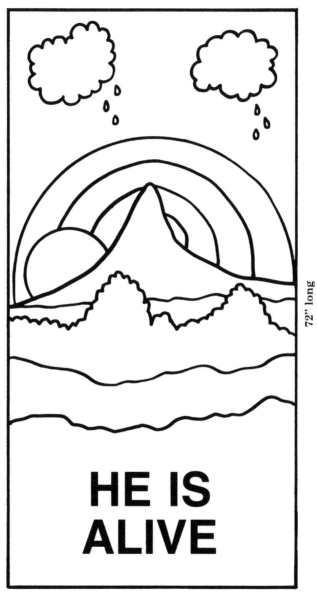

72" long

36½" wide

Workstation 4 — Sermon/Bible Lesson

GETTING READY

Have the children draw the letters freehand or have stencils for them to trace the words that go on the banner: HE IS ALIVE. Use felt or other suitable material for letters. Use sharp scissors to cut felt. Copy and post the following instructions for the children:

> Draw and cut out the letters for the Easter banner that will hang in your church. Make the letters for HE IS ALIVE big — about 5" high and 4" wide.

Workstation 5 — Witness to the World

GETTING READY

The children will build and add the cross to their church for Easter. It should be simple and fit nicely on the top. Provide the wood scraps and other materials, and copy and post the following instructions for the children:

> You are in charge of building a cross to go on top of our church. The cross shows that we follow Jesus. The cross can be plain and simple or painted. It's up to you. Use thin narrow strips or boards from our wood scraps. The center board should be about 12" high and the crosspiece should be about 5" on each side. Attach the cross with a long screw. You will need adult help to attach the cross to the church.

Workstation 6 — Prayer

GETTING READY

Copy and post the following instructions for the children:

> The challenge is still on. See if you can finish all of the "T's" today as symbols of the cross.

Workstation 7 — Benediction

GETTING READY

Have prayers about Peace available for ideas, and post a sign-up sheet for a volunteer to read Matthew 6:33 — today and in the Easter service, and for someone to read the Prayer for Peace — today and in the Easter service. Copy and post the following instructions for the children:

Select or write your own prayer for the Benediction for the Easter service. What do we have to do in order for everyone to live together in peace? How does Matthew 6:33 fit into your idea of peace?

The Worship Celebration

I. Call to Worship — Practice the Call to Worship from the Easter service.

II. Sermon — Read Matthew 6:33.
   A. Unroll a long white crepe paper streamer across the floor. Ask everybody to sign their names and draw simple pictures of what peace means.
   B. Give each person a small 5" piece of crepe paper streamer from the second roll. Have them write PEACE on it and tape it on like a badge.

III. Benediction — Practice the Benediction from the Easter service.

Items to Go Home

Wear the Peace ribbons home. Save long Peace streamer for the Benediction of the Easter service.

SESSION 32
HAPPINESS

Workstations are combined today to play a game, "Outcast."

The Bible Lesson

The game Outcast contains six passages from the New Testament for the children to look up and read. The Beatitudes are included, as are verses on trials, reconciliation, greed, giving, and love.

What the Children Will Learn Today

The object of Outcast is to show that there are consequences to every action. The game lets the children test their feelings and decisions. They see that sometimes a decision can be right but unpopular. Share with them how Jesus likely felt like an outcast when people mistreated him.

Time Needed

The game will take 25 minutes. If a group finishes early, have them go over to the Lord's Prayer banner and embroider all the "H's." Use the remaining five minutes for a brief worship celebration.

Supplies Needed

1. "Outcast" game board for each group of 10.
2. One copy of the rule sheet for each game board.
3. A pair of dice for each game.
4. A set of 3" x 5" Decision and Consequence cards in numerical order for each game board and Bibles.
5. Peanuts or popcorn to use as Chances.
6. 10 different STOP sign markers for each game.
7. Happiness-Anger cards: 3" x 5" cards (or pieces of paper) for the children to write down their responses during the game. Don't forget pencils.

OUTCAST

GETTING READY

Draw the Outcast game board, or get it enlarged and copied at a copy shop. Color the squares in bright, primary colors. Glue the game board to heavy cardboard so you can save it to use again later. Figure approximately 10 players to a game board; you may need to make several.

You may trace the stop sign illustration, cut it out, and use it as a pattern to make paper markers — one for each child playing. Color them in various hues. This is the game piece that will be used to move around the game board.

Copy the Decision and Consequence statements onto 3" x 5" index cards. Then place them in the proper squares on the game board in numerical order. The cards may be used over and over during the game, but it is important to keep them in order so the consequences will match up to the proper decision.

To start the game, count off players in groups of up to 10. Mix the younger children with the older ones so they can help them with reading and playing the game. Each group needs a game board and pair of dice. Each individual needs a stop sign marker, a pencil, a Happiness-Anger card, and 16 peanut or popcorn Chances. (Remind the players to save their Chances to eat after the game is over, and furnish extra for after-the-game snacking.) Copy the following Outcast game rules for each group of players:

OUTCAST RULES

1. Each player rolls the dice and moves the number of spaces indicated. The object is to get to the Happiness square first.

2. You must roll the exact number needed to land on Happiness. If your number is too high, you must go backward the extra number of spaces.

3. Chances: Each player has 16 chances (popcorn or peanuts) with which to play the game. Everyone must pay one chance to play at START.

4. A player who runs out of chances may receive five more by returning to START.

5. Each time a player lands on LUCK, he or she automatically goes forward five spaces.

6. When a player lands on a Decision space, he or she draws the Decision card on the top of the stack.

7. After answering yes or no to the question, the player draws the corresponding Consequence card. Each card is then placed on the bottom of its stack.

8. If young team members cannot read or write, older members

help them when it is their turn.

9. When you land on a space, you must do what it says. Write your answer on your HAPPINESS-ANGER card.

START

As An Individual

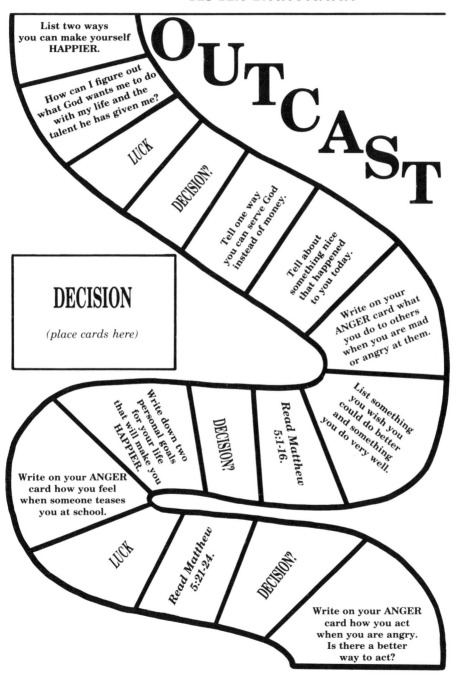

List two ways you can make yourself HAPPIER.

How can I figure out what God wants me to do with my life and the talent he has given me?

LUCK

DECISION?

Tell one way you can serve God instead of money.

Tell about something nice that happened to you today.

OUTCAST

DECISION

(place cards here)

Write on your ANGER card what you do to others when you are mad or angry at them.

List something you wish you could do better and something you do very well.

Write down two personal goals for your life that will make you HAPPIER.

DECISION?

Read Matthew 5:1-16.

Write on your ANGER card how you feel when someone teases you at school.

LUCK

Read Matthew 5:21-24.

DECISION?

Write on your ANGER card how you act when you are angry. Is there a better way to act?

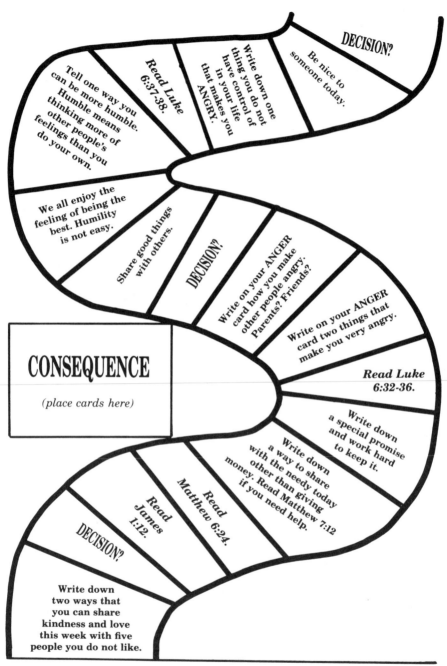

DECISION?

Be nice to someone today.

Write down one thing you do not have control of in your life that makes you ANGRY.

Read Luke 6:37-38.

Tell one way you can be more humble. Humble means thinking more of other people's feelings than you do your own.

We all enjoy the feeling of being the best. Humility is not easy.

Share good things with others.

DECISION?

Write on your ANGER card how you make other people angry. Parents? Friends?

Write on your ANGER card two things that make you very angry.

Read Luke 6:32-36.

CONSEQUENCE

(place cards here)

Write down a special promise and work hard to keep it.

Write down a way to share with the needy today other than giving money. Read Matthew 7:12 if you need help.

Read Matthew 6:24.

Read James 1:12.

DECISION?

Write down two ways that you can share kindness and love this week with five people you do not like.

On the Path to . . .
HAPPINESS

Decision Statements
(To be copied onto 3" x 5" cards)

---

1. Everyone gets angry. We must find a way to show we are sorry and to help those we have hurt. If someone you were rude to earlier today suddenly came over to your table, would you stop playing and tell them you're sorry for how you have acted?

---

2. Have you ever made a promise you did not intend to keep or have you ever broken a promise you truly intended to keep? What happened?

---

3. If you had a choice between being friends with the most popular person in your class at school or a person who no one likes, who would you choose? Why?

---

4. As Christians, we are challenged to share even things we care about or need ourselves. Would you give away one of your toys to a child who has nothing to play with? Which toy?

---

5. It is always much easier to see the faults of others than our own. We tend to like people who are like us. We often dislike those who are different or do not act as we want. How would you feel if someone you were rude to today treated you the same way you treated them? Would you try to talk to the person and think of a way to be friends?

Consequence Statements
(To be copied onto 3" x 5" cards)

---

1. IF YES: Saying you are sorry is not painful. It helps both you and the other person feel better. Good job.

IF NO: It takes more courage to say you are sorry than it does to be rude. Be brave and say you are sorry. Pay two CHANCES. Embarrassment is a small price to pay.

---

2. IF YES: Most of us have. Try to make it up to the person by helping them do something they want to do.

IF NO: Good for you. It's just as bad to not do something you promised you would do as it is to promise when you have no intention of doing what you promised.

3. IF YES: Advance to the nearest LUCK space for being kind.

IF NO: It's easier to be friends with those who are popular than with someone who others treat like an OUTCAST. Read Luke 6:32-36.

4. IF YES: You have made a wise decision. Advance five spaces.

IF NO: It is hard to give things away. But sharing what we have with those who do not have any is what Jesus has asked us to do. Go back five spaces and think about your decision.

5. IF YES: Advance five spaces on your way to HAPPINESS.

IF NO: It's impossible to be friends with everyone, but it's not impossible to be nice to everyone, even those we do not like. Go back three spaces and TRY AGAIN.

The Worship Celebration

I. Select someone with a clear, strong voice to read "One Life to Give."

II. Talk about how it feels to make an unpopular decision.

Items to Go Home

Happiness-Anger cards.

SESSION 33
GRACE

The Bible Lesson

Philippians 4:4 and 4:13 talk about God's acceptance and love.

What the Children Will Learn Today

"Grace" is hard for children to understand. I use the acronym: God's Rare Acceptance Covers Everyone.

Time Needed

Use 20 minuites for workstations and 10 minutes for worship.

Supplies Needed

1. Workstation signs and instructions.
2. Bible-era refreshments (whole grain bread, nuts, dates, olives, grapes, grape juice, raisins, goat's milk or cheese).
3. Bibles and biblical costumes.
4. Large cardboard boxes for the biblical house (or you may use the cave from Christmas, Session 25, Benediction workstation).
5. Furnishings for the biblical house: brown rug to use as dirt, stuffed toy sheep, carpenter tools, clay pottery, or clay lamps (from the Prayer workstation in Session 18).
6. Craft supply basket: usual supplies plus brown paper bags.
7. Seder meal ingredients (apples, lemon juice, honey, salt, water, hard-boiled egg, parsley, dill pickles, Playdough), white paper plates, napkins, and measuring spoons.
8. Pennies or paper flowers to pass out, balloons with messages of peace and love, or newspapers about clown ministry (as done in Session 16, Offering workstation).
9. A piece of cardboard or wood 60" wide and 25" in length, long pole or dowel, four 2 x 4's, coat hanger, paint (optional), woodworking basket.

Workstation 1 — Call to Worship

GETTING READY

Each station this week uses drama to teach about how Jesus lived. Gather large cardboard boxes (like appliance boxes or used moving company boxes) for the house or use the same boxes that you used at Christmas for the cave. Put some furnishings (toy sheep, clay pottery, rugs, etc. by the boxes, along with musical instruments and music to practice for the Easter service. The house can be used as part of your scenery for the Easter service. Copy and post the following instructions for the children:

> You are building a simple house. Make a three-sided, C-shaped structure out of boxes. Cover any writing on the boxes with pieces of paper bags.
>
> Houses in the Bible were made of hardened clay, and often with only one door and one window. Jesus and his followers were not rich.
>
> To make your house a little more interesting, add things like stuffed toy sheep, clay jars and pottery, bread-making supplies, an old brown rug to use as the dirt floor or a small wooden table or workbench. Since Joseph was a carpenter, Jesus would have worked with a hammer, plane, scraps of wood, or saw.
>
> Once you have the house set up, sit down with your musical instruments and practice for the Easter service.

Workstations 2 and 4 — Affirmation of Faith and Sermon

GETTING READY

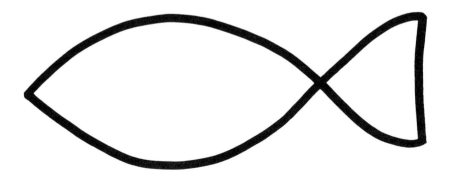

The reader of "One Life to Give" should be ready to practice. Set out your biblical costumes. Use old sheets for extras. Provide a baby doll wrapped in swaddling cloths. The boat is being made at the Offering workstation. Trace the outline of the fish and make a pattern. Set out craft supplies and netting material for a fishnet.

Your clowns have performed "The Good Samaritan" several times (all through Chapter Six on clown ministry, starting with Session 14). They should know it very well. Someone will read the parable as the clowns pantomime along. Using this familiar parable will help the clowns be more relaxed and confident during the Easter service. Post a sign-up sheet (for today and for the Easter service) for actors to pantomime "One Life to Give" (use the same reader as last week) and clowns and a reader for "The Good Samaritan." No clown make-up is needed for today. Copy and post the following instructions for the children:

> The same person from last week should read "One Life to Give," which tells about the life and impact that Jesus has had on our lives. The reading is acted out by costumed Bible characters.
>
> Listen to the words as they are read so you will know when to act out your part. Start with Jesus' birth. Someone dressed like Mary sits beside the house, rocking a baby doll. When the reader says "worked alongside his father," the carpenters should pretend to build with a hammer and nails. When the reader says "preacher," someone acts like he is speaking to the fishermen on the boat. The fishermen should pretend to be fishing with a net. You can even make paper fish to catch.

Workstation 3 — Offering

GETTING READY

Remember to ask for donations of lumber and the old sheet. Set out the woodworking basket. Copy and post the following instructions for the children:

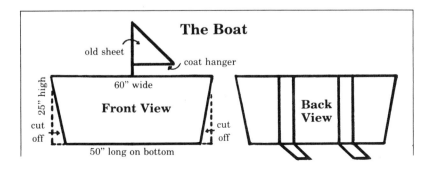

Fishing boats of Jesus' time were not fancy. Use a piece of cardboard or wood about 25" high and 60" long. Cut a right triangle off each end (see drawing). Attach a long pole in the center for the sail. You can tack a triangular shape cut from an old sheet to the top of the pole for a sail and tape it to a straightened out coat hanger so it will hold its shape. Attach two pairs of 2 x 4's nailed together in an "L" shape on the back of the boat for a brace for each side. The boat should now stand up on its own. Paint your boat brown or leave it plain.

Workstation 5 — Witness to the World

GETTING READY

Your clowns should be familiar with "The Sower and the Seed" from using it previously (in Session 14). The clowns can practice without make-up today. Post a sign-up sheet for clowns and a reader to perform "The Sower and the Seed" today and in the Easter service. Copy and post the following instructions for the children:

You are going to practice for the Easter service today. Start with the cross-building pantomime. When the carpenters build the cross, they should just pretend with hammers and nails and the cross made in the Witness to the World workstation a few weeks ago. The clowns will then act out the parable of "The Sower and the Seed" as the reader reads the story from Matthew 13:1-9.

Those not in the clown troupe can hand out pennies, make flowers or balloons with messages of peace and love to pass out, or they may be newspaper reporters handing out newspapers about clown ministry. Make sure that everyone is involved.

Stay in place at the boat until "One Life to Give" is over. Then the clown troupe enters and acts out "The Good Samaritan." You will need a reader to read the story from Luke 10:27-37. Practice all you can today!

Workstation 6 — Prayer

GETTING READY

Copy and post the following instructions for the children:

The challenge is still on. See if you can finish all of the "G's" today for God's never-ending grace.

Workstation 7 — Benediction

GETTING READY

Gather the paper plates, craft supplies and seder meal ingredients and have the biblical snack items ready to be served at the close of the worship service. Post a sign-up sheet for two readers: one to read Philippians 4:4, and one to read Philippians 4:13 (today and also during the Easter service). Copy and post the following instructions for the children:

As we prepare for Holy Week and Easter, remember that Jesus, too, was preparing for a religious festival. Passover was a celebration of freedom for the Jews. Most families had a special meal or "Seder" on the first night of the celebration. Make a "Seder Plate" to sample.

 First, draw a large Star of David on a white paper plate provided. Then mix and place each of the following items on one of the six points of the star: (1) "CHAROSETH" (pronounced "Harroses") reminded the Jews of the mortar they made in Egypt when they made bricks for the Pharaoh. Mix chopped apple pieces with one teaspoon of honey and 1/4 teaspoon of lemon juice. Second, place some horseradish or chopped dill pickles on the plate to be (2) BITTER HERBS representing how hard it was to be slaves in Egypt. Serve parsley for (3) GREENS reminding the Jews of how sweet life was under Joseph in Egypt and the hardships they faced later under other rulers. Place two teaspoons of salt in a cup of water to make (4) SALT WATER to remind everyone of the tears of sadness at the crossing of the Red Sea. A (5) BAKED EGG is placed on the plate to celebrate new life in the promised land. Make a (6) LAMB SHANK BONE out of playdough (since you don't eat bones) and place it on the plate to stand for the love of God and the Jewish practice of making animal sacrifices as part of their worship ritual.

The Worship Celebration

I. Sermon — Practice sermon portions of the Easter service.

II. Witness to the World — Practice the cross-building pantomime and "The Sower and the Seed" clown skit for the Easter service.

III. Snack — Explain the purpose of Seder meal and share snacks.

IV. Benediction — Close with Bible readings from Philippians

4:4 and 4:13 and today's slogan: God's Rare Acceptance Covers Everyone.

Items to Go Home

If your church has the custom of passing out palm branches, try to get a supply so you can give one to each child. Also send home a reminder about your Easter service with the date and time of arrival. You'll want to allow plenty of time to put on the clowns' make-up, gather materials, practice, etc. The reminder should also tell the parents to send the Lenten offerings with the children next week.

SESSION 34
LOVE

Today's session is a joyous celebration for Easter Sunday.

The Bible Lesson

The Bible verses compare the hollow egg used at Easter to the message in John 20:1-2, 8-9, 19, and 29.

What the Children Will Learn Today

The children will learn what Easter really means through the religious symbolism of the Easter egg.

Time Needed:

Use 25 minutes for workstations and five minutes for worship.

Supplies Needed

1. Workstation signs and instructions.
2. Raw and/or hard-boiled eggs (one for each child in your group).
3. Easter egg dye in various colors.
4. Colored chalk and Bibles.
5. Instruments, sing-along tapes, and tape player.
6. Craft supply basket: Usual supplies plus glitter, blunt-nose metal scissors, and a 3" wide white candle.
7. Ear wash bulb or similar syringe to blow out the egg, extra bowls, water, and clean-up supplies.
8. Snack: bread, white grapes, and a potato masher to mash the the grapes to make juice.

WORKSTATIONS

Workstation 1 — Call to Worship

GETTING READY

Use a 3" wide white candle. Ask an adult to supervise. Copy and post the following instructions for the children:

> Your job today is to carve PEACE and LOVE on opposite sides of the candle. The early Christians often carved fish and other symbols into their pottery and jewelry. Use only a *blunt pair of metal children's scissors*. Do not use a knife or sharp scissors.
>
> Write each word on the candle. Press the blunt pair of scissors into the candle until you have carved a little trench for each letter. Put glue in the groove you made for each letter. *Do one word at a time.* Then sprinkle with gold glitter. Let dry, then rub extra glitter off. Repeat process for second word. Your words should show up nicely.

Workstations 2 and 3 — Affirmation of Faith and Offering

GETTING READY

Provide a special snack of bread (try a traditional Easter bread recipe) and grape juice for today. The children will make their own juice using white grapes which don't stain. Copy and post the following instructions for the children:

> Turn in your Lenten offering containers. Then offer a gift to a friend. Read John 20:1-2. Use the potato masher to mash the grapes to make juice. Offer some to a friend. Cut two pieces of bread; give one to a friend.

Workstation 4 — Sermon/Bible Lesson

GETTING READY

Three workstations will be set up for decorating Easter eggs. Place the tables in the shape of a cross. The Bible verses have been coordinated to fit the activity. Ask an adult to supervise. Copy and post the following instructions for the children:

> Have you ever wondered how an egg got to be hollow on the inside? You are about to make one. Read John 20:8-9 in the Bible.
>
> Roll up your sleeves and put on an old shirt or cover-up over your clothes. Pick up one of the raw eggs. With the needle, gently punch a hole, about 1/8" wide, at each end of the egg. Hold the egg over a bowl. Use an ear wash bulb to blow air into the egg through one of the holes. The contents of the egg should flow out through the other hole. Work slowly and carefully. Wash the eggs out with water using the same method.

Workstation 5 — Witness to the World

GETTING READY

For younger children who cannot blow an egg out, decorating a hard-boiled egg is still an all-time favorite. Use the special wax crayon from an egg dye kit or just plain crayons. Copy and post the following instructions for the children:

> Everyone loves to decorate Easter eggs. Today you will decorate eggs with Christian symbols. First read John 20:19 in the Bible. Draw the Christian sign of the fish, cross, the anchor cross, a butterfly, rainbows, or your favorite symbol. Then dye your egg different colors.

Workstation 6 — Prayer

GETTING READY

Copy and post the following instructions for the children:

> The challenge continues, but today you are to sew the first letter of your name. For example, if your name was Jill, you would sew a "J." If you cannot find a letter that your name begins with, sew an "L" for Love.

Workstation 7 — Benediction

GETTING READY

This is the last step with the egg. Make sure you have adult supervision and room to spread out. Mix the colors the way you normally do. For the chalk, crush three or four different colors into fine powder and place in separate bowls. Copy and post the following instructions for the children:

> Before you start, read John 20:29 in the Bible. Then decide what color you would like your egg to be. Dye your egg. While your egg is still wet, sprinkle different colors of chalk dust over the egg. Be careful with your egg until it is dry. When the chalk dust is dry, it will not fall off the egg.

The Worship Celebration

I. Sermon — Explain: The Easter egg is an ancient symbol of life. The hollow egg reminds us of the empty tomb. We dye eggs different colors to celebrate the Good News. We use Christian symbols to identify ourselves as followers of Jesus.

II. Benediction — close with the "He Is Alive" chant from the Easter service.

Items to Go Home

Decorated Easter eggs.

CHAPTER ELEVEN

A JOYOUS PENTECOST

Because Pentecost was a time of rejuvenation within the early church, the children, too, experience new things that help them understand the coming of the Holy Spirit: Pentecost worship in a cozy plastic "bubble," making decorated sugar eggs as an expression of thanks for the Sunday school teachers, and building special kites relating to the wind and the tongues of fire.

SESSION 35

ARE YOU READY?

The Bible Lesson

The challenge is to involve *everyone,* no matter what their age or attendance, so that by the end of "A Joyous Pentecost" all feel wanted and needed as members of the children's church. The children read Matthew 4:18-19.

What the Children Will Learn Today

Children should understand not only what worship means but also the purposes of the church.

Time Needed

Use 25 minutes for workstations and five minutes for worship today.

Supplies Needed

1. Big plastic bubble or a floor rug to sit on in a circle (if you do not have a bubble and wish to make one, purchase four 100" x 300" sheets clear *heavy* plastic sheeting at a building supply store. Also needed: wide strapping tape and a box fan.)
2. Fish windsock supplies, cardboard containers (with the bottoms cut out), and paper.
3. Workstation signs, instructions, Bibles, and a snack.
4. Recipe (see children's instructions, Workstations 3 and 4) and enough sugar and water molding mixture to make an egg to give to all the Sunday school teachers in your church, and plastic egg molds from cake decorating store (any kind of attractive handmade gift idea can be substituted for the sugar eggs).
5. Craft supply basket: usual supplies plus round circles for scales, sequins and glitter, old buttons, and crepe paper streamers.

WORKSTATIONS

Workstation 1 — Call to Worship

GETTING READY

Have sing-along tapes playing and instruments available. Post a sign-up sheet for singers and musicians to lead music in today's worship celebration, and copy and post the following instructions for the children:

> Pick a song for everyone to sing in today's Call to Worship in the bubble.

Workstations 2 and 3 — Affirmation of Faith and Offering

GETTING READY

The children will never forget the year they came to church and made hollow sugar eggs. They are not difficult to make — only three steps are required. You will mold the eggs today, decorate them next week, and present them as gifts to Sunday school teachers on Pentecost. These are special gifts that the children can give with pride, yet these eggs are easy enough for even four-year-olds to help make. Have an adult at this workstation to help.

The egg molds come with complete directions. If you can't find egg molds, you may use egg-shaped cupcake pans or take-apart plastic eggs.

You're just molding the eggs today. Make a few ahead for practice and to use as examples. Let the eggs set for two hours until the outside is dry and hard. Then, hold the dry side of the egg in the palm of your hand. With a spoon, gently begin to scoop out the wet sugar on the inside of the egg. Scoop slowly and gently. Hollow out the egg and then set it on an open shelf to dry. If the egg breaks, just remold it. Copy and post the following instructions for the children:

> You are about to discover an exciting way to make eggs. The egg you make today will take several weeks to finish. The hollow egg represents Jesus' empty tomb, standing for life after death.
>
> To mold a hollow sugar egg, (1) mix two cups of granulated sugar with *exactly* 4 teaspoons of water. Do not add extra water. Measure very accurately. The mixture will feel damp. (2) Fill and press the sugar mixture into your clean dry plastic egg molds. Pack *firmly,* and fill the molds completely. (3) Place a piece of cardboard over the sugar in the egg. (4) Holding the egg and cardboard tightly together, flip the egg onto the cardboard. (5) With the cardboard sitting on the table, lift the plastic egg mold from the egg. You will need to use two egg molds to make one finished egg. Cut an opening with thread — cut the end or top as preferred. Put your two half eggs side by

side so the openings will match up when you put them together later. Then let the egg dry. Your egg will sit on the cardboard to dry for two hours. Do not touch the egg or it will crumble. If you forget and touch your egg or it crumbles or cracks, simply dump the sugar mixture back into the bowl (do not add any water) and start over. Don't be discouraged! These eggs are love gifts, and love takes patience.

The hollow eggs can be kept indefinitely as a reminder of the joy and message of new life at Easter, which was the message the early Christians wanted to send out into the world. You will give your eggs to the Sunday school teachers in our church as a way of saying thank you for all they do.

Packing sugar into the mold

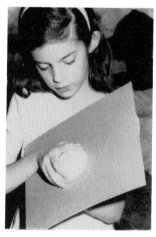

Flipping the egg

Lifting the mold off the egg

Cutting the egg with thread

Finished cut

Scooping out the egg

Workstations 4 and 5 —
Bible Lesson/Sermon and Witness to the World

GETTING READY

There are many plans available for making plastic bubbles, and commercial versions are available in some areas.

The bubble can be used for many years and many purposes. The children enjoy it very much. The bubble is a perfect setting for stories, puppets, singing, and Vacation Bible School.

Have some friends help you before the session. If you do not have room in your regular meeting place, arrange to meet today in the fellowship hall.

Unroll the heavy sheets of plastic across your fellowship hall floor. Use only *heavy* builder's plastic. Tape the plastic together with the strapping tape making two long sheets 200" wide and 300" long.

Fold the plastic over, forming a big pillow. Tape all sides together except for a slit on one side for a door and a corner open for the fan. When all of the sides are taped together, place the fan in the corner opening and tape the sides of the plastic to the fan. You do not want any air leaks except for the slit you left for a door.

Copy and post the following instructions for the children:

> Gently help unroll the bubble. Turn on the fan and watch the air blow your bubble up. You may need to hold the door closed for a few minutes till the bubble fills with air. Always take your shoes off before entering the bubble, and leave the fan running on *low* to keep the bubble inflated. Patch any holes with tape. Then go over to Workstation 7 (Benediction) and make a large fish windsock, using the biggest container. When you're done, tape the windsock inside on the top of the bubble.

Workstation 6 — Prayer

GETTING READY

Copy and post the following instructions for the children:

> We are still embroidering the Lord's Prayer Banner. Sew each "I" you can find for "Involvement" today.

Workstation 7 — Benediction

GETTING READY

This project can be as elaborate or simple as you want. Set out the craft supply basket. The children can draw a fish on paper or they can draw and decorate a fish windsock with round circles for scales, sequins and glitter, or old buttons. The fish windsocks can be made out of plain paper or round cardboard containers. You can use oatmeal cartons or even tissue holders. Post a sign-up sheet for someone to read Matthew 4:18-19 in today's celebration, and copy and post the following instructions for the children:

> Cover your cardboard container with your favorite color of paper. Draw a fish on the sides of the container. You may simply color your fish or use the supplies available and make a very fancy fish. Glue or tape streamers to the bottom of your container when finished. Attach a string to the top of your fish. Now your fish will fly along beside you in the wind as you walk out of church. Read Matthew 4:18-19 together and think about why the early Christians used the sign of the fish.

The Worship Celebration

I. Call to Worship — Gather in the bubble to sing the song.

II. Benediction — Read the Bible verse and close with the Lord's Prayer.

Items to Go Home

Fish windsocks. (Save the big windsock for the bubble.)

SESSION 36

IN THE YEAR 2993

The Bible Lesson

The Bible Lesson for Pentecost is a series of short verses strung together by several readers. Children do not listen to any one reader for long. The Bible verses tell the story of Pentecost: Numbers 28:26; Leviticus 23:17; Acts 2:1-4, 28, 32-33, 44-46 and 4:32.

What the Children Will Learn Today

They will get ready for a big birthday party for the church and will celebrate what it means to be a church.

Time Needed

Use 25 minutes for workstations and five minutes for worship today.

Supplies Needed

1. Big plastic bubble or a floor rug.
2. Handout for Call to Worship.
3. Bibles and pencils for everyone.
4. The sugar eggs that are ready to decorate. (Any kind of special handmade gift idea can be substituted for the sugar eggs.)
5. Royal icing (recipe below) and simple decorating kit. Do not mix royal icing ahead. Furnish the supplies and mix immediately before using.
6. Kite supplies: 33" x 66" thin white plastic, 1⅛" dowel, 3¼" dowels, strong cloth tape, kite string, and red streamers.
7. 72" x 35" red and ½ yard white felt or paper for banner.

WORKSTATIONS

Workstation 1 — Call to Worship

GETTING READY

Have the bubble set up with a box of Bibles inside and pick a secretary (older child or adult). Save the Call to Worship written by the children for the spring service. Post a sign-up sheet for helpers to lead the Call to Worship. They will help both today and next week. Copy and post the following instructions for the children:

Imagine that you are children of the year 2993. You've heard about a celebration in the church long ago called Pentecost. You have gathered in your plastic bubble church to look at old records to see if you can revive this ancient custom.

Open up the box, dust off the Bibles, read the following verses: Numbers 28:26; Leviticus 23:17; Acts 2:1-4, 12, 32-33, 44-46, and 4:32, and then answer the questions as children of the future!

1. What do you think the tongues of fire stand for?

2. What does the wind represent?

3. What does the last verse in Acts 4:32 mean when it says "they were all of one spirit?"

4. Why do we call Pentecost the birthday of the church?

5. What is the Holy Spirit?

Put what you have learned together and write a Call to Worship for your Pentecost celebration next week.

The Call to Worship is an invitation to come and worship together. You may: (1) sing a favorite song, (2) fill in the invitation: "_____ are invited to a _____ to celebrate _____ because _____", (3) read Bible verses, or (4) do all three.

Pentecost was also a kind of invitation, an invitation to come and believe and to show your belief to others by how you lived your life. Remember, you are in the year 2993 and no one even knows or remembers what Pentecost is all about. Keep things lively because, after all, this is a celebration.

Workstations 2 and 3 —
Affirmation of Faith and Offering

GETTING READY

The hollow sugar eggs are to be presented to the Sunday school teachers on Pentecost. If you end up with more sugar eggs than you have Sunday school teachers, you can send the extras to shut-ins.

Mix the royal icing right before you want to use it. Recipe: 3 egg whites, 4 cups confectioner's sugar, ½ teaspoon cream of tartar. Beat with mixer at highest speed for 10 minutes.

Add colors and place the icing in decorating tubes. Allow the children to decorate the eggs. You'll be amazed at their creativity.

Copy and post the following instructions for the children:

> Today's task will be to decorate the eggs. Take the decorating tubes, squeeze the tube, and make simple designs to decorate each egg. You may even add little pictures or miniatures. Use frosting to put the two halves of your egg together. Then set the decorated egg aside to dry. Do not touch the egg until it's completely dry.

Workstation 6 — Prayer

GETTING READY

Copy and post the following instructions for the children:

> We are still embroidering the Lord's Prayer Banner. Sew each "I" you can find for "Involvement" again today.

Workstations 4 and 5 — Sermon/Bible Lesson and Witness to the World

GETTING READY

You will need an adult to help the children build a kite. Set out the supplies, and copy and post the following instructions for the children:

> Today you are going to build a kite. Measure and cut the plastic carefully, following the measurements in the drawing. Fold your plastic triangle kite in half to make sure that each side is exactly equal. Cut and tape down a ¼" dowel 33" long exactly in the middle of the kite. Next, securely tape the 26" side of the keel on top of the center dowel starting at the base of the kite. You will have a 7" gap at the top where the keel does not go all the way to the point. Flip your kite over, cut and tape down the two ¼" dowels to the wing edges, again starting at the base of the kite. Again, there will be about a 10½" gap from the point. That's supposed to be there, so don't panic. Then, measure down 19½" from the point and tape down a ⅛" dowel 30" long. Reinforce the tip of the keel with cloth tape, punch a hole in it, and tie on your kite string. Add long streamers for "tongues of fire" effect. You're ready to fly on Pentecost!

The Tongues of Fire Kite

STEP 1: Cut the plastic

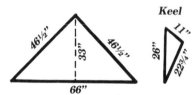

STEP 2: Tape keel and center 33" dowel

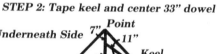
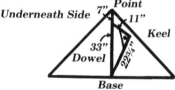

STEP 3: Tape 3 remaining dowels

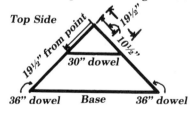

STEP 4: Attach streamers

Workstation 7 — Benediction

GETTING READY

The children are making a red and white banner to hang in their church for Pentecost. They will also make matching bookmarks from the felt or paper scraps. Copy and post the following instructions for the children:

> The fish was a secret symbol of the early Christians. The fish marked the way to the worship service and was a sign of Christian friendship. Today you are going to make a banner marking the way to your Pentecost Service. Make a paper pattern for a large white fish to go in the center of your red banner. Also, make white letters saying, "COME AND FOLLOW ME" to go across the bottom of the banner. When you have everything cut out, glue the fish and letters down with "tacky" glue. Let dry completely. From the scraps, make a simple Bible bookmark with a fish on it.

The Worship Celebration

I. Call to Worship — Gather in the bubble for the special Pentecost Call to Worship.

II. Benediction — Close with the Lord's Prayer.

Items to Go Home

Fish Bible bookmarks.

SESSION 37

ON THE WINGS OF FIRE

The Bible Lesson

The children are reading about Pentecost today: Numbers 28:26, Leviticus 23:17, Acts 2:1-4, 28, 32-33, 44-46, and 4:32.

What the Children Will Learn Today

The Pentecost Celebration is a worship service and birthday party for the church. The children will learn what Pentecost means, experience the excitement, and involve every single person who comes to worship that day.

Time Needed

Five minutes for the Call to Worship, 20 minutes at workstations, and five for the Benediction.

Supplies Needed

1. The bubble or a floor rug and the Pentecost banner (hang in center of church).
2. Call to Worship from Session 36.
3. Bibles with fish bookmarks.
4. Workstation signs and instructions.
5. The hollow sugar eggs to be used as gifts for teachers.
6. Tongues of Fire kite from Session 36.
7. Cake or cookies, napkins, cups, and beverages for party.
8. Craft supply basket: usual supplies plus tissue paper, tempera paint, red construction paper, red crepe paper streamers, paint brushes, painting smocks or old shirts, and clean-up supplies.
9. Red balloons (use helium or regular balloons).
10. "Pin the Candle on the Cake" game: picture of a cake, long strips of paper for candles, yellow construction paper, flame patterns, scissors, glue, pencils, and tape.

The Joyous Pentecost Celebration

I. Have everyone gather at the Children's Church.

II. Start with the children who wrote the Call to Worship.

III. Then send everyone to Workstation 1 to begin.

WORKSTATIONS

Workstation 1 — Call to Worship

GETTING READY

Have sing-along tapes playing background music. Set up Children's Church and bubble.

Tape the balloon strings to the top of the bubble when it is inflated. The balloons float on top and look very colorful. Make sure you have a balloon for each child to take home. Remember donations. Have adult Sunday school classes sponsor the children by providing the money for the number of balloons needed.

Place the hollow sugar eggs on the communion table. Hang the banners. Small paper fish along the walls or floor mark the path to follow just as the early Christians did.

Put a large picture of a cake on the wall where children can easily reach or you may use the cake poster coming up in Session 39 (Sermon), Cut out strips of paper for candles and provide yellow construction paper, scissors, and flame patterns. Copy and post the following instructions for the children:

Read Numbers 28:26, then play "Pin the Candle on the Cake" game. Take a candle and write on it something you wish would happen at our church. Use the flame pattern and cut out and glue a flame on your candle. Close your eyes and, with the help of a friend, spin around three times and with your eyes still closed, go over and tape your candle onto the big cake poster. Look where your candle landed, then go to Workstation 2.

Workstation 2 — Affirmation of Faith

GETTING READY

Set up the learning station tables in the shape of a cross. Provide the frame pattern and supplies. Copy and post the following instructions for the children:

Read Leviticus 23:17. Your gift today is sharing your talents with those who need help. We are making kites today. Here's how: Cut a piece of tissue paper to the size of the construction paper. Fold the tissue paper and one piece of red construction paper together into two equal rectangles, like a book. Next, place the frame pattern on your folded tissue paper, placing the word "fold" on the fold of your tissue paper. With the paper still folded, trace around the inside and outside of the pattern. Then do the same with your folded construction paper. You've made two triangles. Cut only around the outside edge of your tissue paper triangle. Cut both the inside and outside lines to make a kite frame with your red paper triangle. Go on to Workstation 3.

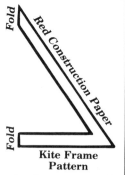

Kite Frame Pattern

Workstation 3 — Offering

GETTING READY

Set out a basket full of pennies so that everyone can have a penny to share. Set out the streamers, hole punch and other supplies. Copy and post the following instructions for the children:

Read Acts 2:1-4. Glue your red kite frame to your tissue paper triangle kite and staple red streamers across the base of the triangle to form the tongues of fire. Punch a hole in the top of your kite, then tie a string through the hole. Stop and help anyone having trouble.

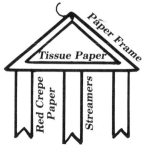

Before you leave, take one penny from the basket. Find someone to share your penny with as a sign of Christian friendship. Tell your friend to share the penny with another. "Pass the Love of God with one penny to everyone." Write your name on your kite and go to Workstation 4.

Workstation 4 — Bible Lesson/Sermon

GETTING READY

Send everyone to the refreshment table after Workstation 3 and then call over four or five painters at a time to Workstation 5.

The children will love it when you tell them the *Cake* is the sermon today. Have a special message on your cake to explain the Pentecost message to the children as they receive their punch and cake. The children may read Acts 2:28 as they wait.

Workstation 5 — Witness to the World

GETTING READY

Set out paints, brushes, water, and old painting shirts. Have the children wait at the refreshment table till you call them. Copy and post the following instructions for the children:

> Paint the mini "tongues of fire" kite however you wish. Your kite should be an expression of you. Share paints. The triangle is symbolic of the Trinity — the Father, Son, and Holy Spirit. Read Acts 2:32-33. Your painting tells others how you feel just as you tell others what you believe by what you do and say. Go to Workstation 6.

Workstation 6 — Prayer

GETTING READY

Copy and post the following instructions for the children:

> Sew each "P" you can find for "Pentecost." Embroidering reminds us that the answers to our prayers are not always immediate. Read Acts 2:44-46, then go to the bubble.

Workstation 7 — Benediction

GETTING READY

Arrange for a time when the children can give the Sunday school teachers the sugar eggs (could be in the congregational service).

Have one person in charge of flying the large "tongues of fire" kite (made in Session 36), but give everyone a turn to launch the kite or hold the string. If there is no suitable area for kite flying, let the children hold the kite on a string and run back and forth with it fluttering.

Provide a blank card with "Peace Be With You" written on the front. Release your "Peace" balloon to go out into the world, then send everyone home with a hug or handshake and the early Christian closing, "Peace Be With You." Copy and post the following instructions for the children:

Read Acts 4:32 in the bubble. Find a card and write a statement or draw a picture showing how a Christian acts toward others. Staple your card onto a red balloon. Then sign your name onto the card which says "Peace Be With You." Follow the "tongues of fire" kite outside for the Benediction.

Items to Go Home

Small tissue paper kite and red balloon for each child.

WRITING THE WORSHIP SERVICE

WRITING THE CHILDREN'S SERVICE

Sunday morning worship takes on a fresh perspective when the children plan and present their own service. Incorporating much of the learning and activities of the past months, the children's service is a treat for worshipers of every age. We're *all* God's children!

SESSION 38

Worship Is . . .

The Bible Lesson

Placed back in time to an early church service, the children can formulate their own beliefs as they answer the question: How does Jesus fit into my daily life? (Exodus 23:1-2, Mark 10:19-21, Matthew 22:36-40, and Luke 10:29-37).

What the Children Will Learn Today

If you dress the children in costumes, put up blinking lights, and pretend they're in a time machine, by the end of the time at the workstations they'll have started writing their service without even knowing it.

Time Needed

Fifteen minutes for worship and 15 minutes for workstations.

Supplies Needed

1. Woodworking basket and scrap wood.
2. Bibles, snack, biblical costumes, hymnal, instruments.
3. Workstation signs, instructions, and extra paper at each.
4. Christmas lights for the tunnel, paper fish, baskets.
5. Large cardboard boxes or biblical house from Easter.
6. Refreshments: round loaves of whole grain bread, nuts, dates, olives, grapes, grape juice, raisins, goat's milk or cheese.
7. Paper sacks, small sticks, and ribbons for scrolls.
8. Screw-in eye hooks and rubber bands or used guitar strings.
9. Two sheets of newsprint: one saying "Christian-Like Behavior" and the other saying "Non-Christian-Like Behavior."

WORKSTATIONS

Workstation 1 — Call to Worship

GETTING READY

Dress up in simple costumes. The early church often held services in homes, so bring out the cardboard house from Easter or at least get a rug to sit on. Use the bubble from Pentecost for a costume shop and time machine. The time machine may be made by hanging blinking Christmas tree lights across a doorway, or you may make a cardboard tunnel with levers, dials, and flashing lights. Cut out and tape paper fish onto the floor to guide the children to each workstation. Also hang the two sheets of newsprint on Christian behavior near your worship area for use in the celebration. Make a list of songs your group has enjoyed singing throughout the year. Save newsprint, song sheet, and scrolls for Session 40. Copy and post the following instructions for the children:

> Hold on to your hats, because we are going to be TIME TRAVELERS today. We are going to set the machine to take us back to Jerusalem after Pentecost, when the followers of Jesus were deciding how to share his message. Put on a biblical costume from our costume shop and then, to get into the time tunnel, write down a favorite song or circle one on the sheet. Walk through the time tunnel to enter Old Jerusalem. Then follow the fishes as they lead you from workstation to workstation today.

Workstation 2 — Affirmation of Faith

GETTING READY

Have scroll-making supplies and a basket ready. Copy and post the following instructions for the children:

> You are frustrated. Every time you try to tell one of your friends about Jesus, they say, "he's dead now and he can't help us anymore." No one believes Jesus can still change their lives unless they see a miracle. You decide that if you write your ideas down, then maybe someone some day will read them and understand. Use one of the brown pieces of paper to make a scroll. Write down on your scroll one way that you think believing in Jesus can change your life. Your idea may be something Jesus said, an action, or a way of acting. Make these ideas or actions something that you can actually do in your own life today, like "Say a kind word each day." Tape straws onto each end of the paper and roll up your scroll. Tie a string around your scroll to keep it rolled. Place your scroll in the basket when you have finished.

Workstation 3 — Offering

GETTING READY

Furnish screw-eye hooks and rubber bands or used guitar strings.

Copy and post the following instructions for the children:

> Pick out a piece of wood and cut to desired size. A 7" x 12" board makes a nice shape to hold and play, but even a 2" x 4" works fine. Place three screw-eye hooks in a row on each end of your board. Attach the rubber bands or tie the guitar strings through the hole and onto the hook. Make sure it is tight. You now have a harp.

Workstations 4 and 7 — Sermon and Benediction

GETTING READY

Have foods set out ahead of time for the meal. The children can arrange them on a plate. Save the secret code that the children come up with for their spring service. Post a sign-up sheet for helpers to lead today's biblical worship service, and copy and post the following instructions for the children:

> Since it was often dangerous to even mention Jesus' name, early followers often hid to worship together. You are going to lead a biblical worship service today for our celebration. Sign up for the part of the service you would like to do. Practice with your friends. Pretend you are in Bible times. Be ready to welcome the guests to your home and lead the service: (1) Start by saying the Lord's Prayer together. (2) Share a meal together. Serve bread, fruit, vegetable stew, or goat's cheese. (3) Next is a lesson from the first five books of the Old Testament: Read aloud Exodus 20:7-17. (4) Back then, someone who had heard Jesus speak would retell one of his stories. Read Matthew 21:28-31. (5) Talk about what the story meant like the early Christians would have. (6) After the discussion, the early Christians would sing. You can, too. Many of the Psalms have been set to music; check your church hymnal. (7) A traditional ending for the services was for everyone to share a Christian hug and kiss with each other person at the service before leaving, and repeat Corinthians 13:13. This was very special; they were never sure when they might be arrested and would never see each other again. (8) If you are not much for hugging, you might decide on a secret code that everyone could use at school or in the neighborhood to say "Hi!" to fellow Christians. You could also choose some actions or ways of living for your group to identify themselves.

Workstation 5 — Witness to the World

GETTING READY

This station is responding to the scrolls written for the Affirmation. Put the scrolls made at the Affirmation workstation in the basket at this station when they are finished. Provide a sheet of newsprint. Save both the scrolls and the list to use in writing the spring service. Copy and post the following instructions for the children:

> Reach into the basket and pull out a scroll. Read it and write on a sheet of newsprint how that message could help you today. Tie the scroll back together and put it back in the basket.

Workstation 6 — Prayer

GETTING READY

Copy and post the following instructions for the children:

> Try your best! We want to finish by next week.

The Worship Celebration

I. Call to Worship — Read the following script to set the mood:

Life in Jerusalem

Life was both hard and simple in Jerusalem when the early church was getting started. Most of a person's time was spent just living. A young man learned a trade in order to support his family. This might be farming, fishing, tending sheep, or building things out of wood, just as Jesus learned to be a carpenter. Young women learned to cook, sew, and take care of the house and children. These things were an all-day job and were essential if a family was to survive. Bread had to be made every day.

The rooftop was a favorite place for the family in this hot, dry region. The roof was flat and usually much cooler than inside the house. People would eat, sleep, grind corn, pray, worship, and do household chores on the rooftop.

The Christians did not have a church for public worship so they would hide and meet in caves or in fellow Christians' homes.

II. Sermon — Have those who signed the sheet begin the service.

III. Benediction — Just as the service ends, have an adult or teenager in costume as a Pharisee enter the room and shout,

"You're all under arrest for being a part of one of those Christian meetings." Have two pieces of newsprint up on the wall saying: (1) Christian-Like Behavior and (2) Non-Christian-Like Behavior. The Pharisee should mention several behaviors, with the group deciding whether such actions belong on the Christian or Non-Christian list. Suggestions are: being kind to others, following the Commandments, hating others, or telling lies.

Fill lists with as many ideas as possible. The Pharisee then says, "Being a Christian isn't so bad after all! Instead of arresting you, I'd like to join your Christian meeting!"

Items to Go Home

Secret code. Encourage the children to try it out this week.

SESSION 39

THE BIRTHDAY PARTY

The Bible Lesson

The Bible Lesson teaches that worship is a time of truth, celebration, and honesty (Psalms 150 and Philippians 4:8-9).

What the Children Will Learn Today

Help the children discover the meaning of each part of the worship service. The party will turn into a worship celebration.

Time Needed

Twenty minutes for workstations and 10 minutes for worship.

Supplies Needed

1. Workstation signs and instructions.
2. Musical instruments, song book, and Bibles.
3. Cake in the shape of a cross and cake poster.
4. Icing (blue, gold or yellow, white, red, and green).
5. Simple cake decorating kit (available in grocery stores).
6. Multicolored candy sprinkles.
7. Washable ink pad and old, light-colored bed sheet.
8. Craft supply basket: usual supplies plus balloons, tempera paint, paint brushes, painting shirts, and permanent markers.
9. Punch, paper plates, napkins, etc. for party.
10. Live tree to plant or just a branch on a wooden stand.

WORKSTATIONS

Workstation 1 — Call to Worship

GETTING READY

Bring out all of the instruments and song books. Post a sign-up sheet for musicians to play and sing in today's celebration, and copy and post the following instructions for the children:

> Make a list of five of your favorite songs. Select one for today's service. Practice.

Workstation 2 — Affirmation of Faith

GETTING READY

Bake a cake in the shape of a cross. Use a cross-shaped cake pan or cut your own cross pieces from a cake baked in a 13" x 9" pan. Cut one 13" x 4" long piece and two 6" x 4" pieces. Put the pieces together with icing. One cake serves about 20.

Make icing colors to remind the children of the liturgical colors they studied earlier: blue for truth and honesty, white for purity, gold for royalty, green for learning, purple for preparation, and red for the Holy Spirit. Either make your own icing or use prepared mixes and food coloring. Have the cake, icing, decorating tips, knives, and sprinkles ready. Have an adult helper supervise to make sure everyone gets a turn to decorate. Copy and post the following instructions for the children:

> Only *five* are allowed at this workstation at a time, and you are limited to five minutes per group. Remember to share and think about the needs of your neighbor. Make sure your neighbor gets a turn.
>
> The cake is in four sections. You are allowed to do only one section of the cake so that each group will get a chance. Spread white icing smoothly with the knives over just your part of the cross cake. Then, using the decorating kit, decorate the cake with liturgical colors and, last, make a stained glass window on top of the cross with the candy sprinkles. Clean the work space for the next group.

Workstation 3 — Offering

GETTING READY

These children are making a "Love Task Tree." This can be a live tree (to be planted this spring) or you may simply use a twig or branch. The branch should be hammered onto a wooden stand made from scraps so it stands upright. Provide the fish pattern and construction paper. Copy and post the following instructions for the children:

Make two paper FISH using the pattern. Use any color paper and decorate as you wish. Punch a hole at the top and tie a string through each hole tying the two fish together to make a "fish card." On the inside of the card, fill out these promises: (1) I will show I care for others by _____. (2) I have _____ that I can share with others. (3) I will do _____ to share God's love. Hang your card on the Love Task Tree to remind you of your promises.

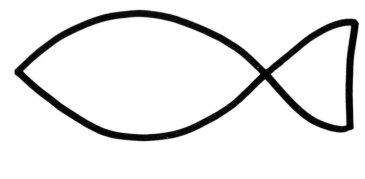

Workstation 4 — Sermon/Bible Lesson

CAKE POSTER

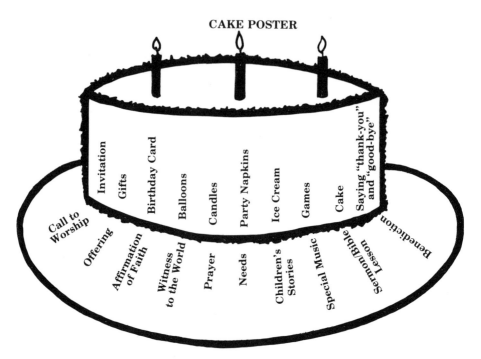

GETTING READY

Make a large copy of the cake poster (see illustration) and place on the wall. The words on the cake describe the different things found in a typical birthday party. The corresponding words on the platter tell about each part of the worship service. Relating the familiar parts of a birthday party to the parts of a worship service makes the concepts easier for the children to grasp. The poster also serves to divide up the work groups for putting the children's service together next week. Copy and post the following instructions for the children:

Read Psalm 150 and Philippians 4:8-9. Then go over to the poster on the wall and place your name beside the three things that are most important at a party. Which of these things do you think are the most important at a birthday party?

INVITATION: inviting friends to celebrate with you

BIRTHDAY CARD: selecting the right words and picture to tell friends how special they are

CAKE: sends a message of love and happiness

CANDLES: to make a wish for something

GIFTS: to give and share with others

GAMES: fun with friends

BALLOONS: a message to send home with the guests

SAYING THANK YOU: before you say good-bye, you always say thank you

ICE CREAM: yummy food to eat when you're hungry

PARTY NAPKINS: to tell something special

Workstation 5 — Witness to the World

GETTING READY

Have an old, light-colored bed sheet cut 71" x 23." This sheet is used to make the handprint rainbow banner which hangs on the lower side panel of the church. Measure about 7" up from the bottom of the banner. Put a piece of tape across the bottom one-third. This tape will serve to mark the dividing line between the rainbow and the line of thumbprints. The children will paint their handprint rainbow across the top two-thirds of the banner next week. This week you want them to only work on the bottom third. Use washable ink pads, markers, and ink pens for the drawings.

HANDPRINT RAINBOW BANNER

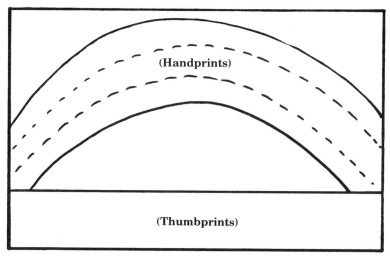

Copy and post the following instructions for the children:

"Thumbs up!" Find a place to sit at the table, ink your thumbs on the *washable* ink pad, place your thumbprints across the bottom of the banner in the area set aside for thumbprints. Do not put your thumbprints on the top part of the banner.

Songs and stories call Jesus our friend. If Jesus were alive today, what kind of friend would he be?

On your first thumbprint, draw a picture using your thumbprint for the person, or just write a description of your ideal best friend next to your thumbprint, giving this person all of the qualities you could ever want a friend to have. Show feelings and character, not looks. On your second thumbprint, draw a picture or write and describe the kind of friend you would like to be to others.

Workstation 6 — Prayer

GETTING READY

Copy and post the following instructions for the children:

Thanks for helping to finish the banner!

Workstation 7 — Benediction

GETTING READY

Set out the craft supply basket. Have extra balloons to replace those that pop. *Only* older children or adults should blow up the balloons. Copy and post the following instructions for the children:

> Decorate a balloon to bring to the birthday party. Use tempera paint, permanent markers, or letter cut-outs. Write one word on the balloon to tell what worship means to you, like Love, Sharing, Peace, or Kindness.

The Worship Celebration

I. Call to Worship — Tell the children that when they picked what they felt were the most important parts of a birthday party, they also picked what was important in a worship service, because worship is a time to celebrate God's love, just as a birthday party is a time to celebrate our love for our friends.

II. Sermon — Compare the parts of a party and the parts of worship:

*The Invitation and the Call to Worship invite us to come.

*The Birthday Card and the Affirmation of Faith tell a message about something we believe.

*Cake and Sermons share a message made especially for us.

*Candles and Prayer are a time to wish or hope for something special. (We pray for understanding and help with our problems.)

*Gifts and the Offering help to make others happy.

*Balloons (sending a bit of the party happiness home) are a way of witnessing and sending messages out to others about our faith.

*Games and Congregational Hymns get everyone involved.

*Party Napkins and Ice Cream are special pleasures, just as Special Music and Children's Stories are ways to sing praises.

*Thank You and Good-Bye are the Benediction — sending everyone out to spread happiness, kindness, and the Good News.

III. Benediction — Serve everyone a piece of cake, sing a favorite song, and close with a love circle and the Lord's Prayer.

Items to Go Home

Balloons.

SESSION 40

THE PARTS OF
THE WORSHIP SERVICE

The Bible Lesson

The children's worship service is largely based on verses from the four Gospels.

What the Children Will Learn Today

Writing and leading their own worship service gives the children an opportunity to explain the life and customs of biblical times, the purpose of worship, lessons from the Bible, and the teachings and parables of Jesus.

Time Needed

Twenty minutes for workstations and 10 minutes for the worship celebration.

Supplies Needed

1. Worship service poster and Bibles.
2. Workstation signs and instructions.
3. Hymnals or song books and a snack if desired.
4. Craft supply basket: usual supplies plus Thumbprint banner from Session 39, tempera paint, and brushes.
5. Newsprint and markers for each workstation.

WORKSTATIONS

Make a large poster with the order of worship on it and a brief explanation of purpose from the celebration in Session 39. Tape the poster up in your worship area ready for the children to add their parts to it during today's celebration.

Workstation 1 — Call to Worship

GETTING READY

Have on hand the "I Believe" puppet workstation signs from Session 1, the Call to Worship written by the children in Session 36, the list of favorite songs from the Call to Worship in Session 38, newsprint, and song books and all of the instruments. Post a sign-up sheet for a volunteer to hang up the newsprint and explain the Call to Worship, and other volunteers to lead the Call to Worship in the children's service. Copy and post the following instructions for the children:

> Look over the Call to Worship that you wrote for Pentecost. Use some of these ideas or write a totally new Call to Worship that invites others to come and celebrate God's love (Psalm 150) for our children's service. This is your service; be creative. A Call to Worship can include music, Bible passages, clown skits, readings, a thought for the day, or poetry. Think of ways that you can include everyone. Use the instruments. Choose a hymn for everyone to sing. Write your ideas on newsprint.

Workstation 2 — Affirmation of Faith

GETTING READY

Furnish the scrolls from Session 38. Post a sign-up sheet for a volunteer to hang up newsprint and explain what the Affirmation of Faith is, and for volunteers to help with the Affirmation in the children's service. Copy and post the following instructions for the children:

> From the time when Jesus first called his twelve disciples until today, his followers have come from many different lifestyles (John 8:31-32), cultures, races, and ideas. Even today we follow Jesus for many different reasons and in many different ways. Think of one of the teachings of Jesus. How can you follow this teaching? Look over the "I Believe" puppet workstation signs and your scrolls. An Affirmation can be a song, Bible verse, or a list of things you believe. Use your earlier ideas or write a new Affirmation for the children's service. Put your ideas on newsprint.

Workstation 3 — Offering

GETTING READY

Set out the Love Task Tree from Session 39, Chapter 12. Post a sign-up sheet for a volunteer to hang up newsprint and explain what the Offering is, and for volunteers to lead and serve as ushers in the children's service. Copy and post the following instructions for the children:

> Remembering Jesus' life and teaching is one way we grow in our faith (Luke 12:13-15). Another way is to show our love for God and our neighbor. Think of a way to share with the needy

other than giving money — maybe collecting food or adding to
your Love Task Tree. Use your earlier ideas or write a new idea
for the Offering for the children's service. Special songs are often
sung during the offering. Write your ideas on the sheet of newsprint.

Workstation 4 — Sermon/Bible Lesson

GETTING READY

Mark some stories in this book for the children to look over in case
they would like to adapt them for the puppets, and place any available
puppets at this workstation. There are several good books on making
simple puppets (see Suggested Reading List at the end of this book). The
children can kneel behind a side panel of the church for a puppet stage.
Post a sign-up sheet for a volunteer to hang up newsprint and explain
what the Sermon is, and for volunteers to help with the Sermon in the
children's service. Copy and post the following instructions for the children:

Sometimes a message comes as a sermon, and sometimes it is
acted out (John 8:1-11). Sometimes it is heard in a song, and
sometimes in the words of a child. Think of a special way to
share God's message for our children's service. Look over the
parables we have used before: Luke 10:30-37, Matthew 7:24-27,
and Mark 4:1-8. Plan to use puppetry, clown ministry, acting
out the parables, or telling a story. Write the sermon on the
sheet of newsprint.

Workstation 5 — Witness to the World

GETTING READY

Set out the statement from Session 12 on how the children share
the "fruits of the spirit" in their lives. Post a sign-up sheet for a volunteer
to hang up newsprint and explain the Witness to the World, and for
volunteers to help with this part of the children's worship service. Copy
and post the following instructions for the children:

We witness through our talents, our gifts to others, our daily
words, and our daily actions. How we react to the problems of
daily life is a form of witnessing (Matthew 13:24-30). Worship
is also a witness to our faith. Look over the Witness materials
that you wrote in earlier sessions. Use your earlier ideas or write

> a totally new Witness to the World. Witnessing can be a statement from Jesus, something you act out, a song, or something you read. Write your plans on newsprint.

Workstation 6 — Prayer

GETTING READY

Set out the Lord's Prayer dialog from Session 29, Chapter 10. Post a sign-up sheet for a volunteer to hang up newsprint and explain the meaning of prayer, and for volunteers to help with this part of the children's service. Copy and post the following instructions for the children:

> We pray for understanding and help with our daily problems (Matthew 6:5-15), for world peace, and for hope for tomorrow. Use some of your earlier ideas or write a new prayer for the children's service. A prayer can be a song, interpretive dance, Bible verse, a prayer you write yourself, or saying the Lord's Prayer together. Write your plans on the sheet of newsprint.

Workstation 7 — Benediction

GETTING READY

Set out the children's version of the "Love Commandment" from Session 12. Post a sign-up sheet for a volunteer to hang up newsprint and explain what the Benediction is, and for volunteers to help with this part of the children's service. Copy and post the following instructions for the children:

> The Benediction is the close of the worship service. It sends everyone out to share God's love (Matthew 7:1-5). Think of a fitting Benediction for your service. Use some of your earlier ideas or write a new closing for the children's service. Select a song to use. Write your plans on the newsprint.

The Worship Celebration

    I. Have the children at each workstation tape their portion of the service up on the wall. The children should have their order of worship complete for their bulletin and service. If there are any problems, correct them now. Compliment them on their hard work.

    II. Have paint and banner ready ahead of time. Have old shirts or costumes for painting. Use the liturgical colors for your rainbow. Draw a curved line showing where the rainbow should begin. Have everyone place their handprints, row after row for the colors of the rainbow, on the banner. Before they wash their hands, have them place their handprint on a piece of paper to take home. Have everybody sign their handprints with a paint brush. When you finish, have everyone's handprint and name on the banner who has helped at any time during the year (including adults). This banner will hang on the one remaining empty side of your church — it's your cornerstone, so put the year and date on the banner at the bottom.

III. Next week you will practice the first half of the service, so tell everyone to be ready.

Items to Go Home

Extra handprint papers.

SESSION 41

PUTTING IT ALL TOGETHER

The Bible Lesson

Children often panic when they have to read the Bible. Yet children are accustomed to reading out loud in school and take great pride in reading. Help the children prepare so that they can read with confidence: (1) Choose an easy translation for children to read. (2) Read the verse together first, practicing any difficult pronunciations. (3) Have the child practice reading with the actual microphones for the service. When children read out loud, they should read slower than usual.

What the Children Will Learn Today

Start with the Call to Worship and practice the first 30 minutes of the service. If you can practice in the sanctuary, great. If not, set up and practice in your usual room, making the setting and circumstances as similar as possible. Practice when to stand and when to sit and how to use microphones. Designate a lay leader to introduce hymns and readings to keep the service flowing. Appoint adult assistants to help the children know when to enter and leave. Simplify the process as much as possible for the children. Where there are problems, help the children solve them. Give the children confidence and encourage them to use their skills.

Time Needed

Thirty minutes of practice.

Supplies Needed

1. First half of Order of Worship from Session 40.
2. Children's church and whatever setup you plan to use.

SESSION 42

LEADING THE CHILDREN'S SERVICE

The Bible Lesson

If some of your readers have trouble, work with them individually. Use lots of positive reinforcement. Don't think of reading the Bible as a performance; this is a worship service. The idea is to share and celebrate God's love together. Most of all, help the children to enjoy reading the Bible.

What the Children Will Learn Today

Practice the second half of the service today. Decide if your group needs additional practice. Make sure your children feel ready and are excited to lead their service. Remind them that there are no perfect worship services. Tell them that adults often make mistakes. Telling your group about a mistake you made once really helps the children to relax. They realize that you can make mistakes and still have everything work out okay. Tell the children how proud you are of them and their hard work. Make sure each and every child is involved and feels like an important participant in the children's service. Plan refreshments or some other kind of treat for after the service.

Time Needed

Thirty minutes of practice.

Supplies Needed

1. Second half of Order of Worship from Session 40.
2. Children's church, costumes, instruments, props, and whatever setup you plan to use.

PART V

WHERE DO WE GO FROM HERE?

CHAPTER THIRTEEN

AN UNFORGETTABLE SUMMER

Traveling back through the ages in their time machine, your ace reporters give the scoop on life in Bible times. A newsletter, radio show, and TV program for KTBT (Key to Bible Times) Network News keep the budding young journalists in search of the who — what — when — where — why behind the customs of life long ago.

For a truly successful program, you need: (1) A totally different than usual program, not just the same old thing you always do, and (2) A program that is both fun and educational. My summertime suggestion is: KTBT (Key to Bible Times) Radio, Television, and Newsletter Network News.

If you just end your Christian education programs when school's out with "Sorry, that's all till next fall," you are missing out on a wonderful experience. Summertime is one of the best times to build up your programs. Parents are often desperate for activities to keep their children from being bored.

Families with children usually move during the summer and want to reestablish in a new church before fall. A strong summer children's program brings families to your church.

Many families also travel and visit different churches over the summer. What does your church offer visiting children? My own children's faces look so sad every time they hear a polite usher say, "Sorry, but we don't have anything for the children during the summer. They can just sit with you if you like." On the other hand, a church we visited several summers ago was filled with children actively involved in worship. Little children, teenagers, and even grandparents participated. It was beautiful, and I have never forgotten the feeling of seeing all ages worshiping together.

Think about what appeals most to children when they are visiting a new church. My three children still talk about the minister at a church we visited two years ago who sat down and immediately sized them up as the "biggest," "littlest," and "middlest." Genuine childlike friendliness touches their hearts. It helps children feel involved and included.

One summer our family visited a church that was very family-oriented. The ushers handed each child a children's bulletin. The opening song was one that the children knew, and they all sang along joyfully. The opening prayer was brief and closed with the entire congregation, including the children, saying the Lord's Prayer together. The offering was taken at the beginning of the service so that the children could also place their offering in with the rest of the congregation. The children's minister called all of the children up front for an active children's story and then cheerfully sent them on their way to a special planned activity during the sermon.

So before you close down your classrooms for the summer, think of all you can offer to the children during the next three months.

SESSION 43
COME AND FOLLOW ME

The Bible Lesson

Summer is a time to have fun. This is also true in Christian education. The Bible verses are used in a crossword puzzle, word scramble, and fill-in-the-blank type games.

What the Children Will Learn Today

The children will see how people lived in Bible times through their workstation activities.

SUMMER SETUP (KTBT NEWSROOM)

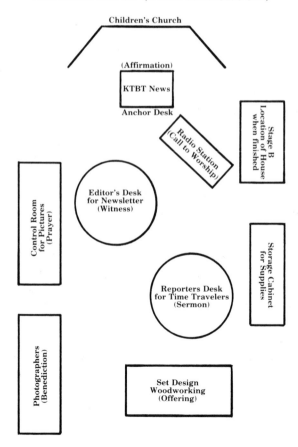

Time Needed

We'll still use seven stations for 20 minutes, but with new sign titles related to news media. Each week throughout the summer the workstations will be the same: KTBT (see summer setup diagram). Therefore, you will not have to change signs or spend time with new setups. The 10-minute worship time is a Morning Devotional Radio Show.

Supplies Needed

1. Woodworking basket and wood to build biblical house (see below). Make sure you have a ruler and framing square on hand.

2. Box for TV camera, round margarine container with hole in center of the bottom, string tied onto a pencil, silver duct tape, aluminum foil, black construction paper, black tempera paint, paint brushes, and cover-ups.

3. Reference books on biblical life, old Sunday school materials and magazines to cut from, Bibles, and a snack.

4. Workstation signs with newsroom titles (see summer setup), and instructions.

5. Table or small desk to be used as the anchor desk for the news.

6. Musical instruments, song book, sing-along tapes, tape recorder with blank tape for recording, and posters.

7. Craft supply basket: usual supplies plus newsprint and name tags.

8. Dress-up clothes — old ties, hats, suits, high heels, etc. for the children to dress up in as they pretend to be at a TV studio.

9. Roll of paper at least 12" tall (butcher paper or newsprint works well).

WORKSTATIONS

Workstation 1 — Call to Worship

GETTING READY

The Call to Worship station will become your DJ's radio station. Hang some posters of Christian rock singers or just provide song books, sing-along tapes, and instruments as usual. Have a blank tape for the group to record music on. Save for Session 49. Key for scrambled words: FATHER, HEAVEN, KINGDOM, FOREVER, WILL, EARTH. Post a sign-up sheet for a DJ to play a tape in today's Morning Devotional Radio Show, and copy and post the following instructions for the children:

> You are the Radio DJ's for Children's KTBT — KEY TO BIBLE
> TIMES Radio Show that airs each day as a Morning Devotional.
> The station manager likes to keep people guessing, so your theme
> for the day is in scrambled code. You must unscramble these
> words to know what kind of music to use for today's program:
> HTFERA, VHANEE, MIDNGOK, VOEFRER, LIWL, and
> RHATE. If you need help, say the Lord's Prayer (Matthew 6:5-15
> in your Bible). Put on some music to play while you work. Then,
> find a song that everyone can sing along with for the Call to
> Worship today that has a similar message to the code words you
> unscrambled. Practice with the instruments. Tape record your
> song for today's devotional. You're ON THE AIR in 20 minutes.

Workstation 2 — Affirmation of Faith

GETTING READY

Set up a desk in front of the children's church with a sign saying
"Anchor Persons Needed for Nightly News (both men and women may
apply)." This will also be the place for your radio show today. You'll need
the craft supply basket and large sheet of newsprint. Post a sign-up sheet
for an announcer to read the thought for the day on today's Morning
Devotional Radio Show. Copy and post the following instructions for the
children:

> You have been hired to fill the KTBT anchor desk for the news.
> Your job is to read the news copy; unfortunately, your page has
> arrived today with several words missing. Read Matthew 7:1-2,
> and fill in the missing words. This phrase from the Bible will
> become your by-line or trademark. Work together and draw a
> big picture explaining what this phrase means. The picture goes
> on the front of your desk. You're ON THE AIR in 20 minutes.
>
> ANNOUNCER: *(Begins as soon as music finishes.)* Good
> morning, and peace be with each of you today. Welcome to
> KTBT's Morning Devotions. Our thought for the day comes
> from Matthew 7:1-2. "_____ not, that _____ may _____ be
> _____ yourselves: for as _____ _____ so you will be _____,
> and the measure you _____ to _____ will be dealt out to
> _____." Next we have a report from our "About Town Re-
> porter" at one of our neighborhood churches.

Workstation 3 — Offering

GETTING READY

Make a sign saying "Set Designers." The house is built in a similar way to the church and is an excellent stage to act out Bible stories or show puppets. Read the "Guidelines for Building a Biblical House." This is a long-term project that you will work on each week. You will be able to finish the house by the end of summer. Keep the guidelines at the workstation and just start up each week where you left off the week before. An adult will be needed to help each week. Copy and post the following instructions for the children:

> The business manager for the TV station thinks ratings and sponsors will increase if the station does an on-location report from Nazareth during Jesus' lifetime. Reporters have been sent back in time to gather the facts. You are to build a biblical house as a backdrop for the on-the-spot reports. Follow the directions of the adult in charge at Joseph's carpenter shop.

Guidelines for Building a Biblical House

THREE RULES: (1) Always measure a board twice before you cut, (2) Ask an adult to check your measurement before you saw, (3) After the boards are cut, use a pencil and write the measurement and location on each board. (Example: Bottom right, 48" long.)

Supplies Needed

a. Lumber, 1" x 2" nominal thickness (actually measures ¾" thick). These are sold as furring strips and often go on sale. You need 8 pieces that are 8 feet long.

b. Lumber, 2" x 2" nominal thickness. These add stability to the bottom. The plans call for 3 pieces of 8 feet in length. You'll have some left over.

c. Lumber, 1" x 3", one board 8 feet in length.

d. One piece luan or other fine plywood 2' x 4' in size and ³⁄₁₆" thick.

e. A box of 1¼" nails. These are short enough that the points won't stick out of the boards.

f. Two 2" hinges for door, and four 3" hinges for house.

g. Tacks to attach carpeting.

h. 2' wide inexpensive roll of carpeting, brown in color, for walls of house. You will need four 47½" long x 24" wide panels of carpeting for the sides, one panel 48½" long by 24" wide to fit next to the window, and the bottom front panel needs to be 70" long x 24" wide (or a total of 8¾ yards). Remnants are often sold 3 yards to a roll.

DIAGRAM FOR
THE BIBLICAL HOUSE

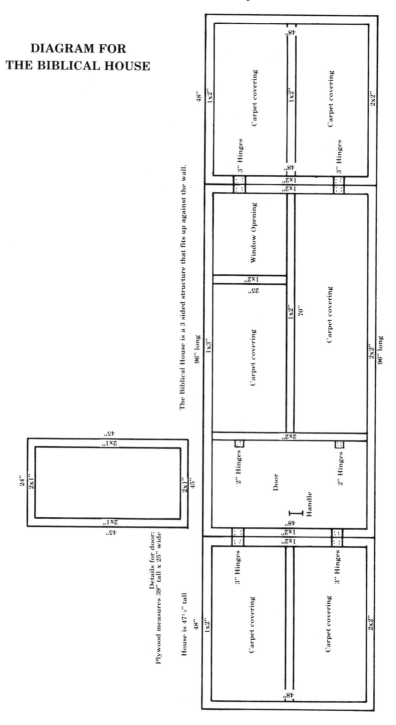

Interior of Biblical House

Sawing

Step 1: Measure and cut *two* of the 2" x 2" boards in half. These will be used to make the two bottom pieces to go on each side of the house and to make the one vertical door piece needed for hinging the door. *Do not cut* the other 2" x 2" board, because you will need the full 96" board to go across the bottom front. You'll have a scrap left over.

Step 2: Measure and cut four 1" x 2" boards 96" long in half for the side panels. You now have all of the boards cut for the side panels. See diagram.

Step 3: Measure and cut one 1" x 2" board in half for vertical front pieces. Make sure each board is properly marked with "front pieces" and 1" x 2".

Step 4: Measure and cut one 1" x 2" board 70" long for the center front section of the house. This leaves a scrap for the window. Again, mark each piece with the measurement and location.

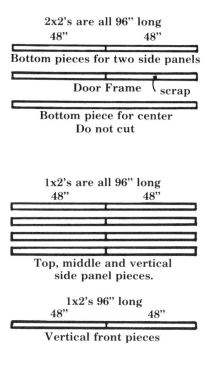

2x2's are all 96" long
48"   48"

Bottom pieces for two side panels

Door Frame ⎰ scrap

Bottom piece for center
Do not cut

1x2's are all 96" long
48"   48"

Top, middle and vertical
side panel pieces.

1x2's 96" long
48"   48"

Vertical front pieces

70"   25"

Middle front   Window
                      frame

Step 5: Do not cut the 1" x 3" board for the top front of the house.

Step 6: Measure carefully and cut one 1" x 2" board as shown in the drawing. You will end up with one 45" board and two 24" boards for the door. Measure and cut last 1" x 2" for the other 45" board for the door.

Step 7: Make your frame *before* you cut the plywood for the door. Then just cut your plywood to neatly fit your frame.

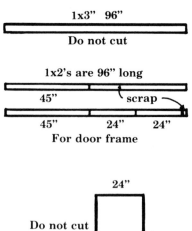

You have now finished cutting all of the boards. Congratulations!

Sanding

Sand all boards until they are smooth. Do not nail any boards together until they have been sanded completely.

Hammering

Step 1: Build the house one panel at a time. Start with a side panel. Lay out the top, middle, and bottom side panel boards on the floor. Nail the vertical side boards on top. Use your framing square to make sure all the corners are the same. Measure twice before you hammer. Don't worry about fancy corners, just hammer each board down securely. Add a little glue to the corners to make the joints secure. Sand smooth.

Step 2: Repeat the same process as above for the other side panel.

Step 3: For the center section, measure with framing square and nail together the 96" top and bottom front pieces to the 48" side boards. See drawing. Then lay out the window. Nail the 2" x 2" into place for door frame. Nail down the 70" long 1" x 2" and then the window frame. See drawing. Measure carefully. Sand any rough spots that remain.

Your house is together. Congratulations to all workers!

Step 4: Attaching the hinges will depend somewhat on the type of hinges you secured. It is best to have an adult attach the hinges and then let the children tighten the screws. *But before you attach the hinges, stand the house up with adult help and test out the placement of your hinges. Make sure the house will fold up.* Lay the house back on the floor.

Step 5: Attach one hinge according to the package directions and then stand the house up again and test for accuracy.

Attach remaining hinges and cheer! Attach carpeting next.

Carpeting

Step 1: Measure and cut carpeting to fit each opening except for the window. Check measurements twice before you cut.

Step 2: Lay the house down flat on the floor. Hammer carpeting into place with small tacks. YOU'RE GETTING CLOSE.

Door

Step 1: I suggest attaching the door last so it is not in your way when tacking on the carpeting. Nail the 24" boards on top of the 45" side boards. Use your framing square, and glue the joint before you nail. Measure very carefully for the exact size of the door panel. Cut your plywood to fit your door frame. Then nail into place. Attach the hinges of the door onto the 2" x 2" vertical door frame board. Again, it's best if an adult puts the hinges in the right place, and then lets the children help tighten the screws. Test to make sure that your door will open and close.

Rejoice! You have completed the biblical house.

Building the Biblical House

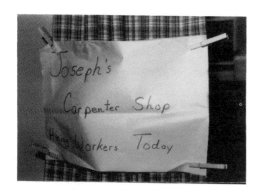

Workstation 4 — Sermon/Bible Lesson

GETTING READY

Make a sign: "Reporters' Desk (Need Reporters for Time Travel Assignment — Experience Required)." Use the bubble or an old cardboard box for your time machine. Have some books available that tell about life in biblical times, paper, and pencils. Save what the children write each week for Session 49. Copy and post the following instructions for the children:

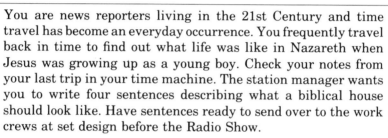

You are news reporters living in the 21st Century and time travel has become an everyday occurrence. You frequently travel back in time to find out what life was like in Nazareth when Jesus was growing up as a young boy. Check your notes from your last trip in your time machine. The station manager wants you to write four sentences describing what a biblical house should look like. Have sentences ready to send over to the work crews at set design before the Radio Show.

Reporter's Notes: Joseph and Mary were not rich, so their house was probably one large room with a raised platform at one end where the family lived. The outside of the house was usually made of hardened clay mud. There was often only one window and one door, since the people were afraid of robbers. A family might keep sheep in the lower level of the house to protect them from wolves and thieves. Jesus grew up in a large family and their house was probably crowded. People would eat, sleep, grind corn, pray, and do many households chores on the rooftop because it was cooler.

Since there was no plumbing, women had to carry water daily from the well in town in large clay jars. Shopping was done at the marketplace. A person could buy food as well as pottery, cloth, and other items in Nazareth.

Workstation 5 — Witness to the World

GETTING READY

Make enough copies of the puzzle for all the children. Make a sign: "Editors' Desk for the Newsletter." Save all puzzles for Session 49. Post a sign-up sheet for an About Town Reporter to read the report from the local church on today's radio program, and copy and post the following instructions for the children:

> You are newspaper reporters writing a summer newsletter to go out to neighboring churches. Your newsletter will have typical story articles about people, a biblical crossword puzzle, and drawings for photographs.
>
> It will be your job this summer to write stories and select one crossword puzzle to use in the newsletter. You'll have a different puzzle or word game to choose from each Sunday. Work the crossword puzzle submitted today first to help you get in the mood to think. Then, write four sentences for the "About Town Report" telling about someone at your church who is a follower of Jesus.
>
> Reporters use: WHO? WHAT? WHEN? WHERE? WHY?

Key to Puzzle on page 299.

Use your Bible to look up the verses and then complete the puzzle.

Across

1. _____ betrayed Jesus. (Luke 22:48)

2. The Last Supper was Jesus' way of saying good- _____ to his disciples. (John 13:1-4)

4. Jesus asked them to find a house with an _____ room. (Luke 22:9-13)

5. Jesus was one of the _____. (Luke 2:39-42)

7. Peter called Jesus _____. (John 13:6 and 13-14)

8. Jesus wants us to _____ to others. (2 Corinthians 9:7)

10. _____ was the Roman Ruler at the time of Jesus' death. (Luke 23:1-3)

12. God is _____. (1 John 4:7-8)

Down

1. A very important teacher. (John 13:13-15)

3. Jesus used _____ as a symbol for his body and life. (John 6:35)

6. Jesus told the woman who was about to be stoned to _____ and not to sin again. (John 8:3-11)

7. Jesus used _____ as a symbol to explain that we would understand the meaning of life better if we listened to his teachings. (John 8:12)

9. Jesus died so that we might understand that there is _____ after death and live our lives as God wants us to. (John 6:51)

11. You reap what you _____. (2 Corinthians 9:6)

See page 298 for puzzle key.

Workstation 6 — Prayer

GETTING READY

Have a roll of white shelf paper or newsprint 20" wide x 6 yards long. You may need to tape two rolls together, because they are often sold 3 yards to a roll. Make a "Control Room" sign. Furnish glue, scissors, ruler, and drawing supplies. This project will take most of the summer to finish, so you will have the same setup each week. Select a cardboard box and check to make sure that your paper will fit easily inside.

TV Monitor and Film

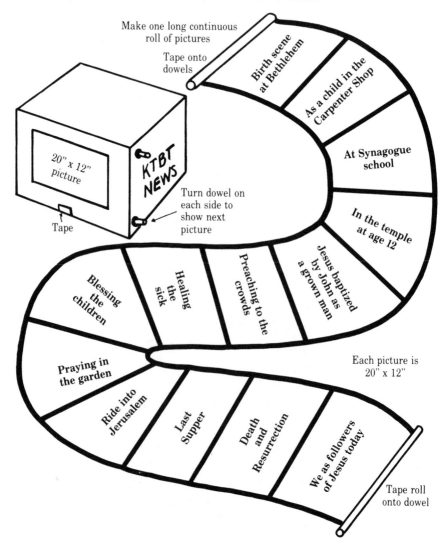

Copy and post the following instructions for the children:

> You are to draw pictures for the KTBT Children's Documentary on the life and teachings of Jesus. These pictures will be one long roll of pictures, like film. Each of your pictures should be 20" wide by 12" tall because that is the size of your TV screen. You will add picture after picture to make a long roll of pictures telling the story of the life of Jesus. You work in the control room. It is your job to cut out or draw pictures and glue them onto the roll in order. Start at the beginning with Jesus' birth in Bethlehem and growing up as a child of a carpenter. Use old Sunday school materials to cut pictures from or draw your own. Remember — only one picture will be seen at a time. Be sure to measure each picture and keep it at a 20" x 12" size so it will fit on the TV screen. The roll of paper in front of you will be filled with frame after frame of pictures telling Jesus' life story. The pictures will be on one long roll — like actual film footage would be.

Workstation 7 — Benediction

GETTING READY

TV CAMERA

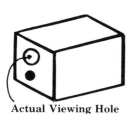

Actual Viewing Hole

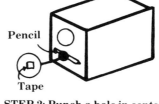

Pencil

Tape

STEP 1: Cut a hole above the lens to actually see through. Cut a small hole in the center for string to go through.

STEP 2: Punch a hole in center of margarine container. Tie a knot in end of strings. Tape string securely so it can't slip through hole. Run other end of string through small hole in box. Tie tightly to a pencil inside to keep from slipping back through box.

Foil

STEP 3: Glue foil onto the front of the lens. Lens should turn easily.

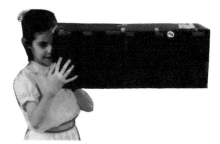

Make a "Photographers" sign and have an adult there to help. Copy and post the following instructions for the children:

> Your job today is to make a TV camera to use in our TV studio. Use the box provided. Cover with black paper and cut out letters to spell KTBT on the side. Paint the margarine container black. Put the string through the hole in the margarine container. Tape securely. Punch a hole in the box where the lens should attach. Put the end of the string through this hole. Pull tight and tie a pencil on the end of the string to hold the string tightly in place. Make sure the lens turns. Glue a piece of foil right in the center for the glass lens over the tape. Cut another hole in the box to actually look through.

The Worship Celebration

I. Call to Worship — Music tape should be played by the DJ as an introduction.

II. Affirmation of Faith — Announcer with Thought for the Day.

III. Witness to the World — Report on followers of Jesus from today's local church.

IV. Benediction — Give everyone a name tag to make press badges.

Items to Go Home

Press badges with name and KTBT NEWS to wear home.

SESSION 44

THE LORD IS MY SHEPHERD

The Bible Lesson

The Fact Finder game includes questions from the four Gospels.

What the Children Will Learn Today

By building a house, children will learn about Jesus' way of life.

Time Needed

Twenty minutes for workstations and 10 minutes for the game show.

Supplies Needed

1. Woodworking basket and wood to build biblical house.
2. Fact Finder game, Bibles, and a snack.
3. Reference books on biblical life, old Sunday school material or magazines to cut from.
4. Workstation signs with newsroom titles and instructions.
5. Table or small desk to be used as the anchor desk for news.
6. Musical instruments, song book, sing-along tapes, tape recorder with tape for recording, and posters.
7. Craft supply basket: usual supplies plus large sheets of newsprint.
8. Dress-up clothes — old ties, hats, suits, high heels, etc. for the children to play dress-up with as they pretend to be at a TV studio.

WORKSTATIONS

Workstation 1 — Call to Worship

GETTING READY

The answers to today's scrambled words are: SHEPHERD, LEADS, ME, GREEN, STAFF, CUP, and HOUSE. Post a sign-up sheet for a DJ to play the taped song, and copy and post the following instructions for the children:

The Station Manager has sent another message in code. Today's words are: HPEDHSER, SLADE, EM, NRGEE, FSATF, UPC, and USHEO. If you need help, look up Psalm 23 in your Bible. Then look through your song books to find a song that tells the same message as the words in code from Psalm 23. Tape your song. You're ON THE AIR in 20 minutes.

Workstation 2 — Affirmation of Faith

Post a sign-up sheet for a game show host and contestants for the Fact Finder game, and copy and post the following instructions for the children:

You will be the game show hosts for today's Fact Finder game in the TV studio. Make a Fact Finder sign with the newsprint in the craft supply basket. Select four teams with three on each team. Answer each question in your own words. The Fact Finder game works best if it is lively and fast.

The rules for this game are: (1) Each team will be asked a question in turn. If the answer is correct, the team gets five points. (2) If the team cannot answer the question, then the other teams have a chance. Go to the next team in turn. The team to answer the question correctly receives two points. (3) If no one can answer, the game show host gives the answer and goes on to the next question. The team with the most points gets to pass out the snack.

FACT FINDER QUESTIONS

1. What do you have to do to be a good neighbor? **Help another person in need (Luke 10:25-37).**

2. If you are humble, forgiving, try to do what is right, and look for ways to help others instead of yourself, you'll be? **Happy (Matthew 5:1-16).**

3. What does "you are the light of the world" mean? **Your actions tell others about your faith (Matthew 5:14-16).**

4. Why did the Pharisees want to kill Jesus? **Because he taught the people that love was more important than rules and laws (Luke 16:14-18 and Matthew 26:57-67).**

5. What was the commandment that Jesus taught? **Love God and your neighbor as yourself (Matthew 22:34-40).**

6. What did Jesus tell the twelve disciples to go and do? **To teach**

the good news to everyone (Matthew 28:16-20).

7. Say the prayer that Jesus taught the disciples. **The Lord's Prayer (Matthew 6:5-15)**.

Workstation 3 — Offering

GETTING READY

Copy and post the following instructions for the children:

> Start where you left off last week.

Workstation 4 — Sermon/Bible Lesson

GETTING READY

Provide the "Fashion Digest" for the children to read. Post a sign-up sheet for the time traveling reporters to read the fashion report today, and copy and post the following instructions for the children:

> Your assignment today is to explore the fashion scene and discover the typical clothing worn by Jesus and his family. Filter through the news of the day and decide what to report. Write three sentences. Be ready to read in today's MOMENT FOR FASHION during the game show. You may dress in costume. You're ON THE AIR in 20 minutes.

FASHION DIGEST

The fashion scene two thousand years ago when Jesus was a boy was far from t-shirts and blue jeans. It was against the law for men and women to dress alike. The rich had many clothes to fit the season, but Jesus' family probably had one everyday outfit and maybe one set of good clothes to wear for special occasions. Jewish men usually wore loose-fitting clothes. They would wear a long linen shirt made from the flax grown around Galilee. Over that, they would wear a loose-fitting, knee-length tunic sometimes made of wool held together by a cloth wrapped around the waist for a belt. This belt was used as a pocket to carry things. When traveling or when it was cold, men would wear a thick cloak which also doubled as a blanket. Squares of cloth tied onto their heads protected them from the heat and sun. Prayer shawls were worn by men on the Sabbath for worship. The poor went barefoot or wore sandals. Women wore linen dresses, usually blue, decorated with ribbons and distinctive embroidery on the yoke showing what village they lived in. Women wore lots of jewelry — necklaces around their necks and rings on their fingers and toes. On their heads, women often wore long veils held on by a chain of coins. Small children wore long, free-flowing shirts as outfits. People often shared or borrowed clothes. Even the poor kept their clothes clean by washing them in streams with olive oil soap or stomping on the clothes in tubs of water.

Clothing was often woven in one piece on a wide loom. A hole was left in the middle for the head. The sleeves could be made any length. Then the garment was folded in half and sewn together along side seams.

Workstations 5 and 6 —
Prayer and Witness to the World

GETTING READY

Setup is the same as last week: roll of paper, magazines, scissors, etc. Copy and post the following instructions for the children:

> Continue working on the pictures for your TV monitor. Read these Bible verses: Luke 2:1-20, Mark 1:16-20, Luke 9:10-17, Mark 10:13-16, John 12:12-15, Mark 11:15-19, Luke 22:14-20, John 19:16-18, and Luke 24:1-7. Cut out or draw pictures to tell about the life of Jesus.

Workstation 7 — Benediction

GETTING READY

Furnish magazines and drawing supplies. Save the finished pictures for Session 49. Copy and post the following instructions for the children:

> You're a roving photographer. Cut out or draw pictures for the upcoming evening news. Show pictures of how someone can follow Jesus (1) at church, (2) school, (3) home, (4) in your local town, and (5) as a world leader.

The Worship Celebration

    I. Call to Worship — Theme music (Psalm 23 song) to introduce TV show.

   II. Sermon — Fashion Moment by the Time Traveling Reporter.

  III. Affirmation of Faith — Fact Finder game show.

  IV. Benediction — Game show ends with the Lord's Prayer.

Items to Go Home

Today's snack should be something cold to eat right before going home on a hot summer day, such as Popsicles or finger jello.

SESSION 45

SHAPES AND COLORS ALL AROUND US

The Bible Lesson

As Christians, we are to witness for God in Christ's name (1 Corinthians 13:1-13). The story gives a simple example to follow.

What the Children Will Learn Today

As you continue the newsroom atmosphere, the children will keep learning about what life was like in Jesus' day. Save the stories and items written by the children because you will need them in Session 49.

Time Needed

Twenty minutes at workstations and 10 minutes for the story.

Supplies Needed

1. Woodworking basket and wood to build biblical house.
2. Pennies, double-sided tape, Bibles, and a snack.
3. Reference books on biblical life to read and old Sunday school material or magazines to cut pictures from.
4. Workstation signs with newsroom titles and instructions.
5. Two medium-sized potatoes, table knife, and ink pads or tempera paint and paint supplies.
6. Musical instruments, song book, sing-along tapes, tape recorder with extra blank tape for recording, and posters.
7. Craft supply basket: usual supplies plus large sheet of newsprint.
8. Dress-up clothes — old ties, hats, suits, high heels, etc. for children to play dress-up with as they pretend to be at a TV studio.

WORKSTATIONS

Workstation 1 — Call to Worship

GETTING READY

Provide copies of the puzzle for the children. Key: PATIENT, SELF-

ISH, KIND, LOVE, JEALOUSY, CHILD, GO, RUDE, NOT, NEW, SLOW, IN, MAN, and ANGER. Copy and post the following instructions for the children:

> There are fourteen words in today's message. See how many you can find. The words may go in any direction. Read 1 Corinthians 13:1-13 for help. Select and record a song to fit the coded message.

```
P  L  O  V  E  N  J  S
A  C  R  N  K  O  E  E
T  K  H  U  O  R  A  L
I  A  I  I  D  T  L  F
E  N  S  N  L  E  O  I
N  G  L  M  D  D  U  S
T  E  O  A  Q  U  S  H
X  R  W  N  V  I  Y  S
```

Workstation 2 — Affirmation of Faith

GETTING READY

Copy and post the following instructions for the children:

> The set design workers need help sanding the wood for the house. Help out today.

Workstation 4 — Sermon/Bible Lesson

GETTING READY

Bring potatoes, regular (not sharp) table knives, and a stamp pad or tempera paint to make the potato coin stamps. An adult helper is needed. Copy and post the following instructions for the children:

On your last time trip back to Nazareth, you noticed that everyone seemed to be using a different kind of money in the marketplace. You decide to get out the travel guide and see if you can figure out what kind of money you should make with your time machine replicator before you go to the marketplace again. If you can't decide, just make a copy of each coin listed. Take half of a potato, carefully carve with only a *table knife* the picture from the coin. Use a stamp pad or tempera paint, then stamp out as many coins as you wish and cut them out.

Biblical Coins
All money in Israel was in the form of
a coin. There were many different kinds
of coins used. It was no wonder there
were so many money changers.

Lepton: A Jewish coin or shekel, a
very small coin and low in value.

Matthew 27:3-5 or
18:23-25

Silver Stater: Greek coin, called a
drachman, often showed the head of
the ruler and was used to pay temple tax.

Exodus 30:11-14
Mark 12:41-44

Denarius: Basic Roman silver, gold,
or bronze coin. Silver coins were used
as a day's wage for a laborer.

Luke 15:8-10

Workstation 5 — Witness to the World

GETTING READY

Save stories for Session 49. Copy and post the following instructions for the children:

Write a five-sentence news article about something nice that happened to you this week. Remember to use: WHO? WHAT? WHEN? WHERE? and WHY?

Workstation 6 — Prayer

GETTING READY

Copy and post the following instructions for the children:

Keep working on the pictures.

Workstation 7 — Benediction

GETTING READY

Set out newsprint and markers. Save the pictures for Session 49. Copy and post the following instructions for the children:

Think of a time when someone was kind to you today. Write or draw a picture of this kindness on the newsprint.

The Worship Celebration

Have double-sided tape on the floor down the center of your Children's Church. Announce Children's Story Hour on KTBT and read "The Lost Penny." Give each child a penny at the end of the story.

The Lost Penny

Michael walked in following his parents and hid behind them as they shook hands and talked with people he didn't know. His mother turned and said, "Michael, wouldn't you like to shake hands, too?" Michael didn't like to shake hands. He just hid his face behind his mother.

Besides, he didn't even know these people, and wasn't his mother the one always saying "don't talk to strangers"?

Michael was so relieved when they finally went into the church and sat down. As Michael sat down, he looked at the floor. There on the floor in front of him was a penny. It was right next to his foot. He reached down and picked the penny up and held it in his hand. The penny was cold and dark and had certainly not been well taken care of because it looked sort of bent.

"Now why would a penny just be lying there on the floor?" he thought. He held the penny in his hand and rubbed it on his pants to see if he could clean it off a bit. There might even be a hint of a shine there.

The penny wasn't his and he knew he was never supposed to take anything that didn't belong to him. But who did it belong to? He looked but there was no one around except his mom and dad.

As he considered what to do with the penny, he continued to rub it back and forth on his pants. A penny is not worth much. As a matter of fact, he couldn't think of anything that he could buy for just a penny. And besides, this old penny was so dull and ugly looking, it wasn't even worth keeping.

Michael was about to put the penny back on the floor where he found it when he looked down at the penny. The same penny he had been holding in his hand and rubbing all this time had changed. The penny was no longer dingy-looking; it was shiny and Michael sat holding the shiny penny in his hand and realized that with just a little time and effort, he had been able to transform an old dingy-looking penny into a pretty new penny that anyone would be glad to own. Michael began thinking again about what he would like to do with this sparkling, new-looking penny he had found, when all of a sudden the offering plate was passed in front of him and he found himself somehow dropping in his penny.

He wasn't exactly sure why he had placed the penny he found in the offering, but it somehow seemed the right thing to do. After all, it wasn't his penny; he had only taken care of it for a little while and had given it a new sense of worth and beauty. Michael felt good about passing the penny on as he did because now the little penny would have a chance to help make someone else happy. Of course, Michael knew that just one little penny alone couldn't give everyone around the world a piece of bread to eat or a cup of clean drinking water when they were thirsty, but as he looked around the church again, this time he looked at all of the people and thought — if everyone sitting here today put just one penny in the offering plate, we could all make a difference. Together we could, with just our pennies, feed those who are hungry.

As Michael sat back in his pew listening to the closing hymn, he smiled. With just a little bit of care and love, he made a dull penny turn bright and shiny. Maybe handshakes weren't so bad after all; they were kind of like that — a little bit of love to brighten someone's day. No, he wasn't going to start shaking hands — that was adult stuff. But a smile — yes, a smile might do just as well. He promised himself he would start smiling at everyone on Sunday morning, and then he'd keep it up all week long.

And as for his penny, he was going to remember to bring a penny every time he came to church to put in the offering plate. And so everyone would know that even a penny was special, he would shine his penny up each day before he placed it in the offering plate. *(Pause)*

Today I have a penny for each one of you. Each penny is different, just like each of you are different. You can do as you like with your penny. You can shine it up nice and pretty and place it in your pocket and take it home, or if you wish you can place your penny on top of the tape down the center aisle. All of the pennies placed on the tape this morning will go to help hungry children have food to eat. So now, just like Michael, you have a penny and you have to decide what to do with your special penny.

Items to Go Home

Let everyone make some coins to take home with the potato stamps and give them an ACTION ASSIGNMENT: Think of a way to share kindness and love this week with five people you aren't friends with.

SESSION 46
A PIECE
OF OURSELVES

The Bible Lesson

John 13:4-5 and 12-17.

What the Children Will Learn Today

The children will learn how Jesus lived by combining dramatics with learning for a meaningful experience. Wearing costumes and making bread add to the fun and involvement.

Time Needed

Twenty minutes for workstations and 10 minutes for interview.

Supplies Needed

1. Woodworking basket and wood to build biblical house.
2. Bread-making supplies: bowls, wooden spoons, foil, 3½ cups of coarsely ground whole wheat flour or oat bran (check health food stores), 2 teaspoons of salt, ½ cup milk (unless you can find goat's milk), ½ cup water, ½ cup butter, 4 packages quick-rising active dry yeast (or use leftover batter from the day before as a starter to get bread to rise).
3. Bibles and a snack of homemade bread and honey.
4. Reference books, old Sunday school material or magazines.
5. Workstation signs with newsroom titles and instructions.
6. Musical instruments, song book, sing-along tapes, tape recorder with extra blank tape for recording, and posters.
7. Craft supply basket: usual supplies plus large sheet of newsprint.
8. Foot-washing bowl, water, two biblical costumes, and towel.
9. Dress-up clothes: old ties, hats, suits, high heels, etc. for children to play dress-up with as they pretend to be at a TV studio.

WORKSTATIONS

Workstation 1 — Call to Worship

GETTING READY

Set out the tape recorder and instruments. Post a sign-up sheet for a DJ to play the tape as an introduction to the interview today, and copy and post the following instructions for the children:

> The Station Manager has requested MYSTERIOUS music to be used at the TV studio for today's "Meet the Experts" talk show. Today's guests are three archaeologists. Your music will be played in the background as the show begins. Practice and record some MYSTERIOUS sounding music with the instruments provided. You're ON THE AIR in 20 minutes.

Workstation 2 — Affirmation of Faith

GETTING READY

Make copies of the interview for each participant. Post a sign-up sheet for the interview participants: the interviewer, and the three archaeologists, and copy and post the following instructions for the children:

> The newsroom is buzzing with excitement. Your noontime "Meet the Experts" talk show at KTBT is hosting three world famous archaeologists today. These archaeologists have uncovered many facts about Nazareth during Jesus' lifetime. Get with your panel of experts and go over the interview. You're ON THE AIR in 20 minutes. Have someone make a big sign saying "Meet the Experts."

Script for the Interview

INTERVIEWER: **Welcome to Meet the Experts! Today we have three famous archaeologists on our show who will help us learn about what life was like in Nazareth when Jesus was a boy. We are very pleased to have** (*Make up and fill in names for each*) _____ (*Archaeologist 1*) **from** _____, _____ (*Archaeologist 2*) **from** _____, **and** _____ (*Archaeologist 3*) **from** _____ **with us in our studio today. Let's begin with a typical day. I believe you told me that six-year-old boys in Nazareth would go to school at the synagogue, but girls would stay at home and learn from their mothers and help to bake bread each day.**

The boys spent half a day in school learning from the first four books of the Bible. The second half of the day they would learn a trade from their fathers or a tradesman. Jesus learned to be a carpenter from Joseph. What others jobs did boys learn?

ARCHAEOLOGIST 1:   There were craftsmen to teach pottery-making and stone masons. There were also shepherds and fruit growers in the area, and even fishing for those near the Sea of Galilee.

ARCHAEOLOGIST 2:   Farming was a family tradition. The boys of farmers would learn to sow the seeds before they plowed the field. They would simply scatter the seed and then plow it under.

ARCHAEOLOGIST 3:   If you did not have enough money to own your own land or to have a trade, you might have been a steward, slave, or laborer. A steward was trusted with important jobs, often involving money, property, or crops. A slave was a member of the household and had a better position than a day laborer. The day laborer did not have a regular job. He just went to the marketplace and hired out each day. Often he would not have a place to live or food to eat unless he could find work each day.

INTERVIEWER: Speaking of food, what did most people eat?

ARCHAEOLOGIST 3:   Stew was the favorite dish of most families for dinner. The stew would be made with beans, lentils, peas, lettuce, cucumbers, squash, onions, or garlic.

ARCHAEOLOGIST 2:   The ordinary people, like Jesus' family, could not afford meat. They usually ate fish or just vegetables.

ARCHAEOLOGIST 1:   Since they did not have refrigerators or grocery stores, the people of Bible times usually salted their meats, fish, and vegetables to keep them from spoiling, and then they would only prepare what could be eaten at one meal.

INTERVIEWER: And I understand that they had to make bread every day. Is that right?

ARCHAEOLOGIST 3:   Yes, they would use leftover sourdough from the day before to get their bread to rise.

ARCHAEOLOGIST 2:   The women would have to carry water from the well each day in order to have water to drink and cook with.

ARCHAEOLOGIST 1:   People living in biblical times did not eat three big meals the way we do. If they ate breakfast at all, it was probably just a piece of leftover bread and fruit. Lunch might be just some bread, olives, or figs. The evening meal when the work was done was the main meal of the day. It was usually stew, sour goat's milk (if the family was lucky enough to have a goat), and bread made fresh in the stone ovens.

INTERVIEWER: Well, that's all the time we have today, but we want to thank each of our guests for helping us learn more about life in Nazareth when Jesus was a boy.

Workstation 3 — Offering

GETTING READY

Copy and post the following instructions for the children:

Keep on building the Bible house.

Workstations 4 and 5 —
Sermon and Witness to the World

GETTING READY

Bring all of the supplies needed to make bread: bowls, wooden spoons, bread recipe (but use oat bran instead of regular flour because it has more of the actual texture), and foil. Heat the milk, water and butter ahead of time. One recipe makes 12 small loaves — double or triple if you need to. Copy and post the following instructions for the children:

Eating together in biblical times was a sign of friendship, trust, and confidence. To betray someone after eating with him, such as Judas did (Matthew 26:23-24) was unthinkable. Bread baked fresh every day was a part of every meal and was even used as a spoon to dip into stew.

Recipe

3 ½ cups of coarsely ground whole wheat flour or oat bran

2 teaspoons of salt

½ cup milk (unless you can find goat's milk)

½ cup water

½ cup butter

4 packages quick-rising active dry yeast (You can use batter left from the day before if you wish, but quick-rising yeast will work faster.)

Heat milk, water, and butter until almost boiling, then let the mixture cool until warm. (This has been done for you ahead of time and is wrapped in a towel.) Add flour or oat bran, milk and butter, salt, and yeast. Mix well. Divide into 12 round balls.

Each person gets a round ball of dough to knead on a flour-covered table. To knead, pull and punch the dough until it is smooth.

Put the bread on greased foil to send home. (Do not wrap up in the foil.) Send bread dough home with each child to bake. Let bread rise for three hours; bake at 350 degrees for about 20 to 30 minutes (depending on the size of your bread).

Workstation 6 — Prayer

GETTING READY

Provide the list of Bible verses from Session 44 for today. Copy and post the following instructions for the children:

> The director for the newscast is coming to the control room to see if the pictures are ready to edit. You have been working hard for several weeks now. Do you have all of the pictures, starting with Bethlehem and ending with Jesus' death in Jerusalem? Check your Bible verses to make sure that you haven't left anything out.

Workstation 7 — Benediction

GETTING READY

Have costumes, bowl, towel, and water at the workstation. Post a sign-up sheet for the talk show participants: the reader to read the script, the camera person to film the show, and two foot-washing actors in costumes. Copy and post the following instructions for the children:

> Get out your TV camera and set up to film in front of the "Meet the Experts" sign for the opening of today's talk show. Read John 13:4-5 and 12-17. Get the bowl, water, and towel. Have volunteers ready to act out the foot-washing. Set up the scene. You're ON THE AIR in 20 minutes.

Script

In biblical times people usually traveled on foot, either barefoot or wearing sandals. It was the custom to wash your feet before sitting at the low tables to eat. Usually a servant would bring a bowl and towel around and wash everyone's feet. Since there was no servant at the Last Supper, Jesus washed the disciples' feet himself to teach us about humility.

The Worship Celebration

I. Call to Worship — Mysterious music and foot-washing scene to open talk show.

II. Sermon — Foot-washing scene.

III. Benediction — "Meet the Experts" interview with archaeologists.

Items to Go Home

Biblical bread to take home and bake for lunch.

SESSION 47

MAKE A JOYFUL NOISE

The Bible Lesson

Learning more about Jesus would not be complete without learning more about the teachings of Jesus as well (Mark 7:7-16, Matthew 18:21-35, and Matthew 21:12-13).

What the Children Will Learn Today

Our purpose is to review, in a fun setting, some of the teachings of Jesus from the Bible and to think about what they mean to us today.

Time Needed

Fifteen minutes for workstations and 15 minutes for the interview.

Supplies Needed

1. Woodworking basket and wood to build biblical house.

2. Wood scraps, nails of varying sizes, extra hammer, and old bolts at least 6" long for nail xylophone.

3. Reference books on biblical life to read, old Sunday school material and magazines to cut from, Bibles, and a snack.

4. Workstation signs with newsroom titles and instructions.

5. Table or small desk to be used as the anchor desk for the news.

6. Musical instruments, song book, sing-along tapes, tape recorder with blank tape for recording, and posters.

7. Craft supply basket: usual supplies plus large sheets of newsprint.

8. Dress-up clothes: old ties, hats, suits, high heels, etc. for the children to play dress-up with as they pretend to be at a TV studio.

WORKSTATIONS

Workstation 1 — Call to Worship

GETTING READY

   To make the nail xylophone, you will need wood scraps, nails, hammer, and old bolts. Post a sign-up sheet for someone to play the nail xylophone to announce the on-the-spot report, and copy and post the following instructions for the children:

> Can you believe it? The station manager wants you to make a nail xylophone to use to announce special reports that come into the newsroom. Find a 12" long board or scrap. Sand the board until it is completely smooth. Next, find nails of varying lengths and sizes. Hammer the nails into the board about one inch apart and *only ½" into the board* in one long line down the length of the board. Leave most of the nail sticking up tall and straight. Look through the collection of long bolts. Take a bolt and run the grooved end up and down the line of nails to make music. Practice so you'll be ready in case any special news reports come in.

NAIL XYLOPHONE

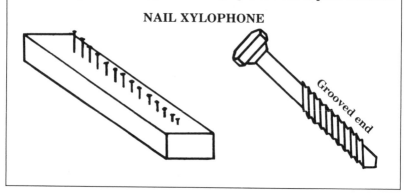

Workstation 2 — Affirmation of Faith

GETTING READY

   Make a copy of the crossword puzzle for each child.
   Key to puzzle: ACROSS — 1. James, 4. Matthias, 7. Bartholomew, 9. Andrew, 10. Philip. DOWN — 1. John, 2. Simon, 3. traitor, 5. Thomas, 6. Paul, 7. Barnabas, 8. Matthew, 11. Peter. Save puzzle and statement for Session 49.

   Copy and post the following instructions for the children:

You need to write a closing statement for the upcoming nightly news which tells what it means to follow Jesus. You only need to write three or four sentences, but you are having a terrible time thinking of what to write. Sit down with some friends and work this crossword puzzle on the disciples to help you get some ideas, then write your statement.

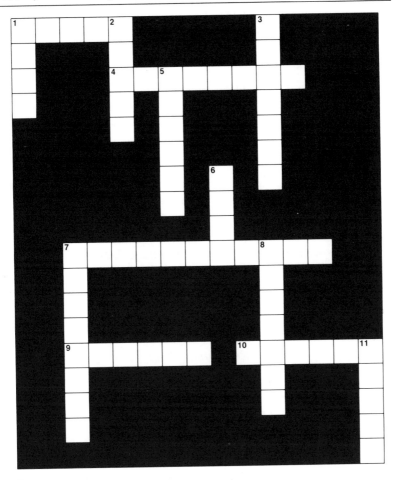

Across

1. John's brother and one of the fishermen. (Matthew 4:21)

4. The disciple chosen to take the place of Judas Iscariot (Acts 1:21-26)

7. He has the longest name of all the apostles. (Mark 3:18)

9. He brought his brother Simon (Peter) to Jesus. They were fishing partners. (John 1:40)

10. He was from the same hometown as Peter and Andrew. (John 1:43-46)

Down

1. Brother of James and partner in the family-owned fishing business. (Matthew 4:21)

2. He was a member of the Zealots, an extremist guerilla group who was changed by following Jesus. (Luke 6:15)

3. Judas Iscariot betrayed Jesus. He is often called the _____. (Matthew 26:15)

5. He was a twin and is often remembered for doubting that Jesus had risen from the dead. (John 20:27)

6. He is often referred to as the "Apostle to the Gentiles" but he was not one of the twelve apostles. He is also called Saul. (Acts 13:9 and 14:14-16)

7. He was often included among the apostles, but like Paul, he was not an apostle. He was believed to be very successful as a preacher and served as a link between the apostles and the church. (Acts 4:36)

8. He was a tax collector for the Romans before joining Jesus. (Matthew 9:9)

11. Andrew's brother and the spokesman of the twelve apostles. His name was Simon, but Jesus called him _____, meaning "rock." (Matthew 16:18)

Workstation 3 — Offering

GETTING READY

Copy and post the following instructions for the children:

> The documentary airs in four weeks; how is the work on the biblical house for the set coming along?

Workstation 4 — Sermon/Bible Lesson

GETTING READY

Set out biblical, newsroom, and futuristic reporter costumes. Post a sign-up sheet for the on-the-spot interview participants, the anchor person, the time traveling reporter, and the biblical character. Copy and post the following instructions for the children:

Set your time machine coordinates for Jerusalem. There is a fast-breaking story happening there. Use the biblical house as the backdrop for today's interview. Dress in costumes if you wish.

On-the-Spot Time Traveling Interview Script

ANCHOR PERSON IN NEWSROOM: We interrupt your regularly scheduled program to bring you this fast-breaking news story outside of Jerusalem with our On-the-Spot Time Traveling Reporter, _____, from KTBT News, about reports that Jesus (the young, thirty-year-old minister from Nazareth) has thrown the money-changers out of the temple. We now go back in time live to _____ in Jerusalem.

TIME TRAVELING REPORTER: Thank you, _____. We are standing here in front of a new house being built on the outskirts of Jerusalem where Jesus and his followers are resting for the night. Yesterday, it was first reported that Jesus rode into Jerusalem on a donkey amid hundreds of Passover pilgrims coming to Jerusalem for the Passover celebration. It was quite a joyous scene. The people spread their cloaks over the road, waved palm branches, and sang "HOSANNA!" over and over.

Today, upon his return to the city, Jesus is reported to have walked right into the outer courts of the temple, which have become like a marketplace with people and merchants everywhere, and turned the money-changers' tables over. The neat stacks and rows of coins on each table rolled everywhere.

It seems that every family must buy a lamb or other animal to offer as a sacrifice when they go to the temple. They must also pay a temple tax. Only a shekel or stater coin may be used to pay the tax, so the money-changers set up rows and rows of tables to change the money of the travelers from all parts of the country into the proper coins. It is fairly common knowledge that these money-changers often exchange the coins improperly, keeping part of the profit for themselves and giving some to the temple priests who allow them to operate this way.

Well, this man Jesus had evidently had enough. He went

in, flipped all of the tables upside down, and said, according to one eyewitness: "This is supposed to be God's house, a house of prayer. You have turned it into a hideout for thieves to sit and steal money from innocent people who cannot afford it." Other witnesses' accounts say he then proceeded to drive the oxen, sheep, and others out of the outer courts of the temple.

Let's speak to one of his followers. *(Turn toward biblical-costumed person being interviewed.)* Thank you for speaking with us this evening. Was it unusual for Jesus to act this way?

BIBLICAL CHARACTER IN COSTUME: Yes, but it was necessary. Jesus has said over and over to uphold the law but not to the point of being unkind to your neighbors. He also said that before you go to pray to God, you need to seek forgiveness from God by offering forgiveness to others and trying to live a better life.

REPORTER: Why did Jesus chase the money-changers out of the temple today?

BIBLICAL CHARACTER: Because he did not think a place of worship should be like a place of business that charges people money.

REPORTER: Thank you for speaking with us tonight, and we're back to you, _____, at the KTBT newsroom.

ANCHOR: Thanks, _____. We will have more fast-breaking headlines as they develop. For now, we'll go back to your regularly scheduled program.

Workstation 5 — Witness to the World

GETTING READY

Make copies of the crossword puzzle for each child.

Key to puzzle: ACROSS — 1. Give, 3. Do, 4. Life, 5. Door, 6. Live, 7. Us. DOWN — 1. God, 2. Jesus, 4. Love, 6. Let, 7. Ur. Save the stories and pictures for Session 49.

Copy and post the following instructions for the children:

Another puzzle has arrived on your desk for consideration. Work the puzzle. Then write a five-sentence story for the newsletter telling about someone who follows the advice of Matthew 7:12 at your school. Remember to use: WHO? WHAT? WHEN? WHERE? and WHY? Draw a picture showing this person following Jesus.

The Good News

Across

1. _____ to others cheerfully. (2 Corinthians 9:7)

3. The Golden Rule: _____ unto others as you would have them _____ to you. (Matthew 7:12)

4. God gives us _____. (John 15:9)

5. "Knock and the _____ will open." (Luke 11:9-10)

6. We _____ each day because of God. (Romans 14:6-8)

7. Give _____ this day our daily bread." (Matthew 6:11)

Down

1. The Creator of all things. (Genesis 1)

2. Author of the Lord's Prayer. (Matthew 6:9-15)

4. God gives us _____. (John 15:9)

6. "_____ others praise you, not yourself." (Proverbs 27:2)

7. Abraham's native place. (Genesis 11:27)

Workstations 6 and 7 —
Prayer and Benediction

GETTING READY

Copy and post the following instructions for the children:

Don't forget you have a deadline to meet. Get some help finishing the pictures of Jesus' life from the photographers.

The Worship Celebration

I. Call to Worship — Play nail xylophone to announce the special report.

II. Sermon — On-the-spot interview.

III. Benediction — Close with the thought: It is always easier to see the faults of others than our own. Think of how you would feel if someone treated you the way you treated them. Jesus taught mercy, forgiveness, justice, and love.

Items to Go Home

Assignment: Go and find someone you can be kinder to this week.

SESSION 48

WORSHIP MUST INCLUDE EVERYONE

The Bible Lesson

The Bible offers "love and kindness" as solutions to the many daily problems we face (Luke 10:25-37).

What the Children Will Learn Today

The scrambled words tell the children how we are to treat outcasts. "There are no outcasts in life, we are all neighbors; therefore, you must go and treat everyone with the same love and kindness."

Time Needed

Twenty minutes for workstations and ten minutes to unscramble the words.

Supplies Needed

1. Woodworking basket and materials for biblical house.

2. Bibles and a snack.

3. Reference books on biblical life to read and old Sunday school material or old magazines to cut from.

4. Workstation signs with newsroom titles and instructions.

5. A large copy of the Scrambled Bible Puzzle on newsprint.

6. Musical instruments, song book, sing-along tapes, tape recorder with tape for recording, and posters.

7. Craft supply basket: usual supplies plus large sheets of newsprint.

8. Dress-up clothes: old ties, hats, suits, high heels, etc. for children to play dress-up with as they pretend to be at a TV studio.

WORKSTATIONS

Workstation 1 — Call to Worship

GETTING READY

Post a sign-up sheet for musicians to perform their song at the conclusion of the game show today. Copy and post the following instructions for the children:

> The station manager likes to think up new song titles. You have just been given the following statement to turn into a new song: "To Know and Feel the Needs of Others." Either write a song to fit the title or select a song that you think fits. You're ON THE AIR in 20 minutes.

Workstations 2 and 3 — Offering and Affirmation

GETTING READY

Copy and post the following instructions for the children:

> Orders have just been delivered: "Need house at Studio B for newscast by next week." Do your best to finish today.

Workstation 4 — Sermon/Bible Lesson

GETTING READY

Provide a copy of the time travel interview at this station. Save the story the children write for Session 49. Copy and post the following instructions for the children:

> Your director wants you to write six sentences describing life in Nazareth when Jesus was a child. You don't need your time machine; you're working at your desk today. The secretary has typed up your notes from the interview you did with one of the housebuilders in Nazareth the other day. Look over the interview and write sentences.

Time Travel Interview With Biblical Housebuilder

REPORTER: What are the houses here in Nazareth made of?

BUILDER: Most of the common people's houses are made of baked mud, bricks, stone, and wood.

REPORTER: Are they large houses?

BUILDER: No, most are just one room with an upper platform for the family and lower level for the sheep.

REPORTER: Where does the family sleep?

BUILDER: Everyone just lines up on mats across the floor; only the rich have mattresses to sleep on.

REPORTER: Why do people keep their sheep in the house?

BUILDER: Sheep are considered valuables; families keep their sheep in the house to keep them from being stolen or killed at night.

REPORTER: Why do you put grates over the windows?

BUILDER: The grates protect the family from robbers because there aren't any locks for the windows.

REPORTER: What are those people doing up on the roof?

BUILDER: In good weather, the family uses the roof of their house for many duties: sleeping, drying fruits and vegetables, praying, grinding corn, drying laundry, and even storage.

REPORTER: What do you do when it rains?

BUILDER: After a rain, you have to get up there and roll the mud on the roof to make it smooth again.

REPORTER: How do the children get up on the roof?

BUILDER: People who can afford to have steps built onto the outside of their houses, and those who can't afford steps just use a ladder. *(End of interview)*

Workstation 5 — Witness to the World

GETTING READY

Post the newsprint containing the large copy of the puzzle. Save puzzle and stories for Session 49. Key to puzzle: JESUS, MARTHA, PAUL, PHILIP, LYDIA, JOHN, MARY, ANNA, and PETER. Copy and post the following instructions for the children:

> The editor wants you to write two five-sentence stories about a famous woman and man in the world today that you would call a follower of Jesus. But you were just about to work on a puzzle. Circle all nine biblical names from the New Testament. The

names may go in any direction and letters may be used more than once for different names. Then, complete your assignment.

```
M P J E S U S
P A E P A U L
A H R T W X Y
J N I T E K D
O Y N L H R I
H T Z A I A A
N M A R Y P X
```

Workstations 6 and 7 — Prayer and Benediction

GETTING READY

Copy and post the following instructions for the children:

The director has set the DEADLINE. You must have all of the pictures telling the story of Jesus' life on the long roll finished and ready for editing. Check your Bible verses and make sure you have not left anything out: Luke 2:1-20, Mark 1:16-20, Luke 9:10-17, Mark 10:13-16, John 12:12-15, Mark 11:15-19, Luke 22:14-20, John 19:16-18, and Luke 24:1-7. Try to finish cutting out or drawing pictures this week. For your very last picture on the roll, draw or cut out a picture to show how Jesus has changed our lives today. How can you show the people in the picture as followers of Jesus?

The Worship Celebration

1. Write the puzzle out on a large sheet of newsprint. Have taped to the wall for the "Unscramble the Words" Game Show.

SCRAMBLED PUZZLE

There are no **stacsuot** _____(Remember the parable of the Good Samaritan or read Jeremiah 30:17). In **eifl** _____, (Luke 10:25) we are all

bsegnhiro _____; (Luke 10:36) therefore, **ouy** _____ (Luke 10:28) must **og** _____ (Luke 10:37) and treat everyone with the **aesm** _____ (Luke 10:37) **elvo** _____ (Luke 10:27) and **nksdiens** _____. (Luke 10:37)

II. Divide into five teams. Have each team designate a Bible celebrity spokesperson for their team. For example, Team 1 is Joseph, a famous person from the Bible.

III. Give each team a chance to solve a word in the puzzle.

IV. To conclude the game show, the musicians should present their song.

V. Ask everyone to write something they wish they could do better and something they do very well on a name tag.

Items to Go Home

The children should wear their name tags home. Remind them to work on what they wish they could do better throughout the week.

SESSION 49

WHAT SHALL WE WRITE?

The Bible Lesson

Jesus gave many suggestions for how we could witness to others (John 8:12).

What the Children Will Learn Today

Humility is not easy. We all enjoy the feeling of being the best. One of the most helpful ways to learn to think about the needs and feelings of others is to work together on a program that includes everyone.

Time Needed

Twenty-five minutes for workstations and five minutes for worship today.

Supplies Needed

1. Woodworking basket and biblical house.
2. All stories, scripts, pictures, and other materials that the children have used this summer for the newsletter and newsroom.
3. Bibles and an easy-to-eat snack as a reward for hard work.
4. Reference books, old Sunday school material, or magazines.
5. Workstation signs with newsroom titles and instructions.
6. Box for TV monitor, two dowels to attach the picture roll, and empty spools of thread for knobs (make sure box fits roll).
7. Musical instruments, song book, sing-along tapes, tape recorder with extra blank tape for recording, and posters.
8. Craft supply basket: usual supplies plus large sheets of newsprint and tempera paint, brushes, and painting cover-ups.
9. Dress-up clothes: old ties, hats, suits, high heels, etc. for children to play dress-up with as they pretend to be at a TV studio.

WORKSTATIONS

Workstation 1 — Call to Worship

GETTING READY

Set out *all* of the songs, tapes, and musical instruments today. Post a sign-up sheet for a DJ to play the tape during the rehearsal and the TV program, and copy and post the following instructions for the children:

> KTBT TV studio wants you to put together music to be played softly in the background during the Children's Documentary News Program. You may reuse previous music you recorded. Choose a theme song to open and close the documentary program. Record your songs on tape and be ready to take the tape to the TV studio in 25 minutes.

Workstations 2 and 6 — Affirmation of Faith and Prayer

GETTING READY

Make all the stories, puzzles, and materials available today. Post a sign-up sheet for an announcer for the rehearsal and the TV program, and copy and post the following instructions for the children:

> The producer wants you to write a five-minute introduction complete with pictures for the Children's Documentary News. The control room engineers have been editing a film telling about Jesus' life story in pictures. Call an engineer over to your office and have him or her help you write your script. Work together and write an introduction that tells the story of Jesus' life. Time yourself reading the script slowly. It must be exactly five minutes. Production meeting in 25 minutes. Start your script with: "Welcome to KTBT's Children's Documentary on the life and teachings of Jesus . . ."

Workstation 3 — Offering

GETTING READY

If the children have already finished the house or if they finish early, have them go and help at another station. Post a sign-up sheet for crew members to set up the biblical house for the rehearsal and the TV show, and copy and post the following instructions for the children:

> Set up the house in Studio B. Make sure everything is ready for the rehearsal next week.

Workstation 4 — Sermon/Bible Lesson

GETTING READY

Have copies of all the materials the children have written and used so far. Have an extra copy at this workstation of the newsletter stories about followers of Jesus at church, school, neighborhood, and the world for the closing. You will need an adult helper to assist the children in putting everything together and writing smooth newsroom-sounding transitions between reports, such as: "From our on-the-spot reporter, we learned firsthand that . . . ," "Our time traveling reporters brought back a most interesting report about . . . ," or, "We turn now to . . ." Work with the children and have fun. Watch a news program for ideas. Post a sign-up sheet for an anchor person to read and for costumed actors to enact the stories, and copy and post the following instructions for the children:

> Your production team has the job of putting all of the reports and stories you have used over the last several weeks on the news together into one 20-minute segment. Pick and choose your favorites. Use costumes and act out the interviews or stories you liked best. Reduce the material down to 15 minutes of news with a five-minute closing on what is happening among Jesus' followers today. For the closing, use the stories submitted to the newsletter. Read one or two of the stories or write your own. The production meeting is in 25 minutes; you must have the complete program ready to show to the director at that time. Time your reports; your segment must be exactly 20 minutes long.

Workstation 5 — Witness to the World

GETTING READY

Decide how large you want your newsletter to be. You can do a simple 8½" x 11" one-sided page that is simply photocopied or whatever you prefer. If at all possible, have the children's stories typed and ready for them to just paste up on paper that is the size you've decided on for the newsletter. Gather together typed stories, pictures that you have drawn, games, puzzles, or anything else that could be used in the newsletter. Post a sign-up sheet for volunteers to help with printing, folding, and mailing, and copy and post the following instructions for the children:

This is it; the editor has called you all together for the production meeting. There is a blank page(s) showing you how much space you have to fill for this week's newsletter. (1) Look over all the stories, pictures, games, puzzles, and anything else on your table. (2) Decide which stories, puzzles, and pictures you want to use. (3) Write new stories if there is something you think your newsletter should tell that is not already written. (4) Arrange the stories and pictures on the page. (5) Tape with one piece of tape (do not glue) each story, picture, or article onto your blank paste-up page. Remember the heading. (6) Make any changes that you want to make. Proofread for errors. Make sure the newsletter is ready to go to the printers. (7) If you plan to mail your newsletter to neighboring churches, make a list and, if possible, include addresses.

Workstation 6 — Prayer

GETTING READY

Send one or two children with the roll of pictures over to the Affirmation Station to explain what the pictures mean. Have the other children stay and help build the TV monitor. Use a box a little bit wider than the paper you used for the pictures. On the widest side of the box, cut out a TV viewing screen that is a little bit smaller than your pictures. Cut the holes for the dowel to fit through. Set out the craft supply basket. Post a sign-up sheet for engineers (at least two) to turn the roll of pictures for the rehearsal and the program, and copy and post the following instructions for the children:

You have to make a new TV monitor for the control room today. Paint or cover the box with paper to make it look like a TV. Leave the front flap open so you can insert the "film" (your roll of pictures) later. Write KTBT NEWS on the side.

Building the TV Monitor

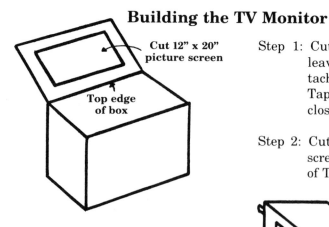

Cut 12" x 20" picture screen

Top edge of box

Step 1: Cut open side of box leaving front flap attached across the top. Tape all other sides closed.

Step 2: Cut 12" x 20" picture screen opening on front of TV.

Step 3: Cut round holes on each side for dowels to fit into.

Step 4: Insert dowels in holes. Tape front closed. Turn dowels to show each picture.

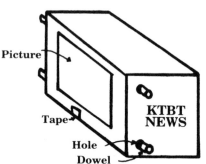

Picture

Tape

Hole

Dowel

KTBT NEWS

Workstation 7 — Benediction

GETTING READY

Set out papers, a ruler, and markers or crayons. Post a sign-up sheet for floor managers to pass out newsletters to the studio audience at the news program, and copy and post the following instructions for the children:

> You have done a great job as photographers and all of your pictures have gone to the photo editor who has only one more request: draw a picture of what you think the church will look like 200 years in the future on a 8½" x 3" piece of white paper. The editor will use your drawing as the heading for the Peace and Love newsletter.

The Worship Celebration

1. Have each workstation give a brief report on what they did.

II. Give the children a snack to be eaten while they listen to the reports.

Items to Go Home

Write a note to go home to parents telling them of the upcoming news program. Ask for dress-up clothes, props, or costumes if needed.

SESSION 50

GO AND TELL THE GOOD NEWS

The Bible Lesson

Each part of this summer news program encourages children to think about their commitment to God. They learn how their lives can reflect his love. (Matthew 5:14-16).

What the Children Will Learn Today

Today is the dress rehearsal for next week's show. Tell the children, "this is show biz." Make sure that everyone is involved and that everyone is having a good time. Learning really can be fun. Most of all, remember: we are still a church, and the purpose of this entire summer program is to share the Good News with children; so don't strive for perfection or push for a perfect performance. Use costumes for reporters of the future, biblical characters, newsroom technicians, newsletter staff, and anyone and everyone. Encourage parents to help their children find old things from home to bring and wear. Use headphones, microphones, and even a video camera (with adult supervision) if you wish to tape your broadcast to show to other Sunday school classes later. Be sure to tell the children what a fantastic job they are doing.

Time Needed

You will have a 25-minute rehearsal and then a five-minute celebration.

Supplies Needed

1. Biblical house and children's church.
2. Snack to eat at the end of the meeting.
3. Newsroom signs.
4. Musical tape.
5. Costumes and props to be used for the program.
6. Scripts.
7. Copies of the invitation to the news program.

Rehearsal

Go through the KTBT Children's Documentary News Program exactly as you plan to do it the next week before your studio audience. Have a snack at the end while you explain the assignment.

The Worship Celebration

I. Give everyone a copy of the "Invitation" to complete.

II. Use your time machine. Tell everyone that their mission is to go into the future in search of a friend. Close with each person going out to invite a new friend to come next week. Emphasize that friendship is not described in terms of "looks" but feelings.

Items to Go Home

Invitations to invite a friend to the TV Program.

Invitation

You are invited to KTBT's Children's News Documentary

Church:

Date:

Time:

We hope you can come.

Early Christians often wor-
shiped in a nearby neighbor's
house. Draw a line showing
where each item would have
been kept in the house.

SESSION 51

FRIENDSHIP DAY

The Bible Lesson

This summer's closing session is a 30-minute "KTBT Children's Documentary News Program." Their "Peace and Love Newsletter" is being sent to neighboring churches (Mark 16:15).

What the Children Will Learn Today

Help the children feel proud of their work, and they'll realize they are capable of doing great things.

Supplies Needed

1. Biblical house, church, newsroom props, and costumes.
2. Refreshments to share with your guests afterwards.
3. Newsroom signs, musical tape, and scripts.
4. Peace and Love Newsletters for the studio audience.

The Worship Celebration

I. Have the children present the KTBT Children's Documentary News Program.

II. Pass out Peace and Love newsletters to the studio audience.

III. Serve refreshments and congratulate all the children.

Items to Go Home

Share kindness, love, and good things with others.

CHAPTER FOURTEEN

WHERE DO WE GO FROM HERE?

This final evaluation session is really the beginning, not the end, of your program. You will receive helpful feedback from the children on what they especially liked and what they would change about the program. With their suggestions in mind, you can prepare for another exciting year of children's worship.

SESSION 52
EVALUATION

Take a moment to reflect on the past year. The children have learned to share and consider the feelings of others while hammering nails together and playing musical instruments. They have learned to settle arguments through compromise and thinking about what each person needs instead of just fighting, yelling, or telling on each other. They also learned all about the different parts of the worship service, but most important they learned that they were needed and important.

There may still be some in your church who think that "children should be seen and not heard." Over time, the success of your program will persuade them that children learn best by working together in a hands-on learning experience.

As you look ahead to next year, don't be afraid to embark on a new building project or to design your own activity. And don't hesitate to repeat favorite sessions. The seasonal sessions are especially conducive for repetition as these special days are tradition-oriented. So it can be with your children's church. Offer a wide variety of experiences to all of your children, because while one child may run to see the music station each week, another child's main reason for coming to church on Sunday morning may be to work with the hammer and nails. Give your children choices.

Remember that you will have a different group of children each year. One year I had children who loved acting out every Bible story but never really got too excited about clown ministry. The next year's group loved clown ministry and wanted to do every Bible verse in full clown regalia. Decide what you liked and what you didn't like. Discuss what they would like to do next year. Make plans that excite the children.

Children need: (1) a family time in the main church service where they are really included, and (2) a special time when they learn about the meaning of worship in a childlike fashion. Children don't absorb much from just sitting and listening; they have to be able to touch, see, hear, taste, and smell what you are talking about. We plant the seed of God's love and then we help it grow by how we structure children's time at church.

When you evaluate your program this year and think about what you are going to do for next year, do more than just hand out the evaluation sheet below. Evaluate the whole program.

The Bible Lesson

Children will not remain children forever. They were not children

20 years ago and will not still be children in 20 years. They are only children TODAY. If we fail to meet their needs today, many of them will not be sitting in the church 20 years from now. Today is the only opportunity we have to MINISTER to the needs of the children of God's church (Mark 10:13-16).

What the Children Will Learn Today

Plan to have a grand party today. Have everyone bring their favorite treats.

Start by passing out the "Survey of Needs" questionnaire. Write down the ideas of those too young to write. Then serve refreshments and play a favorite sing-along tape. If you have pictures in your photo album or possibly a videotape of the service, share them. While everyone is eating, make a master list summarizing the ideas submitted on questionnaires. Look over the list briefly with children. On a separate sheet of newsprint, ask children to list their seven favorite things this year.

Make the seven favorite things the focus of your program workstations for next year. Try to incorporate all the suggestions from the children. Remember that some children will graduate into an older program and new children coming in know nothing about what you did this past year. Plan exciting workstations for the new year ahead which continue to encourage the children to share with each other and that challenge the children to read and use their Bibles.

Children are very creative. They can help you to plan another exciting year of worshiping and learning together in God's church with their suggestions and ideas in this evaluation session.

Supplies Needed

1. Newsprint and markers.
2. Survey of Needs questionnaire.
3. Party refreshments.
4. Pictures or videotape of year's activities.

QUESTIONNAIRE
Survey of Needs

We are planning for children's worship for next year, and we would like to have the ideas of both children and adults. We are very interested in your ideas. Take a minute and write down your response to each statement. Thank you for your ideas. Ideas can be about any of the children's activities that we have done.

Things We Like

Ways We Learn Best

Things We Would Like to Change

Things We Would Like to Do at Church

One Thing We Did This Year That I'm Sure I'd Enjoy Doing Again

The Worship Celebration

I. Distribute questionnaire and refreshments.
II. Compile list from "One Thing . . . I'd enjoy doing again."
III. Write down the children's seven favorite experiences.
IV. Have a sing-along as time permits.
V. Close with a "love circle" (children holding hands) and the Lord's Prayer.

Items to Go Home: Assignment for Next Week

Send everyone out to bring a friend to church next week.

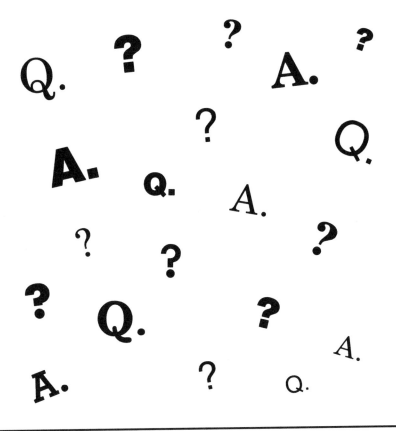

CHAPTER FIFTEEN

QUESTIONS AND ANSWERS

The chapter that follows will help you understand the practical side of pulling these diverse activities together into one program.

Q. How many adults are needed to supervise the children? Can two people handle them with a minimum of chaos?

A. I know from experience that you may or may not be able to count on having four or five volunteers. There must be at least two adults in the room when you are working with wood because at least one adult must stay in the carpenter shop with the tools at all times. Restrict the number of tools at the woodworking station so that you always have an adult overseeing the work of each hammer and saw. Under this policy, I have never had any injuries.

The workstation signs and written directions that are copied and tacked up each Sunday enable older children to work on their own at each workstation so the adults can work with the younger children. Occasionally the "Getting Ready" section suggests extra helpers. Teenagers make excellent helpers.

Q. What are the best ages of children to work with?

A. There is no best age for children's worship. This book is written for ages four through 12. Sometimes four-year-olds have a little bit of trouble, but most churches make the division of ages at four years old. If problems do occur, adding an additional adult usually solves them. It's also fine to let an uncertain four-year-old remain in a younger class. There is nothing wrong with offering separate programs for four- and five-year-olds.

Older children often help younger children on their own initiative. Having older children read directions, write answers, and help younger children with projects was an unexpected joy I encountered when I first conducted this program.

Q. What is the primary purpose of using the sign-up sheets? Does it ever happen that no one signs up to lead a certain area? If so, how did you handle it?

A. The sign-up sheets let you know who will be leading what part of the weekly service. A separate attendance record should be kept. The sign-up sheets allow you to organize the weekly celebrations easily and efficiently. The sign-up sheets let as many children as desire to sign up and lead a part of the celebration. Shy children are much more likely to sign a sheet than raise their hand or volunteer out loud.

In two years, I have never lacked for volunteers. But in such an event, you can ask for volunteers at the beginning of the celebration or a Bible verse can always be read instead of acting it out. Although sometimes children are hesitant to volunteer alone, they are often eager to volunteer alongside a friendly adult who will participate with them side by side. If I notice someone having trouble, I just get down beside them on my hands and knees and join right in.

Q. The offering is not always listed as a collection. Does that mean it is optional?

A. I've never seen a church hesitate to take up a collection. I suggest offering containers and special projects in addition to, not in place of, what your church normally does. Children understand an offering much better when they see something tangible. It is important for children to realize that they can offer their time and talents to God as well as their money. The time and energy given by children often have more meaning in such young lives than money their parents give them.

Q. Do you really think children should use hammers and saws on Sunday morning?

A. Giving the children hammers, nails and saws teaches them about the meaning of worship in the church. They learn about sharing and helping their neighbor as they build their own church, communion table, biblical house, candleholders, and church collection box for the offering. Crayons, oil, and paper help them understand Bible stories as they make their own (paper) stained glass windows to hang in their church. The children embroider the Lord's Prayer on a banner while they learn about the meaning of prayer. I have also taught 40 children at one time to make bread as an introduction to life in biblical times. And there is no substitute for having the children learn about the parts of a worship service by having them write and lead their own children's worship service — with every child involved in a significant role.

Q. How much time do I need to set up each week?

A. The time needed for set-up each week depends upon whether or not you have exclusive use of the room. If you can leave your workstations set up, all you have to do is add the new instructions and items needed at the stations that week. If you have to fold up your church and put everything away in a closet, then it takes a little longer. Using workstation baskets (woodworking, craft, painting, etc.) makes the job of setting up much faster and easier.

Q. Should we save the things the children make each week that they don't take home?

A. Yes, many of the items that do not go home are used later during the special worship services for the congregation, such as the scroll, Peace and Love candle, and others labeled "save." As you collect items throughout the year, you will find it helpful to designate a box or special shelf for the things you are saving.

SIGN-UP SHEET

PROJECT

_____

1	
2	
3	
4	
5	
6	
7	
8	
9	
10	
11	
12	
13	
14	
15	

Note: Sign-up sheet can be enlarged on a copier to 140% io fit comfortably on an 8½"
x 11" piece of paper.

Suggested Reading

Barth, Edna, *Holly, Reindeer, and Colored Lights: the Story of the Christmas Symbols,* New York: Clarion Books, Houghton Mifflin Co., 1971.

Baynew, Pauline, *Thanks Be to God, Prayers From Around the World,* New York: Macmillan Publishing Company, 1990.

Cuyler, Margery, *Jewish Holidays,* New York: Holt, Rinehart and Winston, 1978.

Etkin, Ruth, *The Rhythm Band Book,* New York: Sterling Publishing Co., Inc., 1978.

Giblin, James Cross, *Let There Be Light, a Book About Windows,* New York: Thomas Y. Crowell, 1988.

Kalman, Bobbie, *Early Christmas, the Early Settler Life Series,* New York: Crabtree Publishing Co., 1981.

Lazar, Wendy, *The Jewish Holiday Book,* Garden City, New York: Doubleday and Co., Inc., 1977.

Lindberg, Paul M., *Advent, the Days Before Christmas,* Philadelphia: Fortress Press, 1966.

Litherland, Janet, *The Clown Ministry Handbook,* Colorado Springs, Colorado: Meriwether Publishing Ltd., 1982.

MacLennan, Jennifer, *Simple Puppets You Can Make,* New York: Sterling Publishing Co., Inc., 1988.

Schmidt, Hans J. and Karl J., *Learning With Puppets,* Colorado Springs, Colorado: Meriwether Publishing Ltd., 1989.

Smith, Judy Gattis, *26 Ways to Use Drama in Teaching the Bible,* Nashville: Abingdon Press, 1988.

Thompson, Barbara Balzac, *Passover: Seder, Ritual and Menu for an Observance by Christians,* Minneapolis: Augsburg Publishing House, 1984.

Walker, Les, *Housebuilding for Children, Six Different Houses That Children Can Build by Themselves,* Woodstock, New York: The Overlook Press, 1977.

Walker, Lester, *Carpentry for Children, Young Carpenters Experience the Fun of Building,* Woodstock, New York: The Overlook Press, 1982.

ABOUT THE AUTHOR

Elaine Clanton Harpine, Ph.D., is a program design specialist and group training consultant, specializing in conducting and evaluating youth and children's group programs.

She earned her doctorate in Educational Psychology and Counseling from the University of Illinois, where her research focused on leadership development in the church. She has worked as a Director of Christian Education and youth worker. Her first-hand experience in designing and conducting programs on family relations, marriage communication, leadership development, children's worship, and youth programs has helped many churches enjoy a high level of success in all of these areas.

Some of Dr. Clanton Harpine's published writings include retreats on peer pressure and witnessing; programs about alcohol, coping with failure, parental pressure, cheating, the meaning of Easter, helping your neighbor, suicide, and friendship.

ORDER FORM

MERIWETHER PUBLISHING LTD.
P.O. BOX 7710
COLORADO SPRINGS, CO 80933
TELEPHONE: (719) 594-4422

Please send me the following books:

_____ **No Experience Necessary! #CC-B107**   **$12.95**
by Elaine Clanton Harpine
A "learn by doing" guide for creating children's worship

_____ **Storytelling From the Bible #CC-B145**   **$9.95**
by Janet Litherland
The art of biblical storytelling

_____ **The Clown Ministry Handbook #CC-B163**   **$9.95**
by Janet Litherland
The first and most complete text on the art of clown ministry

_____ **The Official Sunday School Teachers**   **$9.95**
Handbook #CC-B152
by Joanne Owens
An indispensable aid for anyone involved in Sunday school activities

_____ **Get a Grip! #CC-B128**   **$9.95**
by L. G. Enscoe and Annie Enscoe
Contemporary scenes and monologs for Christian teens

_____ **The Best of the Jeremiah People #CC-B117**   **$14.95**
by Jim Custer and Bob Hoose
Humorous skits and sketches by leading Christian repertory group

These and other fine Meriwether Publishing books are available at your local Christian bookstore or direct from the publisher. Use the handy order form on this page.

I understand that I may return any book for a full refund if not satisfied.

NAME: _____

ORGANIZATION NAME: _____

ADDRESS: _____

CITY: _____ STATE: _____ ZIP: _____

PHONE: _____

☐ **Check Enclosed**
☐ **Visa or Mastercard #** _____

Expiration
Signature: _____ Date: _____
(required for Visa/Mastercard orders)

COLORADO RESIDENTS: Please add 3% sales tax.
SHIPPING: Include $1.50 for the first book and 50¢ for each additional book ordered.

☐ *Please send me a copy of your complete catalog of books and plays.*